CW01510538

An interesting group of medals to Qr.Mr.Sjt. William Maxwell, 74th Foot: Military General Service, 1793–1814, with 7 bars; Army L.S. & G.C. (William IV type): Regimental Medal of Merit, 2nd Class, for the Peninsular War, with six battle honours.
(*From the author's collection*).

Plate 1.

# Collecting Medals and Decorations

*by*

## ALEC A. PURVES

*Fellow of the Royal Numismatic Society*
*President of the Orders & Medals Research Society, 1956-60*

POLSTEAD · SUFFOLK
J. B. HAYWARD & SON

TO

MY WIFE

who patiently tolerates the inconveniences

of my enthusiasm for this hobby

FIRST PUBLISHED APRIL 1968
SECOND EDITION 1971
THIRD EDITION 1978

FOURTH EDITION (PAPERBACK) 1983
PUBLISHED BY
J. B. HAYWARD & SON
THE OLD RECTORY
POLSTEAD
SUFFOLK

DISTRIBUTED BY
LONDON STAMP EXCHANGE LTD
5 BUCKINGHAM STREET
LONDON WC2

ISBN  0  903754  99  1

Photography by P. Frank Purvey
Printed in England by Robert Stockwell Ltd, London SE1

# Contents

# Acknowledgements

I should like to express my grateful thanks to the many people who have answered my enquiries, supplied or verified information, or have readily given permission to quote from their writings, and particularly to the following (who are listed in alphabetical order):-

The late Major R. D. Ambrose, MBE., DCM., Royal Norfolk Regt.

The late Brigadier Sir Ivan De la Bere, KCVO., CB., CBE., formerly Secretary of the Central Chancery of the Orders of Knighthood.

Miss L. M. Brown, of Collingwood of Conduit Street, Ltd.

The late Mr H. A. Brading, CBE., Superintendent of the Royal Mint.

Major W. G. Cripps, late of the Royal Norfolk Regt.

The late Mr W. P. Dawson.

Captain K. J. Douglas-Morris, RN.

Mr J. R. Edwards, formerly Area Secretary, Automobile Association, Norwich.

Mr D. W. Greenhalgh, of the Royal Mint.

Mr D. Hall.

Mr G. W. Harris.

Mr John B. Hayward.

Mr J. H. Hine, of B. A. Seaby Ltd.

Mr E. C. Joslin, of Spink & Son Ltd.

Brigadier H. B. Latham.

Mr Julian Loffet.

Lt Col N. W. Poulsom.

The Public Record Office.

Mr James C. Risk of New York.

The Editor of the *Journal of the Royal United Services Institute*.

Sqdn Ldr F. E. Rymills, DFC., DFM.

The late Mr J. G. Silver, Secretary of the Order of St John.

Mr H. A. N. Tebbs, MBE.

Mr C. W. Tozer.

My thanks are due to B. A. Seaby Ltd., for permission to use parts of the text and illustrations which have previously appeared in my brochure, *Some Notes on War Medals*, also for kindly supplying photographs of the *obv.* and *rev.* of the copy D.C.M. (Edward VII).

The reproductions of the Automobile Association awards are by kind permission of that organisation.

# Foreword

THERE are many books available for the medal collector, describing British and foreign awards, with their bars and other insignia, frequently detailing the conditions or circumstances in which they were issued. Sometimes the units participating are listed; occasionally names of some recipients are given.

Most of these books are adequate for the purpose for which they are intended – namely, to describe the medal as, and why, issued. But apart, perhaps, from a brief word about re-strikes, state of preservation, or re-named medals, there is not much about the actual *collecting* of medals; little appears about the work of fakers, die varieties, forgeries, and the many other matters which the beginner has to learn slowly (and sometimes expensively) in the long process of becoming experienced.

It is the object of this work, not to describe the medals (as this information is easily available elsewhere), but to deal with many of the points which do not appear in the majority of medal books, and to assist the collector who is trying to learn the hard way. These notes do not pretend to be comprehensive, and they can only touch on the fringe of what the really experienced collector has to spend a lifetime in learning. And in any case, there is no real substitute for the personal experience gained from handling the medals themselves over a period of years. Lucky indeed is the collector who has the opportunity of regularly examining the lots in medal auctions, coupled with the chance of frequently inspecting the stocks of the leading dealers, who are always ready to advise and assist the genuine seeker after knowledge.

Portions of this work originally appeared as a series of articles in *Seaby's Coin and Medal Bulletin*, later enlarged and revised in my brochure, *Some Notes on War Medals*. This present work covers a wider field, but critics will probably say that British Orders and Decorations have been scantily dealt with, and this is fully realised.

To treat them in the same detail as that given to campaign medals, would have enlarged the book beyond an economic figure, but it is felt that sufficient information has been given to meet the needs of the beginner and average collector, bearing in mind that descriptive and historic data is easily obtainable elsewhere.

Similarly it is quite impossible to deal fully with foreign awards within the space at our disposal, consequently the foreign section is devoted mainly to a general survey of those decorations most frequently seen in British groups.

Finally, in order to avoid the constant repetition of the phrase, *Orders, Decorations, and Medals*, the words *decorations* and *awards* have frequently been used to cover the whole range; also the terms, *bar* and *clasp*, are used synonymously, as is the practice among most collectors (although some use *bar* to indicate the insignia of a second or subsequent award of, say, a gallantry medal or decoration, and *clasp* when referring to an engagement bar).

ALEC A. PURVES

*Brundall,*
*Norwich, Norfolk.*
January 1968

# 1

## Medal Collecting—I

SURELY there cannot be a hobby more fascinating than the collecting of Orders, Decorations, and Medals, with such a wide field of study open to the discerning collector. Unlike postage stamps and coins – both of which offer a most interesting and instructive scope – medals have such a *personal* link. This particularly applies to British awards, where the majority are officially named, and thus you can study the part played by the recipient, his regiment or ship, and even (in the case of officers and those who have won gallantry awards) his individual history.

There is something thrilling and satisfying to have in your collection medals won by men who stormed the fortress at Badajoz, who took part in the battles of Trafalgar or Waterloo, or in the Charge of the Light Brigade, who were present at one of the famous defences, such as Lucknow, Rorke's Drift, or Mafeking, or who formed part of the team which accompanied Scott or Shackleton on their polar expeditions.

But you cannot expect to acquire all these treasures at the start of a collecting career. However, even among the commoner medals, with which the beginner usually starts, there are still many fascinating stories to be found – but you will not find them if you merely accumulate an increasing number of single specimens, just mounting and labelling them with their respective designations, and not bothering to read up the actions and campaigns for which they were awarded.

Naturally, during the early days you will be happy to collect whatever comes your way, British and foreign – perhaps paying too much occasionally, perhaps picking up either a genuine bargain or one which turns out to be not such a bargain through being re-named, faked, or otherwise defective. As in every hobby, you must serve your apprenticeship, but if you start in the right way, this can, perhaps, be shortened and made less expensive.

## The 'Tools of the Trade'

Naturally, you will need some book of reference, and for a start the beginner cannot do better than to buy the latest edition of *Ribbons and Medals*, by Capt. Taprell Dorling, D.S.O., R.N. (There are, of course, other earlier books and plenty of more advanced ones, which will be dealt with in a later chapter). The British medals, in particular, are very fully dealt with – at least, as far as you will need in your early stages – and it is important to have a general knowledge of at least all the more common medals. If you can visit a local museum, regimental or otherwise, which has a reasonable collection of medals, you can see them at first hand, with their respective ribbons, but in addition to knowing what is what, you must also have an idea of how much to pay for them.

Since the first edition of this book appeared, several catalogues of medals and decorations have been published, with approximate values indicated. The collector, be he beginner or advanced, cannot afford to be without at least one of these, and, with the frequent price changes (almost inevitably upwards) it is important to revise or replace the catalogue at intervals. Dealers and collectors alike are rarely in agreement with the prices quoted in these catalogues – some items are absurdly low, while others are far too high – but in the main they give a good *general* indication of how much one should expect to pay.

In addition to such a catalogue – which must of necessity be rather general, usually quoting the price for the commonest bars or regiment, and for the lowest ranks or ratings – the serious collector should really compile his own references, particularly if he specialises in certain units or campaigns. He should study the price lists issued by the leading firms of medal dealers, and from these build up his own price guide. A loose-leaf book is best suited for this purpose, with a page for each medal, noting at the top any useful details, such as the style of naming (often more than one), whether the bars normally read upwards or downwards, the units involved (especially those to whom the medal is scarce), and similar data. You can then enter the prices quoted in the dealers' lists, with a reference as to source and date. Auction records are also very useful, and a subscription to the priced catalogues of Glendining & Co. Ltd. or Sotheby Parke Bernet & Co. (see Appendix B) will prove invaluable, particularly where lots consist of single medals.

The following example of a specimen page gives an indication of how this reference catalogue will look (but please bear in mind that the prices recorded were those quoted shortly before this edition went to press and may well be different by publication date). The references after the prices indicate the sources of quotations, with the month and year. It is, of course, only feasible to take notice of the prices quoted for single medals, as if this medal were included in a group it might be difficult to assign to it a proportion of the total price; similarly, if five of them comprised an auction lot, it would

---

## ASHANTEE – 1873–74

One bar: COOMASSIE. Naming: engraved in roman caps. blackened, with date, 1873–4 or 73–74.

17 Bty.RA; 28 Coy.RE; 2/23, 1/42, 2/Rif.Bde; 1 & 2 West Ind.Regt; Various native units; Naval Bde. from *Active, Amethyst, Argus, Barracouta, Beacon, Bittern, Coquette, Decoy, Dromedary, Druid, Encounter, Himalaya, Merlin, Rattlesnake, Seagull, Simoom, Tamar, Victor Emanuel.*

| No bar: | Naval, RM | NEF | £50 each | H. 3/77 |
|---|---|---|---|---|
| No bar: | Naval | AEF | £78 | CB. 6/77 |
| No bar: | Naval | VF | £50 | CB. 12/77 |
| No bar: | Pte. RWF | NVF | £52 | S. 5/77 |
| Bar: COOMASSIE Gnr.RMA | | VF | £95 | S.5/77 |
| Bar: COOMASSIE Pte. RM | | NVF | £70 | H.3/77 |
| Bar: COOMASSIE Bglr.2RB | | VF | £78 | H.3/77 |

---

not be accurate to take one-fifth of the price realised unless all were in precisely the same condition, and without any variation as to scarcity.

Such records naturally take a long time to compile, and may well be an occupation for winter evenings, but they are very worth while. They not only give an indication of how much to bid for auction lots, but act as a check on prices asked by vendors outside the usual numismatic firms.

A useful piece of equipment is a watchmaker's eyeglass, or a good magnifying glass, preferably one with thee lenses, on arms, so that they can be used in combination. Also essential is a pair of spring callipers (external), for checking the diameter of any medal suspected of being re-named. Naturally this can only be measured against a known unaffected medal, but a very large number of British medals are all exactly the same size, 1·42″ in diameter, so if you have, say, a late Victorian Army L.S. & G.C. Medal in good condition, you can use it to check a Military or Naval General Service, Crimea, Indian Mutiny, and a host of other medals. There are, however, some exceptions, such as Burmah 1823–26, the first Jellalabad Medal, the William IV Naval L.S. & G.C., and a few others; furthermore, among certain issues there are very slight deviations from the exact 1·42″, so it is preferable to check against another specimen of the medal in question. Lay the known medal on a table, and adjust the calliper screw so that the points just touch the edge and the callipers will all but pick up the medal. Then try the callipers on the suspect medal, particularly on that part of the edge where the naming occurs, It is practically impossible to remove a layer of metal from the edge. sufficient to leave no trace of an impressed or engraved naming, without the callipers showing a noticeable slackness. As a check, adjust the callipers to the suspect medal, and if it is re-named or otherwise reduced in size, the points will not fit the correct medal without the use of force. However, it should be remembered that occasionally with late or duplicate issues, a slightly different size collar was used in striking the medals, and this would give a very slightly different diameter.

Another possible accessory is a bottle of concentrated nitric acid, although you will only occasionally require it, to satisfy yourself if a suspect decoration is of base metal when it should be of silver or gold. This sometimes applies to foreign orders and other awards, often enamelled. These are frequently made commercially for jewellers specialising in this market, and are bought by recipients and collectors alike. Naturally, various qualities are available; most of these are in gold, silver-gilt, or silver, but sometimes also in bronze-gilt or some form of white metal, and you will not want to pay 'precious metal prices' for these last. To make the test, clean an inconspicuous spot on the decoration, and just touch it with a *tiny drop* of acid from the glass rod supplied with the bottle – and use an old rag, not a handkerchief or your finger, to remove the acid, otherwise severe burns will follow at once. Base metal will cause the acid to turn bright green or yellow, while gold will leave it colourless; silver will turn it blackish, the exact extent depending on the quality of the silver. It is a good plan to make some tests on defective medals or coins – most of our ordinary silver medals are of 0·925 fineness (the same as British hall-marked silver), whereas the Turkish Crimea Medal and many continental medals are only 0·800 silver, and you can note the difference in the reactions. Then try the acid on a modern cupro-nickel coin or the 1939-45 War Medal, and a green reaction will be seen.

## Methods of Collecting

As with philately, one usually starts as a general collector, and there is surely no better way of getting an all-round knowledge of the subject. But do not be persuaded to collect merely single specimens, refusing groups, for two reasons; first certain medals usually come in pairs or trios, and while one of the pair (or trio) might be awarded by itself, the other might not – for example, the King's South Africa Medal for the Boer War is *always* accompanied by the Queen's Medal, although one could get the latter without the former, consequently a 'lone' King's Medal is of little value, as it is virtually incomplete. Similarly, the 1914 Star (or 1914–15 Star) is always accompanied by the British War Medal and Victory Medal, and the (British) Victory Medal always has at least the British War Medal with it, but the last *can* be awarded by itself. Secondly, a group of several medals to one man frequently has a higher value than the same separate medals, and certainly has a greater interest, showing a period of service in various campaigns, perhaps in many countries, possibly showing a chain of promotion. Remember, too, that such items as the D.S.O., Military Cross, D.C.M., and similar awards almost certainly have other medals 'in tow'. It is not always possible to obtain the recipient's other medals, and a D.C.M. should not be refused on this account, but if you have the choice between a single D.C.M. and one in a group, choose the group. Of course, if you already have a single D.C.M. of the same reign, and do not wish to keep more than one, you can always dispose of it if a group turns up.

In these early days you will probably not mind very much to which regiment, or even to which branch of the services, the medals have been awarded. Some are cheaper than others: a Crimea Medal with four bars to the Guards will cost you more than a similar medal to one of the departmental corps, but much less than one to a man who took part in the Charge of the Light Brigade. But even the cheapest of these has a most interesting story behind it. The recipient shared in the terrible conditions of the Russian winter, in the various battles and the assaults on the fortress of Sebastopol, so this one medal alone can provide you with plenty of ideas for background reading.

During this stage, take every opportunity of examining medals at first hand. If you live within easy reach of any of the leading dealers, or can attend the viewing days of an auction sale, you will be able to handle plenty of medals. The dealers are always very willing to assist the *bona fide* collector, and beginners particularly will find patient attention given to their many questions. Museums are rather less forthcoming, but often if an approach is made to the curator for the opportunity to examine the style of naming on the various medals (having convinced him that a knowledge of these styles is essential to the student and collector), you may be afforded every assistance. But remember that museum collections may well include some re-named medals, especially if their object is to depict the range of medals rather than to exhibit the collection of an experienced collector (but it does not always pay to point out the 'duds').

In due course you will probably feel the urge to specialise, perhaps in just one or two regiments in which you have a special interest; they may be units in which you or your family have served, regiments associated with the counties of your birth or residence, regiments which particularly appeal to you for their fine fighting record; if your interests have maritime leanings, then the medals of the Royal Navy or Royal Marines may strike your fancy.

There are several ways in which you can build up a specialised collection. First, you can make it subsidiary to your general collection, choosing whenever possible groups and single medals to the units of special interest, but retaining other medals for campaigns in which your units did not participate. Secondly, you can concentrate strongly on your specialised items, and only include such other medals as happen to come your way. And, finally, you can collect *only* items to your particular units. Quite a number of collectors follow this last method, but I do feel that it has serious disadvantages unless the scope is very wide. For instance, suppose you limit yourself to two regiments; you may find that only one of them was entitled to the Military General Service Medal, 1793–1814, and only gained two or three bars, while neither was at Waterloo or any of the earlier Indian campaigns; on the other hand both were in the Crimea and the Indian Mutiny and so on. This means that a large number of interesting medals will automatically be excluded from your collection, but this can be avoided to a large extent by having a wide group of specialised interests, such as all Scottish or all Irish Regiments (infantry and cavalry), or Royal Artillery, or one of the corps such as the Royal Engineers, R.A.M.C., or R.A.S.C. (with their predecessors and associated units).

When specialising you should also collect, whether in groups or as single items, awards to your units for gallantry and life-saving, including those of semi-official bodies such as the Royal Humane Society, also regimental medals of the type given for merit during the Peninsular War.

Another quite popular method of collecting, is to group the collection into countries, continents, or subjects, with special attention to say, Indian or African campaigns, or concentrating on Defences and Reliefs. Other collectors try to build up a set of medals covering all the regiments or ships participating in specific campaigns, *e.g.* Waterloo, China 1842, or the B.E.F. of 1914, while some choose medals to regiments which gained battle honours in each action.

### Records – Accession Book; Card Index; Catalogue of Collection

Three types of records are really desirable, particularly when the collection begins to grow in size. First, you should keep an accession book, in which you briefly enter particulars of every medal or group as you acquire them, such as date, medal, name and unit of recipient, price paid (in code, if you prefer), and where bought. For example: "29.11.76. Grp. of 3, Sgt. W. Smith, RFA: Geo.V MM, BWM, Vic. £28. X & Co."

It is useful to carry this book with you wherever you go (mine lives permanently in my brief case), as frequently it is necessary to refer to it, when contemplating further purchases, when discussing medals with another collector, and so on. It can, of course, be a loose-leaf section of the price reference catalogue already described, and many collectors keep it in this way.

Secondly, keep a card index with fuller details; the above example will expand into: "Group of 3 ot Sgt. W. Smith, RFA: (1) MILI-TARY MEDAL (Geo. V). Impr. narrow caps. 123456 BDR. W. SMITH, 84 BDE.R.F.A. (2) BRITISH WAR MEDAL. Impr. square caps. 123456 SGT. W. SMITH, R.A. (3) VICTORY

MEDAL. Impr. as previous but narrow caps. Oakleaf on ribbon for M.I.D. MM. *London Gazette*, 9.2.16. MID. *L.G.*, 16.2.16. All about EF, on brooch as worn. 29.11.76. £28. X.& Co."

Later you can compile a full catalogue, with each item on a page, neatly set out, with any further information which you have found. Perhaps the recipient was wounded or killed in action, or (in the case of officers' medals and the higher awards for bravery) you have been able to trace his services, with promotions, or the citation for an award. Family details might perhaps be found in *Burke's Peerage*, *Kelly's Handbook to the Titled, Landed and Official Classes, Who's Who* (these books are always worth buying, secondhand), or other sources. You may have found a portrait of a recipient, or extracts from a regimental history concerning him or the actions in which he won his medals, and all this can go into the catalogue. Sometimes information is scanty, but with patience and diligence it is surprising how much detail we can often discover. Some collectors like to photograph their medals, or at least the more important items, and prints of these can be used to illustrate the catalogue. If the record is a loose-leaf one, new entries can easily be inserted in the correct chronological (or other) order, while pages relating to items disposed of can be extracted – often a purchaser will be pleased to have your notes.

### Buying from Dealers

Among beginners there is sometimes a tendency to feel that buying medals from the recognised numismatic dealers is liable to be very expensive, but the experienced collector will have somewhat different views. One must admit that the leading dealers have a pretty good idea of the value of each medal (as indeed they should) and the chance of picking up a real bargain is somewhat slender – but it does occasionally happen. Their prices, however, carry with them a guarantee which you will never get with a medal bought at an antique shop or a junk store. And although you may not get a cheap bargain, you will never be 'stung' by the leading dealers. The scarcer medals have often been verified with the medal rolls, and should subsequent investigation – even some years afterwards – prove that a medal bought from them was falsely named or otherwise defective, they will take it back and allow you the purchase price in full. They will always give you a receipt identifying medals bought, and collectors would be wise to file these for reference. Furthermore, if after some years you tire of a certain medal or group – you may acquire a better specimen, or revise your method of collecting – the dealer from whom you bought it will usually give you a very good price for it, especially if you offer it in part exchange or for a credit note. It would be a very different story if you took a medal back to the local antique shop.

But this does not mean that you should not look out for local bargains, although frequently the prices asked by miscellaneous vendors are very high, often much higher than those of numismatic firms. This is often due to ignorance, the fear of selling something too cheaply, and the practice of making too high a rate of profit; one provincial antique dealer regularly buys medals from one of the well-known London medal firms, and puts them in his window at exactly double the purchase price. During recent years, several lots of defective medals – renamed or repaired – have been bought at medal auctions by small antique dealers and junk shop owners, and quickly appear in their shops or stalls, ready for the gullible beginner.

Bearing in mind the guarantee behind the prices of the leading dealers (plus the fact that they will include a new piece of ribbon if at all possible), you should not pay more than about two-thirds, or at the most three-quarters, of their prices when buying in an unknown market, and certainly many collectors buy and sell among themselves on approximately this basis. For this reason it is as well to compile your price reference list in a notebook of convenient size to carry in a pocket or brief case, and substantial enough to stand constant reference.

## Auction Sales

Auction sales provide a most useful training ground, both on the viewing days and at the actual sales – if you can take the time off to attend. Several sales of medals and decorations are held each year by Glendining & Co. Ltd., and by Sotheby Parke Bernet & Co., while Messrs. Wallis & Wallis, of Lewes, Sussex, also frequently include a number of medal lots in their sales of weapons, uniforms, etc.

As regards buying, there are three ways of doing this, namely, by personal attendance, by instructing the auctioneer, or by instructing an independent agent, preferably one of the leading dealers. If you are able to attend personally, you can examine each lot for yourself, or at any rate those lots which interest you. For the benefit of those who are not experienced bidders, perhaps some advice may prove useful. In the first place, keep very quiet about which lots you intend bidding for – even among medal collectors, all's fair at auction sales, and many mark their limit figures in code in their catalogues, so that their very good friends (but keen rivals) shall not know how far they are prepared to go. It is prudent to decide in advance what your limit bids are to be, and then see that the auctioneer is getting your bids. You can bid by voice, by a wave of the catalogue (don't do this to welcome the entrance of a friend, or you may find yourself the buyer of an expensive unwanted lot), by lifting a pencil, or by various other means which the auctioneer will recognise when you become a 'regular'; but in the early stages stick to one of the first two. Avoid shouting eagerly, or everybody will know you are dead keen to get the lot, and make sure you do not get 'auction fever', being tempted to continue bidding way above your limit.

When a rare medal is going very cheaply, be very wary; all the lots have usually been carefully examined before the sale by many experts, both collectors and dealers, and it is unlikely that they will all keep quiet if a genuine medal is being offered.

If you are unable to be present at the sale, although you may perhaps have seen the medals on viewing day, you can give or send your bids to the auctioneer. There is an order form in the catalogues obtained direct from the firm, and if you mark your limit bids, together with any special instructions, the auctioneer will bid for you and obtain the lots as cheaply as possible, having regard to the reserve price and other bids received or made at the sale. Glendining's and Sotheby's conditions of sale include a proviso that a lot can be returned within a certain time if it should prove to be not as described; this is a valuable safeguard, and not always to be found at other sales.

If you are unable to view or to be present, the best method is to place your bids in the hands of *one* of the leading dealers. Admittedly, they charge you 5 per cent. of the purchase price for their services, but as they examine each item with expert knowledge, they will not buy an item for you if there is any doubt as to its genuineness. Also, if you are interested in only one or two medals of a large lot, they can sometimes arrange for you to have these advantageously, especially if another client is interested in a different part of the same lot.

Medals with a story

(*Left*) Naval General Service Medal, 1793–1840, to Midsn. A. F. Parr.

(*Right*) Military General Service Medal, 1793–1814, to Pte. Charles Fraser, 92nd Foot.

Plate 2.

Medals with a story
(*Above*) Arctic Medal, 1818–55, to William Mumford, HMS *Resolute*.
(*Below*) Pair to T. H. Treagus, AB., RN. – Royal Humane Society's Silver Medal and Naval Long Service & Good Conduct Medal.

Plate 3.

No matter how much you want a certain lot, do not ask your agent (whether auctioneer or dealer) to accept an unlimited bid – somebody else may have sent the same instructions to another agent, and then comes the problem of who is going to stop first. For this reason, most agents will not accept a 'no limit' bid.

If you personally attend a sale, make a note in your catalogue of the prices realised (also the buyer's names – this information may come in useful at a later date), and as soon as possible transfer those which are relevant into your reference book. It is sometimes said that current auction prices reflect the true values of medals, but this is true only to a limited extent, the prices depending largely on how many people want a particular medal, and how badly they want it. Some years ago I sent a pair of medals for auction, which would normally have made between £6 and £8; to my surprise (and delight), they made £18. However, this did not mean that the true value of the pair was £18, but merely (as I learned later) that two retired officers of the regiment concerned both wanted the medals, and neither would give way to the other. If a similar pair of medals had appeared later in the same sale, or at a subsequent sale, they would probably have fetched only the normal price, as one of the two chief contestants would, presumably, have been satisfied.

For those interested in foreign medals, it might appear likely that buying at foreign auction sales could be advantageous. However, there are several possible snags which can arise. First, in most European countries the buyer (in addition to the vendor) has to pay the auctioneer a commission, which can be as high as 15 %. Secondly, in some countries there is a tax imposed on purchasers (in addition to the commission), although sometimes this only applies to nationals of the country concerned. Thirdly, postage, packing and insurance charges are likely to be higher than in Great Britain, consequently the total cost, including bank charges (not to mention the possibility of customs charges), of any successful bid will be significantly higher than the 'knock down' figure. Furthermore, at the time of writing the low value of the pound sterling means that the normally rather high continental prices are even higher to British buyers.

Unless one is able to attend personally, it is only possible to send a postal bid, although for some of the more important continental sales a few British dealers usually attend (and advertise the fact in their price lists), and they will act as agents for any of their customers, usually at a fee of 5% of the purchase price (this is in addition to any other charges already mentioned, but at least is a safeguard against buying rubbish). With these foreign auctions it is not always possible for postal bidders to return incorrectly described items (including forgeries or defective pieces), and consequently, while undoubtedly some advantageous purchases can be made, the less experienced collector is advised to weigh up all the pro's and con's before involving himself too deeply.

## Selling Medals

If you have medals to dispose of, any of the leading dealers will be glad to make you an offer, unless the items are very common. There will not be much difference in their quotations, and rarely is anything gained by visiting each in turn, hoping to get a better offer. If you bought any of the scarcer items from one of these firms, it is probable that the dealer concerned will give you the best price. One advanatge of selling to a reputable dealer is that he will be prepared to make allowances for any special feature – perhaps one medal is particularly scarce to a certain regiment, or the recipient later became a famous General.

An alternative method is to sell at auction. You may well receive a higher price although it is, perhaps, something of a gamble. In recent years, however, sales have not been very frequent and prices have been fairly high – at any rate for the better class items. You can safeguard the risk of low prices by putting a reserve figure on each item, and the auctioneer will then not sell a lot unless the bidding reaches at least this figure. It is, of course, unwise to stipulate too high a reserve, as if the bidding does not reach this figure, you will have to pay a small commission, usually 5 per cent. of the reserve price. Generally speaking, medals of any consequence make their full market value, as with the increase in the number of collectors and a shortage of better class material, the demand exceeds the supply. It must be remembered that lots sold are subject to a commission of $12\frac{1}{2}$ per cent. or 15 per cent., and consequently you should consider if the net result is likely to bring a better price than would be obtained from a reputable dealer. Remember, too, that unless you are selling a large collection which justifies an immediate cash advance, you will have to wait some time before settlement; this will depend largely on how soon the auctioneers are able to include your lots in a sale, and you can expect settlement in about two to four weeks after that date.

A third way of disposing of medals is to offer them direct to other collectors, either by writing personally to collectors known to you, or by advertising in suitable journals such as *The Exchange and Mart*. By this means you will probably realise prices somewhere between what a dealer will pay and his selling price. It takes time, of course, and there may be a risk of incurring bad debts. Collectors will expect to pay you appreciably less than they would pay a dealer, even if you are prepared to give the same guarantee as the leading dealers give – but this is balanced by the similarly lower prices which you will probably enjoy when buying from other collectors.

Finally, whenever selling medals be careful to point out any defects. Even if these have been taken into account when quoting the price, the buyer may well feel dissatisfied when he finds them out for himself. Although there is a well-known latin tag, *caveat emptor* (let the buyer beware) there has been, in the past, a code of honour among numismatic dealers and collectors which did not have to rely on such a warning. But in recent years several instances have occurred in which collectors have had occasion to be very dissatisfied with some of the lesser dealers. It is known that some dealers have been impressing names on unnamed (as issued) medals, particularly Crimea – not only 'named' to known participants in the charge of the Light Brigade and Heavy Brigade, but to others as well – and Baltic medals (to Royal Sappers & Miners); others have been buying up unnamed medals with *S.E. Asia 1945-46* and *Bomb & Mine Clearance 1945-49* bars and naming them in what looks like an official style; Military Crosses for both wars have had genuine names engraved on the *rev.*, and those for 1939-45 have been offered for sale with the appropriate stars and war medals added. Copy medals have made their appearance, cast from genuine medals, so that even the naming is copied; while these are not very dangerous, they might easily deceive beginners, so when buying "bargains" from barrows, market stalls, and railway arches, and also from junk shops and miscellaneous dealers who seem to "specialise" in medals, one should always be suspicious and carefully examine *all* medals before buying – there are even copies of Defence Medals and War (1939-45) Medals! – and there is no chance of such vendors refunding your money if you try to return any "dud" medals bought from them.

# Medal Collecting – II

## Housing and Mounting the Collection

Advice is often sought on the best way to house and mount a collection of medals, but like so many questions on collecting, there just is no 'best way'. So much depends on circumstances, individual tastes, the scope of the collection, and other factors.

The two most popular methods are (1) in cabinets having fairly large trays, and (2) in glazed wall cases. Briefly summarised, the former method is more compact, while the latter is more spectacular; but let us consider further their respective advantages and disadvantages.

The choice of size and workmanship of the cabinet necessarily depends on the funds available, and it will be found more economical to have comparatively few large trays, rather than twice the number of small ones; also the larger trays enable one to make a more attractive display. A very suitable size is $18'' \times 15''$ by at least $\frac{1}{2}''$ clear internal depth ($\frac{5}{8}''$ is better if there are likely to be foreign orders with rosettes, etc.). The floor of the trays should be of fairly soft wood (not cedar), and covered with a fine quality green baize, thin felt, or velvet, of a suitable colour. Some collectors of medals to Scottish regiments cover the tray with material of the respective regimental tartans.

## Making a Cabinet

It is by no means difficult to build a cabinet, at a fraction of the cost of a new or secondhand ready made one, especially as nowadays one can easily get attractively veneered timber from DIY shops, with veneer strips to finish off sawn edges, and moulding to embellish the top and base. The following instructions are purely basic, and exact sizes will have to be determined by individual requirements. For the purpose of illustration, we are assuming a cabinet of, say, fifteen trays, each $18'' \times 15''$, to be built in mahogany veneered board (which is made under various trade names), $\frac{1}{2}''$ thick (*Fig. 1*).

Components: base board and top board, each $19\frac{1}{4}'' \times 16\frac{1}{2}''$
2 side boards, $16'' \times 13\frac{1}{8}''$ Back board, $18\frac{1}{4}'' \times 13\frac{1}{8}''$
2 doors, each $9\frac{5}{8}'' \times 13\frac{1}{8}''$
(all the above, $\frac{1}{2}''$ thick)
30 running strakes, $15'' \times \frac{3}{16}'' \times \frac{3}{16}''$
15 trays of plywood (or similar), $18'' \times 15'' \times \frac{1}{8}''$
30 pieces of soft wood, $18'' \times \frac{1}{2}'' \times \frac{1}{8}''$
30    ,,       $14\frac{3}{4}'' \times \frac{1}{2}'' \times \frac{1}{8}''$
(Alternatively these can be $18''$ and $15''$ long, respectively, and mitred)
4 brass hinges, $1\frac{1}{2}'' \times \frac{1}{2}''$
30 (or 15 if desired) brass button knobs with $\frac{3}{8}''$ screw fitting.
2 brass sliding tongues for top and bottom of one door.
1 brass lock for door (or alternative, as below).
Sufficient moulding, $\frac{1}{2}''$ deep, for front and two sides of top and base, and veneer strip, $\frac{1}{2}''$ wide, for exposed edges.

First glue and pin (or screw) the running strakes to the side pieces, at exact intervals of $\frac{7}{8}''$ (i.e. from the *bottom* of one strake to the *bottom* of the next), the lowest being flush with the bottom of the side piece. This gives a gap of $\frac{11}{16}''$ between each, to receive a tray with a total height of $\frac{5}{8}''$. See that the strakes run from $\frac{1}{2}''$ from the front edge to $\frac{1}{2}''$ from the back edge.

The two sides should now be glued and screwed to the back, with countersunk screwholes to be filled with plastic wood and covered with a circle of veneer (this can be made with a punch or a gouge of suitable size). The top and base should then be similarly glued and screwed to the back and sides, making sure that the base protrudes $\frac{1}{2}''$ at the front to allow for the doors; see constructional details in Fig. 1.

It is essential that the doors are hinged *onto* (and not *inside*) the side pieces, so that they will open cleanly to allow the trays to come out. The brass slide stoppers should first be fitted into the top and bottom of the right hand door, and the appropriate sockets drilled into the top and base to receive the pin when slid closed. Also the lock must be fitted into the edge of the left hand door, either in the centre of the right edge (to lock into the other door) or in the top of the door, near the right side (to lock into the top of the cabinet); if the latter method is preferred, then two locks will be required, one

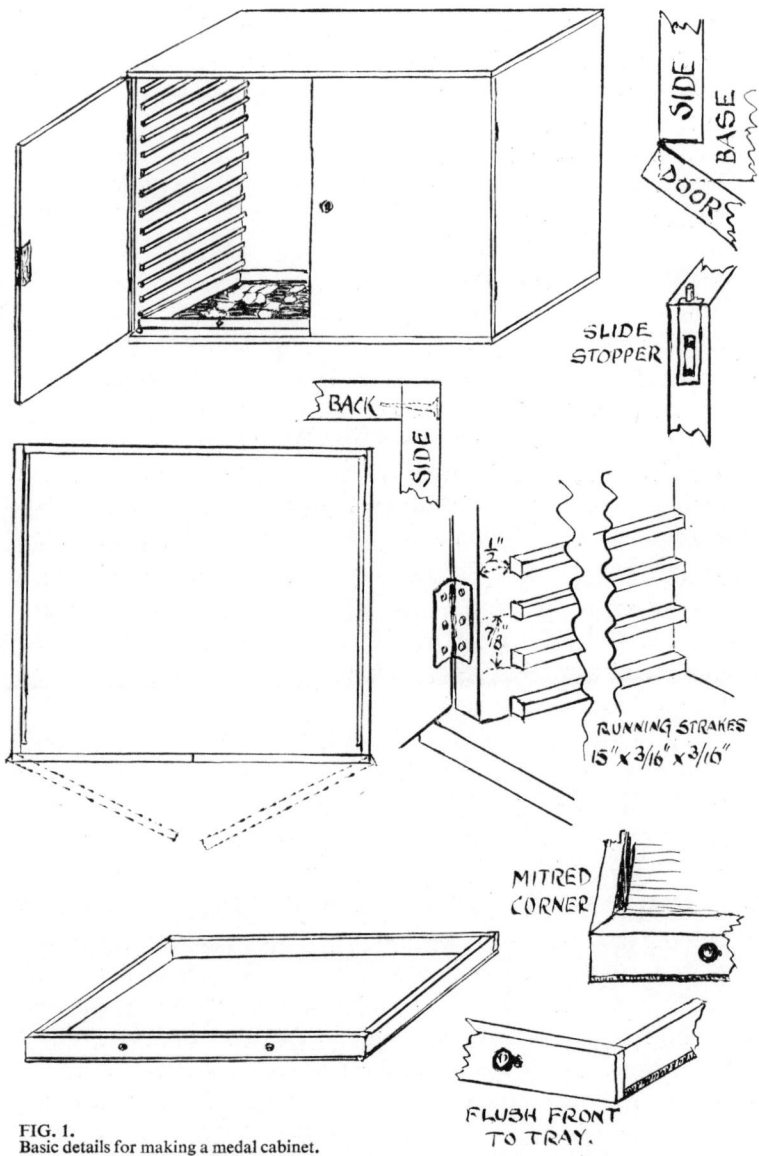

SIDE

BASE

DOOR

SLIDE STOPPER

BACK

SIDE

$\frac{1}{2}''$

$\frac{7}{8}''$

RUNNING STRAKES
15" x 3/16" x 3/16"

MITRED CORNER

FLUSH FRONT TO TRAY.

FIG. 1.
Basic details for making a medal cabinet.

for each door, and instead of fitting a slide stopper to the top of the right door, it should be put at the bottom of the left door. For those who cannot fit a lock into a door, an alternative is to have two rings with a nut-and-bolt fitting, one on each door near the edge, and secured by a good quality (small) brass padlock.

The moulding (not shown in Fig. 1) should be mitred and fitted round the top, bottom and sides. Similarly, if desired, a very narrow moulding can be applied to the doors. All exposed sawn ends should now be covered by veneer strip, glued in position.

The trays are also simple to make, with the sides glued, and pinned from below. The four sides can either be mitred for a neat finish, or can be cut square, the front and back running the full $18''$, while the side pieces will be $14\frac{3}{4}''$ long. However, if it is desired to have the front of the tray flush (i.e. without the base showing), the base will have to be $18'' \times 14\frac{7}{8}''$, and the front $18'' \times \frac{5}{8}'' \times \frac{1}{8}''$ (the back strip will be $18'' \times \frac{1}{2}'' \times \frac{1}{8}''$ as before).

The floors of the trays can be covered as desired, with velvet, green baize, art felt, or other suitable material, fixed in position with Copydex or other fixatif.

An existing cabinet can be similarly converted, but if (as usually is the case) the doors are hinged *inside* the walls, then the trays cannot pull out. To overcome this it will be necessary to fit panels or false sides (with the running strakes, as above) of sufficient thickness to allow the trays a clear run. Even if the doors are hinged correctly for our purpose, it will still be desirable to fit a plywood panel, suitably stained, to each side, with the running strakes already in position. By this means you can not only make sure that each pair of strakes is accurately lined up, but since they can be pinned *through* the panel to the strake, this will be much easier than trying to fit them into an already constituted shell.

A collection mounted in wall cases provides a more spectacular display, and is very suitable for the collector who is fortunate enough to have his own 'den' or medal room. Such cases can, of course, be used in conjunction with a cabinet, in order to show to advantage some of the more interesting groups, perhaps those of family connections or special tributes to certain regiments. The cases themselves will probably vary considerably in size, as opportunities arise to acquire them, but it is as well to keep to one type of wood – mahogany is the most usual, but avoid oak and cedar. Wall cases, like cabinets, are expensive to have made, but they can frequently be obtained at auction sales, including local sales of house furniture, where you might find cases containing collections of butterflies or beetles going cheaply and quite suitable for medals. Again, the handyman can improvise by buying suitable picture frames, which can be deepened by adding strips of wood at the back, so that the 'tray' is sufficiently clear of the glass to accommodate decorations as required. The only disadvantage of converted frames is that it is usually necessary to remove the back to get at the contents, whereas proper wall cases have the glass front hinged so that it can be opened from the front. Another point to bear in mind is that if any of the walls are exposed to sunlight, the ribbons will fade more quickly than those in a cabinet, and thus the cost of occasional re-ribboning must be borne in mind.

As regards the actual mounting of medals in the tray or wall case, most collectors use a best quality brass drawing pin (solid brass is better than brassed or plated ferrous metal, to avoid the damage caused by rust), and a small strip of stiff card, slightly shorter than the width of the ribbon and about $\frac{1}{2}''$ deep; the pin is pushed through the centre of the card, and then through the ribbon from the back. This is then turned over and pressed firmly into the tray, so that the medal hangs squarely and cleanly. A little practice will enable you to position a row of medals so that they all lie evenly. Occasionally you will have a medal with only a short piece of ribbon which is impossible to replace; this can often be adjusted to give a satisfactory appearance, either by having the ribbon single (apart from the bottom portion which goes through the suspender and is stitched neatly at each side), or – if it is nearly long enough – double, with the portion which turns over 'assisted' by using stiff gummed paper to make an extension just holding the edge of the ribbon (*Fig. 1a*). The drawing pin can then be pushed through the paper extension, which should be trimmed so that the sides do not show. When mounting medals in a wall case, it will probably be necessary to use tiny pins in strategic positions to prevent swinging when the case is vertical.

For those who must perforce aspire to a cabinet or wall cases at a future date, the problem of temporary housing is a little difficult.

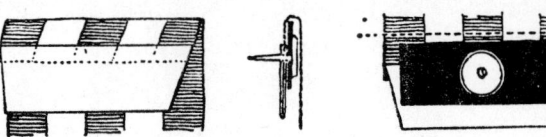

FIG. 1a.
Lengthening a ribbon, and method of mounting.

If, through limitations of accommodation, you just have no other facilities, you may have to resort to a file of envelopes, each containing one medal or group (with each medal protected by a tissue wrapping), but usually something better can be devised. Even a series of shirt boxes, or other shallow 'tray-like' boxes, can be put to good use, or a pile of wooden boards, say fourteen inches by ten, covered with velvet, can be used as a temporary 'cabinet', but if they are to be stacked, some provision must be made for keeping them apart so as not to damage the medals on the tray below.

Another problem which sometimes arises is the 'overflow' question. Our cabinet is, perhaps, crowded to the limit, and we just cannot afford another. One solution is to weed out a few items, and a start can be made on some groups which contain frequently duplicated medals. For example, in a group containing a Queen's South Africa, the 1914–18 trio, and an Imperial Yeomanry Long Service Medal, you could keep the first and the last in the cabinet, with a note on the little descriptive label (which I write in indian ink on white card, and affix with tiny map pins) that the group also includes the 1914–18 trio; these can then be relegated to an envelope marked with the name and contents, and a cross reference to the two medals in the cabinet. The same procedure could be used for D.C.M. groups and similar items. You may wish to keep duplicated items because they relate to one particular regiment; it is then practical to show the more interesting item, and provisionally store the duplicate away, thus leaving a little more room for subsequent acquisitions.

## Groups of Medals

Mention has already been made of groups of medals – by which we mean two or more medals to the same recipient, or to members of the same family (referred to as family groups) – and perhaps it would be as well to discuss the part these play in a collection.

Beginners frequently refuse groups, as they are aiming primarily at securing an example of each medal, arranged in chronological order, and in their opinion a group often upsets this idea, or results in duplication. Some have even been known to split a group, keeping the medals not yet represented in the collection and disposing of the remainder. To the experienced collector this is almost a criminal act, and many of us have medals – singles or groups – where we know that others are missing; sometimes they are medals for which we have been searching for years; sometimes we can trace that the group was complete some years ago, when it appeared in a dealer's list or sale catalogue, but now it exists shorn of one or two items.

As the beginner progresses he will realise that groups of medals have a greater personal interest. They not only show a series of campaigns in which the recipient served, but often show his rise in rank. As the medals begin to tell their story, perhaps with an award for gallantry or merit, so you will appreciate the greater value of the group, both historically and financially.

If you keep a reference list of all your medals in an indexed note-book, under the names of recipients, you may sometimes be lucky enough to find missing medals. Quite a number of Naval L.S. & G.C. medals (William IV and 'wide suspender' Victorian types) can be found to pair up with the Naval General Service Medal, particularly with the last three bars – *Algiers*, *Navarino*, and *Syria* – and with the China 1842 Medal, but beware of assuming that two medals named to such persons as, say, John Brown, William Smith, James Turner, and suchlike, are genuine pairs. If the N.G.S. medal roll shows John Brown as Sailmaker in H.M.S. *Penelope*, and the same rating and ship appear on the L.S. & G.C., then you are probably safe, as you are if the name is more unusual, say, Francis Fogg, even if rating and ship are different. Similarly, an *Algiers* bar to Pte Richard Lawson, R.M., can safely be paired with a long service medal to a Sergeant of Marines of the same name, but almost certainly not to one described as Ordinary Seaman, Landsman, or even Boatswain's Mate or Blacksmith (unless you can find evidence of a transfer in the ship's muster rolls in the Public Record Office, or other satisfactory verification).

With officers' medals it is usually much easier to check groups, *e.g.* from records of service in army and navy lists, regimental histories, and elsewhere. If you have a group with a medal missing, or suspected missing, which you bought from a recognised dealer, it may be that the missing medal was inadvertently detached and may still be among his stock – anyway, it is always worth while asking!

### Arrangement of Groups

What order should be used when arranging the items of a group in a collection? There is no complete answer, since we are free to please ourselves, but the choice usually lies between the correct order at the date of the last award, the revised order which may have been introduced while the recipient was still serving, and the actual order which authentic portraits (photographs or paintings by reliable artists) show that he adopted – frequently incorrect. For example, I had a group of three medals to a Vice-Admiral, which a photograph showed him to be wearing in the following order: India General Service, 1854 (bar – *Pegu*); Arctic, 1818–55; and Baltic, 1854–55. By modern regulations he should have worn the Arctic Medal last, but as he qualified for them in that order, that is how he wore them (even if, as I suspect, he received the Baltic before the Arctic Medal), and that is how they were arranged in my collection.

Evidence of paintings shows the Military General Service Medal worn sometimes before, sometimes after, the Waterloo Medal although the majority seem to be in favour of wearing the Waterloo Medal first. For many years the Victoria Cross and the D.C.M. were worn *after* the relative campaign medal, while frequently officers wore their medals to show a 'balanced' effect; thus a group to a General is shown in a painting (and also came up for auction with an obviously contemporary mounting) as follows: Cabul, 1842; Sutlej 1845; French Legion of Honour (on a longer ribbon); Crimea; Turkish Crimea. Thus the foreign decoration (which should have come after British medals, and before foreign medals) was deliberately misplaced in order to achieve a more artistic effect – but it would be a brave man who would reprimand a General who was also Governor of a Colony. It was not uncommon, judging by portraits, to find senior officers with their medals 'straying' well over to their right – presumably to avoid overlapping, while officers and other ranks alike sometimes wore a Victoria Cross in the centre of the left side, with four medals worn separately, to the 'north-west, north-east, south-east, and south-west' of it.

Until the First World War, Coronation and Jubilee medals were worn before campaign medals, and should be shown thus if the recipient was not serving after the alteration. Similarly the Army L.S. & G.C. ribbon with white edges, should be used on Victorian and Edwardian medals if the holders served long enough to have worn them thus. The same applies to other medals where the ribbon has been changed, such as the Reserve Decoration, R.N.R. Long Service Medal (and others), the Royal Humane Society's Silver Medal, and the various insignia of the Order of the British Empire. In the last case, however, the recipients have the right to retain the earlier ribbon with the first (Britannia) type insignia if they so desire; the present type insignia *must* have the pink and grey ribbon.

Another problem in arrangement is whether to show a group overlapped as worn, or adjacently. Again, you can please yourself; if pressed for space, or if the group is still stitched to the brooch (and you do not want to disturb it), you can display it overlapped, but take care to see that your trays are deep enough to accommodate them without danger of the medals being damaged through contact with the tray above or the dividing slats of the cabinet. If you have adequate space, the group looks better mounted without overlapping, and the risk of damage is avoided – overlapped medals acquire scratches very easily, both in wear and in collections. Some collectors have a strong objection to disturbing 'the original brooch as worn by the recipient', but unless you purchased the group from the recipient himself (with a sworn statement that the medals have never been disturbed since last worn) you cannot be sure that they were not neatly sewn on the brooch by a fellow collector who preferred them that way. Admittedly in most cases they are still just 'as worn', but does it really matter – does it really detract from the interest or value – if you decide to re-mount them, perhaps replacing dirty or worn ribbons, providing *you* are better pleased with the result?

As mentioned earlier, it is generally recognised as a 'crime' to split up groups of medals, and I am always rather disappointed to see in a dealer's stock, groups of medals with pieces of ribbon indicating where items have been cut off. Admittedly not all dealers indulge in this practice, and when they do, it is usually such items as a D.S.O., M.C., Coronation or Jubilee medals, or foreign awards, which are concerned. None of these, even if privately named, can be *positively* identified as the original, and from the more prosaic (and, perhaps, commonsense) point of view, these decorations can always be re-placed if desired – one Military Cross is just like another! But the purist will have none of this, preferring either the original or nothing, although if the dealer replaces the missing item before the buyer has ever seen the group, the latter is none the wiser and perfectly happy. After all, if you buy a group direct from the recipient or his family, you cannot *prove* that the D.S.O. or the Legion of Honour is the original – he may have lost or damaged it many years ago, and purchased a replacement. Surely the answer is that we must just use a certain amount of commonsense in our hobby. But if the recipients of decorations issued unnamed would have them named (where possible) at the time, many of these would not later be detached for sale as separate items.

On the question of naming, another very controversial point often arises. It is well known that some collectors have had the recipients' names and particulars engraved on unnamed decorations, etc. In many cases there is absolutely no doubt whatsoever that (a) the decorations really did belong to the respective recipients, and (b) the collectors concerned are completely honest and trustworthy. In a few cases there is no doubt that neither (a) nor (b) applies, and thus there are times when a prospective purchaser cannot feel entirely satisfied. Consequently a collector should seriously consult his conscience before having decorations named. One cannot lay down any law, and in certain circumstances the practice may be justified. My own feelings on the matter are generally against it, although I must admit that I have twice had medals named – once by permission of the recipient, and once at the request of the recipient's widow; in both cases the medals came to me direct, and my conscience was quite clear, but I would strongly deprecate the practice as a regular habit.

This question is particularly pertinent in view of the recent disturbing situation, where it has been discovered that unnamed Crimea, Baltic, and other medals have been *impressed* in a style almost undetectable from the genuine naming, and sold to both collectors and dealers as genuinely named medals.

In view of this, many collectors are, quite rightly, completely against buying or selling any medals which are not genuinely and *contemporarily* named, in the official or regimental (or "Depot") impressing or engraved either officially or in an undoubtedly recognisable style of the period, such as that undertaken by a local jeweller who named a whole batch of medals for a particular regiment – an example of this is the Cabul 1842 Medal to the 9th Foot, issued unnamed but usually found engraved in an easily recognisable style (see Fig. 4c), and unquestionably executed at the time (see also the notes on Unnamed Medals, p. 31).

### The Condition of Medals

By the term 'condition' we mean the state of preservation, and in everything of value which is collected, condition has an important bearing on desirability, value, and price, Really fine items are usually much scarcer than worn or defective ones (although not so much in medals, as in coins and antiques), and the prices, or market values, vary accordingly.

The present system of grading condition, used by most dealers and collectors in Great Britain, is as satisfactory as any, for the better grades, but the lower terms do not mean quite what they say – except *Poor*, which usually means *terrible*. The grades are:

FDC – (*Fleur de coin*), *Mint*, or *Brilliant:* in pristine condition, with no scratches or blemishes.

EF  – *Extremely fine:* a really nice medal, only just falling short of FDC.

VF  – *Very Fine:* no major defects, but perhaps with a few minor scratches, edge knocks, or contact marks.

F  – *Fine:* rather scratched, marked or worn, or perhaps would be graded higher but for a rickety suspender.

*Fair*, *Good* and *Poor* usually mean progressively poorer conditions; I would prefer the last four grades to be read as *Not very good*, *Poor*, *Bad* and *Terrible*, while many medals described as VF can really only be designated as fine or fair, in non-numismatic language.

In practice, there are so many differences in condition, that it is not easy to stick firmly to the official gradings, and so we often find a slightly better state listed as *Good EF* or *Good VF*, while a little below standard may be shown as *Nearly EF* or *About EF*. It is also usual to make reference to bars or suspender, if damaged on an otherwise satisfactory medal, e.g. EF, *but top bar has been re-soldered*.

Condition affects the prices of coins more than medals, but nevertheless a medal in poorer condition does usually mean a somewhat lower price. There are some collectors who prefer medals showing some signs of wear (for which, no doubt, they expect to pay correspondingly lower prices) on the grounds that they have graced a hero's breast, while the FDC or EF example may never have been actually worn! I must confess I like my medals to be in as fine condition as possible, but bearing in mind that the earlier medals of a group will often be in poorer condition than the later ones, and medals to cavalrymen and field officers of infantry regiments frequently show contact scratches and other wear marks from jangling.

Brooch marks are another source of worry – and devaluation – for the collector. In the middle and late nineteenth century particularly, it was fashionable for the wives or widows of soldiers and sailors to mount the medal itself, usually shorn of its suspender and bars, as a brooch. These medals are often seen nowadays, with melted or filed solder marks at the 'east and west' points, where the pin-hinge and catch have been removed; they have usually regained their suspenders (and bars, too), and one wonders if perhaps these have never been removed, or if the wearer had carefully kept them for future replacement. Failing either of these unlikely explanations, one is forced to conclude that somebody has fitted the medal with a new suspender and bars; if the bars are those to which the recipient was entitled, the medal may be considered as acceptable (at a reduced price) until a better specimen comes along, but many collectors would prefer to let it pass them by.

Another method of brooch adaption is more difficult to spot, and therefore more dangerous; this is the silver ring, usually ornamental, with the hinge and catch soldered to the back, thus avoiding the need of disfiguring the medal; the medal is set in the centre of the ring, with pivot pins fitted at the top and bottom. When re-constituted, the upper pin hole is occupied by the mount, while the lower one is neatly plugged with a piece of silver rod, and the naming (if affected) perhaps engraved to match. Sometimes this is difficult to spot at first glance, but a careful examination with a magnifying glass will show it. The most usual medals found with this defect include the Naval General Service, Military G.S., Army of India, China 1842, and campaigns up to the Crimea and Baltic, but occasionally later medals were also treated in this way.

### Unnamed Medals

British medals, although usually named, are not necessarily so, and beginners do not always need to refuse medals with a plain edge, Unnamed medals fall into three categories: (1) Those issued unnamed, but some of which are found subsequently named, either officially or privately; (2) Those which are proofs or 'specimens', but not marked as such, and (3) Those from which the name has been erased. Let us consider each category separately.

(1) Quite a number of medals were issued unnamed, including Burmah 1826, Ghuznee 1839, Candahar, Ghuznee, Cabul, Jellalabad, Crimea, Baltic, China 1857 (to Navy), Arctic 1818–55, NW Canada, and several others. Of these, the Burmah 1826 is rarely found named, while that for Ghuznee 1839 is frequently found with the name, rank, and regiment engraved either on the edge or in the reverse field.

Some of the other Afghan War medals were engraved or punched, probably under regimental arrangements, since the styles are often the same to men of the same regiment, but unnamed ones are frequently found and command a somewhat lower price. The Crimea Medal could be returned for official naming, and many are found so impressed, in the same style as the M.G.S., while others are punched in irregular letters – often termed 'Depot named' as one style is common to a particular regiment and it would appear that they were all done by the same man. Others are engraved, again frequently in a style common to a regiment, and these were either done privately or taken to a local jeweller. It is important to learn the styles of lettering employed at various periods for the regiments in which one is interested, but do not overlook the fact that even a roughly engraved medal may be perfectly genuine, as Pte. Jones might have engraved his own medals if he felt that he could handle a graver or some similar tool.

Baltic Medals were sometimes privately engraved, while about a hundred to the Royal Sappers and Miners were officially impressed (See Chapter 6).

It is, of course, well known that the Campaign Stars and Medals for the 1939–45 War were issued unnamed as regards British and Canadian personnel; those to Australian and South African troops are usually found named.

(2) Some medals are never seen unnamed, unless they are 'specimens', remainders, or re-strikes. The first often have the word *Specimen* impressed in tiny letters, either on the edge or in the field of the medal, but not always; they are occasionally produced by the Royal Mint, either for official reference purposes or for the use of approved museums. Sometimes, in common with remainders, they get out onto the market instead of being melted down if no longer required officially. These include some of the East India Company's medals for long service, etc. They are useful to fill gaps in a collection, especially if rare, but are worth much less than a named medal. Another class of medal which is often found unnamed is that manufactured for sale in the jewellery and tailoring trades; these are exact copies of, mainly, modern medals, but are without the designers' initials in the appropriate places. They include such items as the George VI and Elizabeth II D.C.M., M.M., Efficiency Medal, Jubilee and Coronation Medals, the R.A.F. decorations, and others. They have a high retail price, but are worth very little to

collectors; if named, they are unofficially engraved, but are normally offered for sale with plain edges.

(3) Medals are often found with the name, etc., wholly or partly erased. This may have been done for one of several reasons; unfortunately, relatives often erase the name when disposing of medals, ignorant of the fact that they are thereby reducing the value to scrap metal price; perhaps the medals have been used as replacements by entitled persons who did not want the expense of having them re-named; sometimes an officer, commissioned from the ranks, erased the lower rank shown on his earlier medals.

Some medals with the name erased have a value above the silver price, because they are rare, but generally speaking they have no appeal to the serious collector.

## Re-Named Medals

Perhaps the biggest snag which the collector encounters is the problem of re-named medals. Generally speaking, these originate through a recipient losing his medals – perhaps having them stolen – and obtaining replacements. Unless he is entitled to obtain an official re-issue (*q.v.*), he will probably buy the appropriate medals from a jeweller, military tailor, or medal dealer, having the original names erased and his own substituted. Unfortunately, from the collector's viewpoint, the value is thus reduced to the same level as those with names erased.

These medals are nearly always engraved – only rarely are they impressed – and it would be quite a coincidence if the lettering matched the original style. Such re-naming is not intended to deceive collectors. If the original is a medal which is *always* impressed, such as the Waterloo Medal and many others, then an engraved one *must* be re-named, or at any rate, not an original issue.

When examining a medal for evidence of re-naming, the state of the edge, where the original name has been erased, at once catches the eye; it is usually slightly rounded instead of being dead square in section (*Fig. 2*), and the narrowness of the rim in the lower segment is plainly noticeable. Also since it is usually 'buffed-up' on a machine, it acquires a polished appearance quite different from a normal edge that has not been so treated. Sometimes the re-naming is very neatly executed, but even so it strikes one immediately as 'wrong', provided one knows what the correct naming should look like.

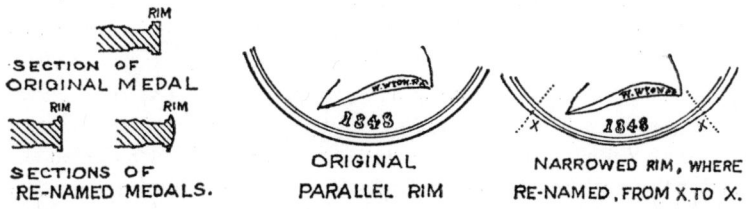

FIG. 2.
Features of a re-named medal. In practice, the narrowed rim usually occupies a longer arc than is shown.

Unfortunately, there is another category of re-named medals, designed to deceive, and here we can include false naming on 'unnamed as issued' medals, such as those for the First Afghan War and the Crimea. Some years ago an unscrupulous gentleman prepared a set of punches very similar to the lettering of the Military and Naval General Service Medals, Army of India Medal, etc. Luckily there are several features by which these can be recognised; sometimes the alignment is not dead straight (but this is not a certain test as some of the genuine naming is also badly aligned); the false naming is often uneven in depth, usually erring on the heavy side (but again some genuine medals have the lettering more deeply impressed than normal). But in addition to these features, the letters themselves show differences, particularly E, F, and N (*Fig. 3*). There have been other 'false impressers', but not to the same extent as the one mentioned above, and further details will be given under the medals concerned.

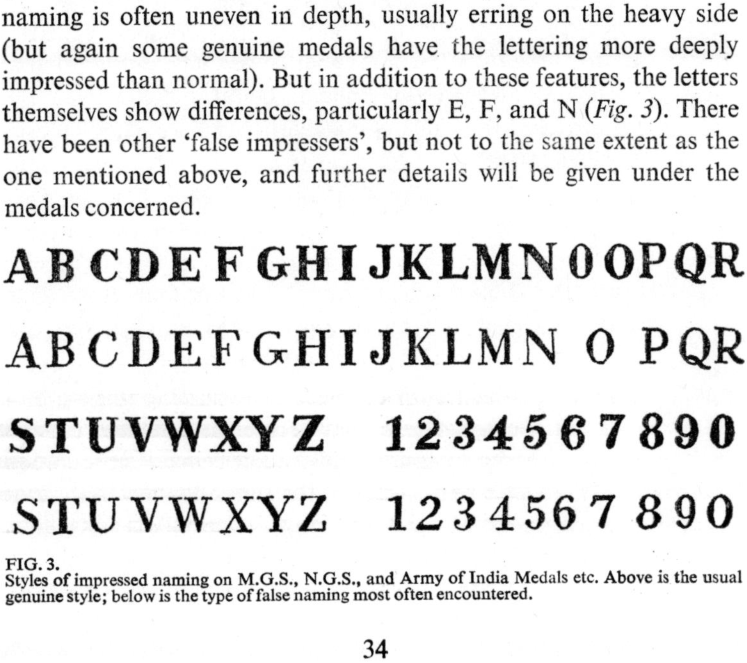

# A B C D E F G H I J K L M N 0 O P Q R

## A B C D E F G H I J K L M N O P Q R

# S T U V W X Y Z    1 2 3 4 5 6 7 8 9 0

## S T U V W X Y Z    1 2 3 4 5 6 7 8 9 0

FIG. 3.
Styles of impressed naming on M.G.S., N.G.S., and Army of India Medals etc. Above is the usual genuine style; below is the type of false naming most often encountered.

34

The best way of learning to spot re-naming, is to be familiar with the style of naming normally used with each medal. Sometimes this is not difficult, but in several cases a variety of styles exists. For example, the India G.S. 1854 varies considerably, both in impressed and engraved styles, according to the bars; the Zulu War Medal, 1877-79, has several styles of engraving, while the Queen's and King's South Africa Medals have two or three styles of impressing and several of engraving (and a pair of these last may have one medal engraved and the other impressed). The George V D.F.M. and A.F.M. boh have a rounded edge and are usually rather poorly engraved, so that in this case the *genuine* medal looks exactly like a 're-named'.

## Other Defective Medals

When buying a medal, from whatever source, always take care to examine every part of it, including the mount, suspender, bars, and rivets. Sometimes repairs are hidden by the ribbon. and if this can be removed for inspection, so much the better. Not every re-soldered bar is a sign of fiddling; sometimes a bar has 'sprung' and has been neatly repaired, in which case it has very little effect on either the price or the desirability. Perhaps the mount has been repaired; this may be a genuine repair to a genuine medal, but you should not overlook the possibility of a fresh mount, suspender, and a set of rare bars, having been fitted to a normally common medal. A medal which should normally swivel should be checked to see that, in fact, it does so. Do not, however, force a medal which is on the tight side, also remember that some modern medals, such as the Naval L.S. & G.C. (George V), Army and R.A.F. General Service (George VI and Elizabeth II), and several others, can be found both swivelling and non-swivelling, so be careful not to damage the latter by too eager a test – in point of fact, you can spot the presence or absence of the swivel pin, and the slightly different types of mount, by close inspection.

Some of the early medals, with steel clips or ring suspension, were later fitted with a plain or ornamental suspender, usually of silver. One reason for this was that the steel rusted, and consequently marked the uniform; another was that some of the early suspenders were very ugly so, not unnaturally, something better looking was preferred. It is not usually considered that such medals are defective (as would be the case if, say, a Boer War Medal were fitted with a scroll suspender) but they are not in original condition. Since they are often improved by this treatment, and were widely worn thus, most collectors are quite happy to accept them, but others prefer the less attractive original fittings.

Rivets securing the bars must be watched, also the pin bar through which the ribbon passes, as bad rivets *may* be a sign of unentitled bars having been added. Again, one must not be too dogmatic, as in many cases bars added later are quite genuine, but the work may have been carried out by local craftsmen, perhaps in India or Africa, where the regiment happened to be serving when the additional bars arrived. Genuine medals exist, such as the India G.S., 1895, with later bars affixed by silver rings, or with a pin bar from rivet hole to rivet hole, but most collectors would prefer to wait for a better specimen.

Certain bars were issued much later than the medal, and will usually be found with rivets slightly different from the others, e.g. *Sebastopol, South Africa 1901* (and *1902*), and many bars issued with the modern general service medals. Sometimes these bars are found loose on the ribbon – safe so long as the ribbon is stitched to a brooch. They will be perfectly genuine in most cases, but if possible should be verified. In some instances they were awarded posthumously, and have been slipped on by relatives, but never attached. An example of this is Dr E. A. Wilson's Polar Medal, in the Scott Polar Research Institute at Cambridge, with its original bar, *Antarctic 1902–04*, and, loose on the ribbon, the bar, *Antarctic 1910–13*, which, of course, he did not live to receive.

As a general rule, defective medals should be avoided, including those where the swivel mount has broken and has been repaired by soldering into a fixed mount; also in the undesirable class are those which have been mounted as menu holders, if the medals themselves have been soldered; sometimes the contraption has been devised so that it can be removed without damaging the medal, but perhaps leaving solder marks on the back of the bars. Such treatment would merit a reduction in price, and the medal could well be included in a collection if it has a particular interest – I would certainly keep it if it were to a 'Light Brigade' or Rorke's Drift man.

## Official Re-Issues

Official re-issues of medals, including late issues applied for many years after the normal date, sometimes cause confusion

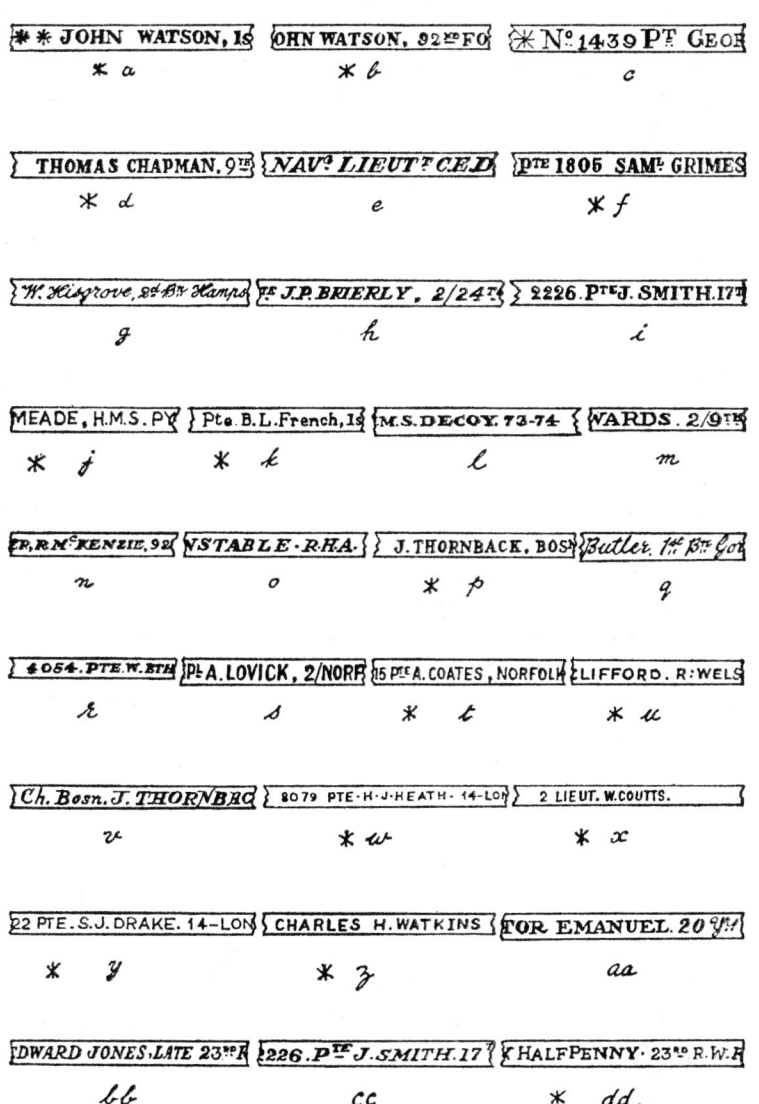

FIG. 4.
Types of impressed and engraved naming found on British medals (see under individual campaign medals, long service medals, etc.). *indicates impressed namings; all others are engraved.

37

among collectors when the style of naming differs from normal.

In certain circumstances a recipient may be entitled to obtain duplicate medals, either as a free issue or against repayment, but if the re-issue is made during the period when the original style of naming is in use, it is impossible to distinguish it from the original (unless marked *Duplicate* or *Replacement*, as is done nowadays). But if the medals were issued many years later, the then-current style of naming may well have been used.

In the case of the Indian Mutiny Medal, originally named in small impressed capitals, like those on the M.G.S., the regimental number was not given, and medals to privates had no rank shown. Re-issues are often seen, however, impressed in taller, thinner capitals (like the Naval L.S. & G.C.), giving the regimental number and 'PTE.' where applicable. Medals for the Ashantee War, 1873–74, are on a somewhat thicker flan than the later (but otherwise identical) E. and W. Africa Medal; the former are usually *engraved* in squat sloping capitals with the date, 1873–74, and blacked in; although some re-issues appear on the thick flan, others (presumably issued after 1892, when the E. and W. Africa Medal was authorised) have been seen on the thinner flan, with *impressed* lettering and no date.

Thus it would appear, and reasonably so, that re-issues are usually named in the style current at the time of re-issue, and this is a useful guide, especially if the original was engraved and the later one impressed.

From the financial point of view, opinions differ as to whether the re-issue is of less value than the original. In the first place, it is not usually known if the piece is actually a re-issue or an original issue to a late applicant; secondly, the medal itself is genuine enough; and where common medals are concerned, it is probably safe to say that an official re-issue has a value only a little, if any, below that of the original piece. On the other hand – and this applies more to rare medals, especially those for gallantry – if two pieces exist named to the same man, then collectors are apt to fight shy of them. This is particularly the case where an award such as the Victoria Cross is concerned. In the past there has been no way of distinguishing which is the original V.C. and which the duplicate (where two exist, both genuine); in some instances the makers have been able to distinguish between them, but I understand that it has not been so in every case, although there is reason to believe that this situation is unlikely to arise as regards future issues.

**Copy Medals**
In the section devoted to unnamed medals we have already mentioned copies of modern medals manufactured for sale in the tailoring trade, but in addition to these, a new trade seems to have boomed in recent years – that of producing copies of all types of medals (in the same way that the market is flooded with copies of arms, armour, and militaria in general). The vendors justify this by saying that the originals are now so expensive that the only way to have them represented in one's collection is to obtain copies.

For many years copies of the Victoria Cross, in various grades of quality from downright poor to very dangerous replicas, have been available, and many collectors have bought one just to show what a V.C. looks like. They are also popular with regimental museums, who can display them instead of the originals, which are kept in safe custody elsewhere.

One series of these copy medals consists of well produced cast copies, from Waterloo and NGS onwards, with the original naming of the genuine medal (i.e. all the copy Waterloo medals bear the same name), and these are offered for sale with replica suspenders and their correct ribbons. Some of these horrible things are marked COPY, and people have tried (sometimes successfully) to erase this, but in the main they are unlikely to deceive anybody but the complete novice. They become a bit more dangerous when they are fitted with an old piece ribbon instead of the new ribbon usually supplied (and when included in a group of genuine medals), and one should always be wary of medals or decorations offered for sale in official cases (particularly items such as the Military Cross, DSO, DFC, and similar awards) on market stalls and barrows, or under railway arches – the cases are probably genuine, but the occupants frequently are not!

In the foreign field copy medals are particularly rife in the awards of the Third Reich, and also Imperial Germany, Austria, etc. Items like the Knight's Cross of the Iron Cross, the Prussian order, *Pour le Mérite*, the 1813 and 1870 Iron Cross are particularly dangerous. Many German as well as Spanish and Portuguese copy medals are on sale in Spain and Portugal, and collectors on holiday are advised really to know their medals before buying what might appear to be good bargains.

In a rather different category are copies of orders, particularly the

Order of the Garter and other great orders, British and foreign. For generations recipients have had copies made for their own use (and for passing on to their descendants, since the original insignia often has to be returned at death). Sometimes a jewelled star or badge was purchased, made by the court jewellers, and these occasionally come onto the market. Foreign orders and decorations have been made by jewellers in all the capitals of Europe, for sale both to entitled recipients (who often have to buy their insignia) and to collectors, but they cannot really be classed as copies, since they are officially recognised. On the other hand, when these foreign jewellers offer for sale locally made insignia of British orders, these are undoubtedly copies and usually vary slightly from the genuine article.

## Cleaning Medals

Although one must not clean coins (except within certain narrow limits), the big majority of medal collectors prefer to clean their medals, but not polishing them with the enthusiasm of the Brigade of Guards or the King's African Rifles. Many, like myself, have served in the forces, and would not think of going on parade with dirty medals; similarly, we do not like to have dirty medals in our collections.

There are a few collectors who love that deep indigo toning which some medals acquire, but this is only the result of impurities in the air having a chemical reaction on the metal – in other words, a form of dirt – and I would rather put the medal straight into Goddard's *Silver Dip* for a few moments and then immediately wash it in warm soapy water. Despite what some people say, I cannot accept that cleaning in this way, or even giving a silver medal a slight rub with an impregnated soft cloth, can do it any harm. Certainly medals so treated over forty years ago show not the slightest sign of any ill effects. Most bronze medals will also look a little better if lightly brushed with a soft clothes brush and similarly washed in soapy water.

Enamelled badges of orders can be lightly brushed with an old toothbrush (with soft bristles, not modern nylon or other artificial bristles) to loosen any dirt which may have collected in the recesses and corners.

**Ribbons**

The question of whether or not to clean or replace ribbons is also one on which opinion is divided. Some dealers and collectors seem to set great store on 'original ribbons', but what is an original ribbon? Admittedly, if one has a Naval or Military General Service Medal in its original box of issue, obviously never worn, one can be fairly sure that the clean, unfaded, and neatly folded length of ribbon is the original, but can one say the same of a dirty, faded ribbon on, say, an Indian Mutiny Medal, hanging from a typical 19th century silver brooch, obviously 'as worn'? Prior to 1914 medals were worn much more frequently than today, and an Indian Mutiny veteran probably renewed his ribbon several times. Perhaps the ribbon on the medal was put on in 1876, nearly twenty years after the mutiny but despite its now being over a hundred years old, it is certainly not 'original' and probably barely contemporary.

But talking of contemporary ribbons, there are a few points worth noting. We have already mentioned the NGS ribbon: the original, or contemporary ribbon had a rather closer weave than its modern counterpart, and was $1\frac{3}{16}''$ (31 mm.) wide, with $\frac{3}{16}''$ edges of a rather dull blue, slightly greyish in tone, as compared with the dark blue usually seen in modern weaves, ($1\frac{1}{4}''$ wide), while the original white was not the 'brilliant white' of today's ribbon.

Contemporary Crimea Medal ribbon was also of a close weave, with about sixty 'rows' to the inch instead of the modern forty; it was only one inch wide, in a *very* pale blue, with $\frac{1}{12}''$ (2 mm.) pale lemon edges, not at all well adapted for a medal made to take a ribbon $1\frac{1}{4}''$ wide.

Several medals originally had ribbons with *corded* edges, including the Baltic Medal ($1\frac{1}{4}''$, or 32 mm., pale lemon yellow, with $\frac{5}{32}''$, or 3·5 mm. slightly greenish-blue edges), Arctic Medal, 1818–55 ($1\frac{1}{2}''$, watered white), the allegedly proposed China 1857 ribbon (in five stripes), Sudan 1896-7, Natal Rising, 1906, the Edward Medal, and the Honourable Artillery Company's special ribbons for the Volunteer Decoration and the Long Service Medal. All these ribbons have since always been made with normal edges, and are, or course quite acceptable as they were used by recipients who renewed their ribbon, but if one can obtain a piece of the contemporary corded ribbon in satisfactory condition, so much the better.

Quite a number of Victory Medals for the Great War were issued with a ribbon just under the usual $1\frac{1}{2}''$ wide, 37 mm. against 38 mm. Some UN Korea Medal ribbon had corded edges, but not all.

When I buy a medal, unless the old ribbon is still in a good state (and it can often be 'improved' by turning it inside out), I would much prefer to have a new (or newer) piece. To this end, if the dealer selling the medal provides a new piece of ribbon (as several do, automatically, if at all possible), and the existing piece is not too bad, I do not throw the old piece away, but keep it in stock in case I need a piece at a later date.

It is difficult to clean ribbons, but they can be improved by rubbing with benzine or other pure spirit. They can sometimes be washed, but one runs the risk of spoiling the silk or having the colours run.

3

# Sources of Reference

*Building a Reference Library      Sources of Reference*
*Libraries, Organisations, Etc.*

## Building a Reference Library

There are, presumably, collectors who feel that they are getting the most out of medal collecting, with no books of reference apart, perhaps, from an old copy of Taprell Dorling's *Ribbons and Medals*, in the same way that there are many stamp collectors who struggle along with just an out-of-date Gibbons' *Simplified Catalogue*.

The financial aspect cannot be ignored, and one realises that collectors of limited means (which includes most of us) just cannot afford to spend pounds on books, when what little they have available they want to use to add medals to their collection. Nevertheless, the beginner and more advanced collector alike would do very well to consider allocating a proportion of his available funds to the gradual building-up of a reference library. By having such books at hand, he will benefit enormously, from the background reading, by being able to verify medals, and by enlarging his knowledge of the hobby, both in general and in detail. Let us have a look at the categories into which these books fall (a select bibliography is given in Appendix A):

(1) *Books on Medals as such.* Naturally, these will come first, and from the books available, the choice will largely depend on funds and opportunities. For those who collect mainly British awards, the recent enlarged and revised editions of Taprell Dorling's *Ribbons and Medals*, are a useful guide for the beginner, particularly as a number of foreign decorations are also included, thus giving an introduction to a wider scope; but the field is limited, and the book does not pretend to cater for the more advanced collector.

The fourth edition (1971) of Major L. L. Gordon's *British Battles and Medals*, revised by E. C. Joslin, is perhaps the best book yet produced dealing with campaign medals only (it does not include Orders, decorations, gallantry awards, long service medals, etc.). He gives some description of the campaigns, and considerable other

43

information, including a list of the units receiving each medal and each individual bar. Provided the collector does not fall into the error of regarding the work as infallible, or rejecting a medal solely because the recipient's regiment or ship is not listed therein, he will find this book extremely helpful. Earlier works on a similar basis, but with much less 'unit' detail, are also useful, and include W. Augustus Steward's *War Medals and Their History* (1915) and his later *A.B.C. of War Medals* (1918), also D. Hastings Irwin's *War Medals and Decorations* (the 4th edition, 1910, is the best). For those who want to know all about the documentation of medals, with much information about their institution, J. H. Mayo's *Medals and Decorations of the British Army and Navy* (2 vols., 1897) is the standard work. Two books which not only deal with medals, but give much background history up to the late 19th century, are T. Carter's *Medals of the British Army* (sometimes found in the first edition as three volumes, but the later 1893 edition is the best, reprinted 1971) and W. H. Long's *Medals of the British Navy* (1895). The last is extremely good and generally reliable for lists of ships participating.

Although most of these books are out of print, they are nearly all fairly easy to obtain, as they frequently appear in the dealers' lists and in auction sales; it is, however, often cheaper to hunt them out in second-hand bookshops. A useful tip is to buy extra copies of any medal books which you may see going cheaply (having made sure that they are intact, with all plates); they can frequently be exchanged with other collectors, while the dealers are often willing to buy them if their stocks are low. Also a spare copy enables one to lend a book without having to part with one's 'best' copy.

For those who collect foreign awards, the scope is very wide, provided one has some knowledge of foreign languages, but very restricted if one is limited to works in English. Again, Taprell Dorling's *Ribbons and Medals* provides a basis, while Robert Werlich's modern large work, *Orders and Decorations of All Nations*, is useful, despite a large number of errors. Some valuable use can be made of older works, such as Burke's *Book of Orders of Knighthood and Decorations of Honour* (1858), which is a translation of a foreign work, and contains a number of mistakes. Another interesting old book is Elvin's *Handbook of the Orders of Chivalry* (1892), which also includes medals, and several bits of 'out-of-the-way' information.

Two foreign works are outstanding, but expensive, The first is L. J. Trost's *Die Ritter- und Verdienstorden* (1910), which is well illustrated, and since the bulk of the data is tabulated, can be readily understood with a smattering of schoolboy German and a dictionary. The second is the Italian work, in three volumes, *Motti degli Ordini Cavallereschi, delle Medaglie e Croce Decorative di tutto il Mondo e di tutti i Tempi* (1908), by C. N. Padiglione; a long title, but an ambitious work, rivalled only by Trost.

There are several books in French, notably *Ordres et Décorations*, by C. Ducortial, published in 1957. Many countries are comparatively rich in literature about their own medals, particularly Germany, the Netherlands, and the Scandinavian countries, but the limitations of space do not permit mentioning them here.

(2) *Books for verifying medals.* In sale catalogues or dealers' lists, reference is often made to medals as 'verified from the medal roll'. Copies of medal rolls – that is, lists of recipients – are clearly most useful volumes to have, but how does one get them? Perhaps the most important are those for the Military General Service (1793–1814), Naval General Service (1793–1840), and Army of India (1799–1826) Medals, so let us consider them first. Until 1947 there were no *printed and published* rolls for any of these three medals, but in that year the late Lt Col Kingsley Foster published a printed edition of the M.G.S. Medal Roll. This is not an official publication, and claims to be no more than a copy of a copy of the original manuscript roll – which itself is acknowledged by the War Office to contain many inaccuracies. This printed edition was privately published, in Germany, and contains a number of obviously 'Germanic' mistakes, such as 'A. of J.' for 'A. of I.' (where reference is made to the Army of India Medal), but despite these few errors, it is most useful.

From time to time one comes across typescript or manuscript copies of all three rolls; sometimes they are offered in the dealers' lists or at medal auctions, and they are good investments as they can save your wasting money on a 'dud' or suspect medal. *It must always be remembered*, however, that with the continual copying and re-copying that has gone over the last hundred years, *omissions and mistakes are bound to have occurred* – initials may have been misread; *James* (or *Jas.*) has become *Joseph* (or *Jos.*); *Horner* gets copied as *Homer*, while cross-references to other bars may be omitted or copied against the previous or following entry. So when checking a medal, if it does not completely verify at first glance, look a little further and make allowances for likely errors before turning it down – and remember that in one 'edition' of the N.G.S. roll, fairly frequently encountered, the recipients of a few of the bars are given alphabetically *under each ship*, the ships themselves being in alphabetical order, whereas the major part of the roll lists all names in alphabetical order for each bar, with the relative ship shown against each name.

The Royal Highland Regt (The Black Watch), published in 1913 a regimental medal roll, covering the period, 1801–1911, and this is occasionally obtainable from medal dealers, while in 1928, the Royal West Kents (50th and 97th Foot) produced Part 1 of their Medal Roll, covering 1793–1881. The edition has now become exhausted, but copies are sometimes available from dealers. Unfortunately the second part has never been published in book form, but was printed in the monthly issues of *The Queen's Own Gazette* during 1933.

Several regiments, such as the 28th London (Artists' Rifles), have published a Roll of Honour for the First World War, with a full list of awards for gallantry, mentions in despatches, etc., and copies of these can often be found in secondhand bookshops.

Quite a number of 1914–18 groups include the insignia of one of the classes of the Order of the British Empire, and these can be verified, if awarded not later than February 1921, from Burke's *Handbook to the Order of the British Empire*. Officers' medals are generally not too difficult to verify, and for Waterloo Medals, Dalton's *Waterloo Roll Call* (1890 or 1904 editions, the latter reprinted, 1971) is a valuable little book, giving details of all officers present.

For those interested in Artillery medals, the *List of the Officers of the Royal Regiment, 1716–1899*, and the revised *Vol. II, 1862–1914*, are particularly useful, as not only do they give records of service, but also campaign medals and bars.

*Hart's Army List*, published from 1840 until World War I, provides much valuable information of officers' services and medals, while the *unofficial* Navy Lists (*Haultain's*, 1839–45; *Allen's*, 1846–56; and *Lean's*, 1878–1916) give similar information on the naval side. The *Official Navy Lists* are also useful, but do not give individual services and awards, although an officer's career can be traced from the ships in which he served, and some issues give lists of gallantry and lifesaving awards. If they are priced fairly cheaply, they are always worth picking up, as are volumes of the *Official Army List*. As regards the last, for details of holders of *temporary* commissions during 1914–18, you must refer to the *Monthly Army Lists*, as the normal quarterly ones give only regular officers.

In addition to those mentioned, there are numerous miscellaneous lists, sometimes a single issue, sometimes published for a few consecutive years, which are well worth searching for in secondhand bookshops. Examples are *The Arctic Navy List, 1773–1873*, published in 1875; *The Indian Marine List*, from 1884 to 1911: *Whitaker's Naval and Military Directory*, published in 1898, 1899, and 1900.

Collectors will probably find my *Bibliography of Orders, Decorations and Medals* useful, as this lists, with full details, many hundreds of books on medals, including verification sources.

(3) *Books providing background information*. Perhaps one first thinks of regimental histories in considering background reading. Naturally, such books are numerous, from brief pamphlets and short 'popular' surveys to multi-volumed, lavishly illustrated official histories, often containing lists of awards, mentions in despatches, etc. The collector who is interested in a particular regiment should have no difficulty in discovering what books are available. In case other enquiries fail, a letter to the editor of the regimental magazine (enclosing a stamped addressed envelope for reply) will usually put you on the right track. There are several 'omnibus' books which contain short histories of a number of regiments, and the general collector will find them helpful. The two outstanding ones are: *The Records and Badges of the British Army*, by Chichester and Burges-Short (2nd Edition, 1899, reprinted 1970), and *Short Histories of the Territorial Regiments of the British Army*, edited by R. de M. Rudolf (H.M.S.O. 1905). The first deals with all units – cavalry, artillery, infantry, and departmental corps – with plates of uniforms and colours, and profuse line drawings of badges. The second covers infantry only, from the Royal Scots to the Royal Dublin Fusiliers, and gives *inter alia* details of the winners of the V.C. and lists of D.C.M. holders; the term, *Territorial*, refers, of course, to the county naming of regular infantry regiments, after the numeral system was discontinued in 1881, and not to what we nowadays mean by 'Territorials'.

Many collectors concentrate on medals to units which particularly distinguished themselves in various actions (including ships), especially those in which official battle honours were won, and they will derive considerable assistance from C. B. Norman's *Battle Honours of the British Army* (1911, reprinted 1971); this book deals with each battle in turn, with a short history of the action, a list of the regiments winning battle honours, and tables of casualties, killed and wounded (but these figures are often only approximate, and do not always agree with regimental records). The naval side is dealt with by Oliver Warner, in his *Battle Honours of the Royal Navy* (1956).

There are numerous books on campaigns, and these can often be bought cheaply on the secondhand market. Even common medals have an interesting story when something is known of the campaigns involved, and for those whose finances are limited, Conan Doyle's *The Great Boer War* (especially the later and larger editions, with maps) will bring a new and added interest to your South Africa medals. Similarly, *The Relief of Chitral*, by G. J. and F. E. Younghusband, will enable you to appreciate more fully the 1895 India General Service Medal.

These are but two examples of the many hundreds of such books, ranging from official histories and autobiographies of famous admirals and generals, to personal experiences of the rank and file – and these last give, perhaps, the most accurate and vivid picture of the conditions under which the recipients of our medals lived, fought, and died. One such lies before me as I write – *The Autobiography of Sergeant William Lawrence*, of the 40th Foot; any collector owning a Military G.S. or Waterloo Medal will value it all the more if he reads this remarkable book by a veteran who survived to receive ten bars with his M.G.S. Medal.

Another type of book which can often be picked up cheaply, yet contains much of interest to the medal collector and student of uniforms, badges, and customs, is the large (folio) volumes published at the end of the nineteenth century, and early this century, often in series. These include *The Navy and Army Illustrated*, *With the Flag to Pretoria*, *After Pretoria*, and similar books. Although they contain a lot of extraneous matter, 'popular' articles, and suchlike, the illustrations can be very useful, and more than once I have found photographs of, or reference to, the actual recipients of some of my medals. In modern times, present and back numbers of *Soldier* often provide items of interest to medal collectors.

### Sources of Reference

How do we set about using these sources of reference? Where do we go for the information, and what use can we make of it when we

(*Above*) Distinguished Flying Cross: *Left* – Genuine; *Right* – Copy.
(*Below*) Air Force Cross: *Left* – Genuine; *Right* – Copy.
Genuine crosses kindly lent by John B. Hayward, Esq.
Plate 4.

Distinguished Conduct Medal (Edward VII):
(*Above*) Genuine: *Left* – obverse; *Right* – reverse.
(*Below*) Copy: *Left* – obverse; *Right* – reverse (kindly lent by
B. A. Seaby, Ltd.)

Plate 5.

have got it? Just let us have a look how this research and background reading works out in practice. Here is a list of a few medals from my own collection, as they would appear in my 'catalogue' without any research:

(1) *Naval Genl. Service, 1793–1840:* 4 bars – *Nile, Egypt, Trafalgar, St Domingo.* To A. F. Parr, Midshipman. (*Plate 2*)

(2) *Military Genl. Service, 1793–1814:* 5 bars – *Egypt, Corunna, Fuentes d'Onor, Vittoria, Pyrenees.* To Chas. Fraser, 92nd Ft. (*Pl. 2*)

(3) *Arctic Medal, 1818–55.* To W. I. Mumford, H.M.S. *Resolute,* 1852–54 (Engraved naming). (*Plate 3*)

(4) Pair to T. H. Treagus, A.B., R.N. (*Plate 3*)
   (a) *Royal Humane Society's Silver Medal,* dated 18th Aug. 1923.
   (b) *Naval L. S. & G.C.* (Geo. V – Coinage head); H.M.S. *Whitshed.*

Although they may look interesting in their own right, that is the sum total of the original information at our disposal, except, of course, that we all have some knowledge of Trafalgar and the Peninsular War. But with some research, the catalogue entries give much more interesting details. These have been considerably condensed here, but will give an idea of what can be done to bring out the *personal* appeal of British medals:

(1) Alexander Forsyth Parr[1] was born on 7th October 1786, and was one of five brothers, four of whom became officers in the Royal Navy. He entered the Navy on 20th October 1796, at the age of ten, as 3rd Class Volunteer in H.M.S. *Swiftsure* (of which ship his father was Gunner). He experienced his first major action at the age of 11, as a powder monkey at the Battle of the Nile. In October 1805 he joined H.M.S. *Agamemnon,* and served in her at Trafalgar. After the battle he was sent on board the damaged *Colossus,* under tow; during the storm the tow parted, and it was largely due to his efforts that the towrope was secured and the ship saved. After the action off St Domingo, he was promoted to Lieutenant, and served in various ships until 1831, when he went on half-pay. Lieut Parr died at Haslar Hospital in 1856.

(2) Pte Charles Fraser[2] was born at Ardersier, Inverness-shire, and enlisted on 7th June 1794, at the age of 16 (height 5′ 3″). He was on the original Muster Roll of the Gordon Highlanders at its embodiment at Aberdeen on 24th June 1794, as the 100th Regiment of Foot, under the command of the Marquis of Huntly, son of the Duke of

Gordon. In 1798 the regiment was re-numbered as the 92nd Regiment.

Each of the five bars on Pte Fraser's medal represents one of the regiment's early battle honours. He served in Egypt and took part in the Battle of Mandora, where the regiment particularly distinguished itself; returning to the U.K. in 1802, the 92nd served at Copenhagen in 1807 (for which no medal or bar was given), and went to the Peninsula in 1808, taking part in the Battle of Corunna in January 1809 and subsequent actions.

(3) William Mumford[3] served as Carpenter's Crew, on the second voyage of H.M.S. *Resolute*, in search of Sir John Franklin, Capt. (later Vice-Admiral Sir Henry) Kellett commanding.

The first winter was spent at Dealy Island, while the second was spent in pack ice. Various sledge expeditions were undertaken, and William Mumford took part in two of these. His first sledge expedition was a twenty-four-day journey, 4th–28th April 1853, when eight men under Richard Roche, Mate, went to place a depot on Cape Mudge; their sledge flag bore a six-pointed star, and the motto, *Mon Dieu est ma Roche* (H.M.Sledge *Beauty*). They covered 173 miles, at temperatures between 10° and —29°F. The following month he took part in a twenty-one day journey of 208 miles, in H.M.Sledge *Murchison* under Lieut Bedford Pim (sledge flag – an anchor; motto – *Hope on, hope ever*). On 19th May 1853, they left the ship to carry a depot and cart across Melville Island for the use of Commdr McClintock's party; during this expedition they took a copy of Parry's record from the cairn on Point Nias, deposited there in June 1820.

William Mumford also had the Naval General Service Medal (which is missing), with bar, *Syria*, serving as A.B. in H.M.S. *Edinburgh*.

(4) "On 18th August 1923, a severe typhoon swept over Hong Kong, during the progress of which H.M. Submarine *L.9* broke adrift from the buoy to which she was moored. Lieut Thomas H. Dickson, H.M.S. *Titania*, jumped on board to try to secure her, but failing, was unable to get back ashore. There was a heavy sea running,

The sources of information for the above are as follows:
[1]N.G.S. Medal Roll: O'Byrne's *Naval Biographical Dictionary* (1849); Navy Lists; *The Times*.
[2]M.G.S. Medal Roll; Muster Rolls of the 100th and 92nd Foot, 1794-1800 (in the Public Record Office); Regimental History of the Gordon Highlanders.
[3]Captain Kellett's official account of the 1852-54 voyage of H.M.S. *Resolute*. (In the Admiralty Library). N.G.S. Medal Roll. Arctic Medal Roll.

and Tom Henry Treagus, A.B. in H.M.S. *Tamar*, went overboard from S.S. *Ginyo Maru*, which was moored to the dockyard wall, taking a line, and after a severe struggle he succeeded in reaching Lieut Dickson; both were then hauled back on board."[4]

Naturally one cannot go to such lengths for every medal in the collection – time and opportunities just do not permit – but some medals and groups justify more time being spent on them, and every collector can do something, if only to read up the details of each action in books borrowed from the public library, to discover the story behind his medals.

## Libraries, Organisations, etc.

In addition to the books and places already mentioned, there are several other sources of information which collectors may find profitable to explore, and perhaps this is a convenient point to stress the fact that *when writing to ask for information, whether to an individual, a dealer, an organisation, a library, or any other source, always enclose a stamped addressed envelope, or, at least, a stamp for reply.* If writing to an overseas source, you should enclose an *International Reply Coupon* (which you can buy at a post office). In addition, when you receive a reply, please write a letter of thanks – simple, not effusive – remembering that often the writer has had to go to quite a lot of trouble on your behalf, even if the result proves unsuccessful. You may think that your simple enquiry does not take up much time or expense, but the person replying may have had several, even dozens, of similar enquiries, and postage bills mount up. Naturally, when you are making enquiries of another collector who is a personal friend and regular correspondent, this formality is usually dropped by mutual consent, but during the last few weeks, I have had no fewer than nine enquiries about coins and medals, all from complete strangers, of which two enclosed a stamp, and only one has so far bothered to write and thank me for the information supplied.

If you have a local regimental museum, it will probably have a reference library of military books, and it will certainly pay to make friends with the curator or officer in charge. It may well prove that you will be able to reciprocate by helping him on some point.

Public libraries (municipal and county) can be used to a much

[4]Citation by kind permission of the Royal Humane Society.

larger extent than is generally realised. Although each library has only a few books on medals and allied subjects, the librarian has facilities for obtaining, from other libraries, almost any book published in Great Britain in comparatively modern times (nineteenth and twentieth centuries, and sometimes earlier). However, this does not usually extend to Army Lists, the *London Gazette*, or similar reference works, but the librarian can tell you where such publications can be consulted.

The Medal Rolls in the Public Record Office, Chancery Lane, London, WC2., are a most useful source of verification, as are the early Muster Rolls (both Army and Navy). Some years ago the War Office transferred all of their older War Medal Rolls from Droitwich to the P.R.O., covering most of the campaigns from 1801 until early in the present century; rolls of the Army L.S. & G.C. to certain units during part of this period are also available. They also have naval medal rolls prior to 1914. The volumes run into several hundred, and collectors and students can study three or four of these rolls at a time, by applying for a Reader's Ticket, which can be obtained by filling up a form issued by the P.R.O. When rolls are to be consulted, the Office should be given at least three days' notice, as many of them are stored out of London, and have to be brought in especially for inspection. Generally speaking, research work of this nature must be undertaken by a personal visit, as the P.R.O. cannot cope with postal enquiries owing to insufficient staff.

Lists of the Army rolls available, with their reference numbers, are given in *Seaby's Coin and Medal Bulletin*, January 1953, pp. 14–17, and May 1958, p. 196.

The Royal Mint Reports (officially entitled *Annual Report of the Deputy Master and Comptroller of the Royal Mint*, and published by H.M.S.O.) are well worth studying, as frequently reference is made to new medals and bars, and much other interesting information is given.

As far as is known, the *Orders and Medals Research Society* was the first organisation in Great Britain dealing *solely* with this hobby. At the time of writing the society normally meets about twelve times a year, on Saturday afternoons, at its own premises in the Duke of York's Headquarters, King's Road, Chelsea, London SW3., and publishes an excellent quarterly journal. Occasionally meetings are held elsewhere. For further details see Appendix C.

The *Birmingham Medal Society* was founded in 1964, and now

meets regularly, while the *Military Historical Society*, whose members' interests include medals, uniforms, badges and buttons, and regimental history, also holds frequent meetings, including visits to regimental depots and museums, and it publishes an excellent quarterly journal. For further details of both of these societies, see Appendix C.

Some numismatic societies have a number of medal collectors in their ranks, and include occasional papers of medal interest in their programmes. Since medals are a branch of numismatics, collectors are advised to join their local numismatic society, even if at the moment there are no other fellow enthusiasts – if you are the first medal collector to join the society, you can perhaps tell the others something of our side of the hobby, and may be able to encourage other local medal collectors to join.

There is, of course, another alternative: find but *one* fellow collector living within reasonable distance, and form your own local medal society.

# 4

## Orders and Decorations

INSIGNIA of the British Orders of Knighthood provide a most picturesque section of the collection, and although the collars, badges, and stars of the higher classes are expensive items, quite a number of badges of the lower classes can be found (frequently in groups with other medals) at reasonable cost.

It is important that collectors should use the correct terms in connection with Orders – one leading military museum had, until recently, several exhibits labelled "Commander of the Bath", a grade which does not exist, as the abbreviation, *C.B.*, indicates a *Companion* of the Order; this is, however, often confused with *K.C.B.*, which is *Knight Commander*.

The two Orders formerly associated with India – the Order of the Star of India and the Order of the Indian Empire – do not have Knights Grand *Cross*, but Knights Grand *Commanders*, since many of the recipients were not Christians, and insignia or titles associated with a cross would be inappropriate.

The correct title for a Knight of the Garter is 'Knight Companion', while *O.B.E.* does not mean 'Order of the British Empire', but *'Officer* of the Order of the British Empire'.

It is interesting, too, that our Orders have their own distinctive adjectives in their formal titles; thus, while the Order of the Garter is *Most Noble*, that of the Thistle is *Most Ancient and Most Noble*, and the Order of St Patrick was *Most Illustrious*. The *Most Honourable* Order of the Bath is followed by the *Most Exalted* Order of the Star of India, while the Order of St Michael and St George and the Order of the Indian Empire, are respectively, *Most Distinguished* and *Most Eminent*. The *Royal* Victorian Order has a different form of designation, as, although the two highest classes confer knighthood, it is in a somewhat different category, having been instituted to reward personal services to the Sovereign and the Royal Family. Strangely enough, the most junior Order, that of the British Empire, has perhaps the highest title of all – *Most Excellent* – which appears to be grammatically incorrect, since, surely, there can be no comparative or superlative of excellence.

## The Victoria Cross

Only two British decorations take precedence over the Orders of Knighthood – the Victoria Cross and the George Cross. Of the former so much has been written, both historically and otherwise, that there is little to add here, except some small details which do not usually appear in medal books.

Ever since its institution in 1856, the cross has been made by the same London firm, Messrs. Hancocks & Co., of Vigo Street, the well-known jewellers. Strangely enough, they do not make any other decorations. The crosses are cast (unlike most other awards, which are struck from dies) and then finished by hand. The War Office supplies the gunmetal as required, but as the chemical composition of this varies slightly from time to time, so the colour and the contraction of the cooling metal also vary, consequently there are minor differences in the size and colour of the finished article. When copies are made (as they frequently have been) using a mould taken from a genuine cross, it follows that this mould will be slightly smaller than the original mould, and when the copy cross contracts on cooling, the result is a specimen noticeably smaller than the original.

Of the many copies which exist, some of these cast ones are the most dangerous, especially if the naming is well done, but the potential purchaser can always ask the makers for their opinion; Messrs. Hancocks can almost invariably say if the example is genuine or not. Furthermore, since the whereabouts of a large proportion of Victoria Crosses is known to various dealers and collectors, it is not difficult to find out if the one offered is 'known'. Some copies are struck from dies, but these, together with many cast ones, are poorly executed and would deceive nobody – in fact, they are not intended to deceive, but are made merely to fill a gap in collections. They are usually unnamed, and nearly every unnamed specimen can be automatically classed as a copy (but at least one *genuine* unnamed example is known). On the originals the name and other particulars of the recipient are engraved on the *rev.* of the suspender bar, while the date, or dates, on which it was won will be found on the cross itself, in the central circle of the *rev.*

For the majority of Victoria Crosses there should be at least one corresponding campaign medal. In many cases these are already with the cross, in family hands, in private collections, or in regimental or other museums. But this is by no means always so, especially as in 1902 King Edward VII decreed that the V.C. could be awarded posthumously to officers and men who were killed in the Boer War, while in 1907 this was made retrospective and several crosses were issued to surviving relatives, but often the campaign medals had disappeared. It is worth while having a working knowledge of the names and units of the winners of the V.C., in case you should ever come across some other medal to the same recipient – it may well be the nearest that you will get to having a V.C.

Until the advent of *Queen's Regulations for the Army, 1881*, there seems to have been no set rule of where, among the recipient's awards, the VC was to be worn. From early photographs and paintings, it would seem that some wore it, like the DCM, immediately after the relative campaign medal, while others, with four or more medals, wore the VC in the centre with the other medals round it at points "north-west, north-east, south-west and south-east". In 1881 it was directed that the VC was to follow the Order of the Indian Empire, while in the *Dress Regulations for the Army, 1900*, it was to follow the Royal Victorian Order (and thus, in both cases, before all campaign medals). It would seem that in 1902 King Edward VII changed this, directing that the VC should come before *all* decorations worn on the bar brooch on the left breast.

It is, of course, well known that with the formation of the RAF in 1918, the blue ribbon for naval VCs was discontinued, and the army's crimson ribbon was adopted for all three services. This alteration was subsequently incorporated into the consolidating Royal Warrant of 22 May 1920. Before this, however, a small amendment was made to the ribbon. Army Order No. 290 of September 1916, provided that a recipient of a bar to the VC should wear a miniature cross on the ribbon strip when the cross itself was not worn. This was amended by Army Order of April 1917, which provided that army recipients were to wear the miniature cross on the ribbon strip to indicate the *first* award, and a further miniature for each bar.

Certain amendments to the original statutes have made civilians eligible for the VC. In *Gallantry*, by Wilson and McEwen, it states that a white ribbon was prescribed for civilians, but we have been unable to trace any authority for this, neither have we seen it mentioned in any authoritative publication.

## The George Cross

Instituted by Royal Warrant of 24 September 1940, the original terms strangely provided that the ribbon should be $1\frac{1}{4}''$ wide, although the suspender of the cross was made to take a ribbon of $1\frac{1}{2}''$ wide. The $1\frac{1}{4}''$ ribbon was actually made (and some ribbon collectors have been fortunate enough to secure a piece), but the correction of ribbon width was made in the Royal Warrant of 8 May 1941.

Naming is by engraved upright capitals on the *rev.*, with the date of publication in the *London Gazette* (not the date of the act of gallantry). Miniature crosses are worn on the ribbon strip as for the VC (*q.v.*).

Holders of the Empire Gallantry Medal (Medal of the Order of the British Empire for Gallantry) could exchange this for the George Cross, but collectors seem to prefer those won after the date of institution, despite the fact that the earlier awards were just as gallantly earned.

## The Orders of the Garter, Thistle, and St Patrick

From the ordinary collector's point of view, there is not much to be said about these three senior Orders, since the statutes require the insignia to be returned on the death of the recipient. However, the sovereign occasionally allows the widow to keep part of the insignia, and consequently original items are sometimes available, but they are naturally extremely rare. More frequently the badges of these Orders which come onto the market are additional pieces, usually made by the same firms who made the originals, purchased by entitled recipients. It has long been the practice for recipients to provide themselves with beautifully made badges at their own expense, which cannot be classed as fakes, since they were made for use by the knights in accordance with the customs of the times. Furthermore, metal stars for British Orders were not furnished by the Crown until 1858. Before that time embroidered stars were the official issue, but metal ones were often privately purchased for all the Orders, and it was not unusual for a man to have several, which were frequently inherited and worn by his descendants when appropriate. This custom is still practised by some of the present K.Gs, for example. A very few copies of badges and stars, made for collectors and mainly foreign in origin, are known; it should not be difficult to detect these, as although usually correct in design, they often depart somewhat from the originals; this is not surprising, since over the years even official stars and badges of British Orders have appeared in various sizes and detail.

Very occasionally a specimen of the Garter itself is seen, but since the 'issue' Garter has to be returned at death, such examples are rarely, if ever, originals. It is only in fairly recent years that Knights Companions have made a general practice of using the investiture Garter (and even now some reserve this for only the most formal occasions), and hitherto 'informal' Garters, embroidered in gold thread, were purchased from firms supplying gold and silver lace goods, for less formal occasions. These examples are often of corded silk, and of a lighter blue than the dark blue velvet investiture Garter, with its gold letters, buckle, and tabs. In the past many Knights Companions have had Garters set with precious stones, and frequently heavily jewelled examples have been presented to foreign sovereigns.

### The Order of the Bath

From its institution in 1725 to its re-constitution in January 1815, the Order of the Bath had only one class, and the badge of the Knights of the Bath (K.B.), worn from a red sash ribbon, was similar to the Civil G.C.B. – the oval gold badge, pierced, bearing the device of the Order. The Civil G.C.B. can be distinguished by the hall-mark, as the K.B. badges were rarely, if ever, hall-marked.

The Statutes of January 1815 make reference to the re-constitution 'commemorating the auspicious termination of the long and arduous contest in which this empire has been engaged'. This indicated the apparent end of the war in 1814, when Napoleon was sent to Elba, but some writers state that the re-constitution took place after Waterloo, as if the phrase referred to the actual end of the war.

The design of the insignia – at that time only in a Military Division and Civil Grand Cross – was the same as today. The Companion's badge, the one most often encountered, was in 22ct. gold, and was approximately $1\frac{3}{4}''$ across, compared with the present $1\frac{7}{8}''$ in silver-gilt, while the ribbon was 2″ wide (usually made as $1\frac{15}{16}$″), instead of the modern $1\frac{1}{2}$″. It would seem that a large number of badges were made for the 1815 re-constitution, as examples with the London hall-marks of 1814–15 and 1815–16 (T or U in a shield, a lion *passant-guardant*, the King's head, and the makers' initials; there was no carat mark for 22ct.) were still being awarded to those decorated for services in the Crimea and the Indian Mutiny.

In 1847 the Civil Division was extended to include Knights Commanders and Companions, with the same oval badge as for Grand Cross, but in smaller sizes.

It appears to have been difficult to establish exactly when the Companion's ribbon was reduced to $1\frac{1}{2}$″, and it has generally been thought that the change was made somewhere between 1875 and 1890 – judging by the information given by earlier writers: even the Central Chancery of the Orders of Knighthood were unable to supply the answer. However, the answer can be found in the Statutes of 31 January 1859; under Statute 21 it states that the width of the ribbon for Companions is $1\frac{1}{2}$″. This is a much earlier date than was generally believed (although it has been there for over a century, for all to see), and unless any authentic document can be produced showing an earlier one, we can accept this as definite.

Another difficulty has been to place a definite date to the change from gold to silver-gilt. The second (1899) edition of D. Hastings Irwin's *War Medals and Decorations* says of the insignia: 'In accordance with a recent order, these are now given in silver-gilt, instead of pure gold.' Unfortunately he does not say how recently the order appeared, but no mention of silver-gilt appears in his first edition, 1890. However, I am indebted to Mr James C. Risk, of New York, for evidence that official instructions were given in 1887, for insignia of the Bath, St Michael & St George, and the D.S.O., to be made in gilt. He tells me that he has a Civil G.C.B. set in gold, hall-marked 1887, and a gilt badge hall-marked 1889.

Until 1st June 1917 the badge of a C.B., Military or Civil, was worn on the left breast, from a straight suspender and with a buckle on the ribbon. Since that date, in common with the equivalent third-class badges of other Orders, it is worn round the neck, by ring suspension. Modern groups containing a C.B. badge should be checked to see if the suspension is correct. For those awarded before June 1917 (where the recipient served, or would have worn the insignia, after that date) the badge will probably show signs of

FIG. 5.
Suspension rings of badges of Companions of the Order of the Bath. (Left: early gold type – Waterloo period; centre: pre-June 1917 type, adapted for wearing at the neck; right: modern type, since June 1917.)

having been altered from a bar suspension to a ring, while those awarded after the change should have an original ring fitting. Apart from a few old badges which may have been awarded already converted, before the new ones were ready, the two types may be distinguished by the fact that the pre-June 1917 badges have the ring at the top of the badge *at right-angles* to the design, so that a second connecting link is needed to bring the larger ribbon ring into alignment; the modern badge has the small fixed ring *in line* with the design, thus the ribbon ring needs no intermediate link (*Fig. 5*).

While it is not possible to guarantee that a badge of this Order, with a hall-mark of not later than the date of the award, was the recipient's original insignia, almost certainly one with a *later* hall-mark must be a replacement.

For full details of this most interesting order, collectors are strongly recommended to buy a copy of James C. Risk's excellent book, *The History of the Order of the Bath and its Insignia*, with coloured frontispiece and 28 plates (several in colour).

### The Order of the Indian Empire

When originally instituted by Royal Warrant of 31 December 1877, this order was in only one class – Companions, who wore a badge similar in design to the present one, but much larger (about the size of the present Knight Grand Commander's badge), with the five petals lettered, respectively, I.N.D.I.A. This badge was known, facetiously and irreverently, as the 'Jam Tart'. In August 1886 the order was enlarged to two classes, while by Letters Patent of 1 June

1887 it was further extended to three classes – Knights Grand Commanders (who wore the badge from a sash), Knights Commanders (wearing a slightly smaller badge at the neck), and Companions (who wore a still smaller badge on the left breast). The letters no longer appeared on the petals of the rose, and from June 1917 the Companion's badge, in common with the third classes of other British orders, has been worn at the neck.

The ribbon of the order has always been described as 'Imperial purple', but has always been made in a very dark blue unwatered silk.

### The Order of Merit

The badges, military and civil, of this Order – which confers neither knighthood nor precedence, but yet is so very highly prized – are adequately described in medal books, although several do not mention that the royal cipher changes with the sovereign, and are, to some extent, misleading as although published comparatively recently, they show an example with the cipher of Edward VII. The firm which makes the insignia confirms that the present badges bear the cipher, E II R.

The early badges were numbered on the edge of the lower arm of the cross, up to no. 26. Mr James C. Risk, who has made a specialised study of British Orders, confirms that this last numbered example was awarded in 1908, and at the same time another recipient received an unnumbered badge. Since then the badges have not been numbered. As so very few are awarded, it is unlikely that the average collector will be offered one, numbered or otherwise, but if an unnumbered one is encountered, it should be remembered that it *might* be a copy (possibly continental in origin), especially if it is not part of a verified group.

### The Royal Victorian Order

Although now administered by the Central Chancery of the Orders of Knighthood, this Order used to have its own Chancery, as, unlike the other British Orders, it is in the personal gift of the sovereign for services rendered to the Royal Family. The insignia, too, have a distinctive feature not enjoyed by the other Orders (except the Order of Merit, *q.v.*), in that they are all numbered, impressed and with class initials for the higher classes (G – Kt. Grand Cross; D – Dame Grand Cross; K – Knight Commander; C – Commander); also the same number and letter should appear on the case. Actually some slight discrepancies can occur here, presumably since cases can easily get mixed at investitures, but known examples show only a few figures difference, such as C.540 on the badge and C.536 on the case.

Apart from royal G.C.V.O. badges (British and foreign) awarded probably up to the end of Edward VII's reign, all badges are numbered by the makers before they are sent to the Chancery. Consequently any unnumbered specimens are likely to be copies.

Until 1958 this Order also possessed another distinctive feature; it was the only British award which, when given to foreigners, carried a continental type rosette on the ribbon of the Fourth Class (*Fig.* 6), and a tiny bow on the ribbon of the Fifth Class* (*Fig.* 6*a*).

FIG. 6.
Rosette formerly used on ribbon of M.V.O., 4th Class, when awarded to foreigners.

FIG. 6a.
Bow formerly used on ribbon of M.V.O., 5th Class, when awarded to foreigners.

FIG. 6b.
Bar to Royal Victorian Medal.

In addition, the cases for these awards included a corner compartment holding a rosette or bow, mounted on a stud for buttonhole wear. These distinctions have, however, now been dropped to bring this award into line with the other British Orders.

When arranging groups for display in a collection, it should be noted that if one of the lower classes of the R.V.O. is included together with the Imperial Service Order, the latter comes *after* the M.V.O. Fourth Class, but *before* the Fifth Class.

There are three grades of the Royal Victorian Medal, namely silver-gilt, silver, and bronze (we understand that the last bronze award was made in 1949, and presumably it has now been discontinued), and these are worn after campaign medals (and polar medals, if any), but before the Imperial Service Medal. Not only can the recipient of more than one grade wear them both, or all, but if he should subsequently have the Order conferred on him, he can continue to wear his Royal Victorian Medal(s).

*This information was supplied by the makers, Collingwood of Conduit Street, Ltd.

During the brief reign of King Edward VIII, two medals were awarded, bearing his effigy and titles on the *obv.*, and are thus among the rarest of British medals.

Since October 1951, medals awarded to foreigners have had a distinctive ribbon, with a white centre stripe, one-eighth inch wide, added to the normal 1¼″ ribbon.

Bars can be awarded for further service, but these seem to be very rare. The only one I have seen was a plain silver rectangle, 29 mm. × 5 mm., with the incised letters, E — R, at the ends, and the date, MAY 1910, in raised letters on a sunken panel (*Fig. 6b*). Unlike other bars, it is neither affixed to the suspender (as this is a ring), slipped over the ribbon, nor sewn on, but is secured to the ribbon by two pairs of sprigs, bent outwards, like paper fasteners.

### The Order of the British Empire

Unlike the Order of the Bath, which has different designs for the badges of the Military and Civil Divisions but sharing the same ribbon, the Order of the British Empire uses the same badge for both divisions, but distinguishes the ribbons by adding a narrow centre stripe for the Military Division.

Insignia of the first (Britannia) type are often found with 1914–18 groups, and most of these can be verified by reference to Burke's *Handbook to the Order of the British Empire*, published in 1921 and listing awards up to February of that year. In many cases short biographies are given, while the chronological lists are useful in confirming whether the award was in the Military or the Civil Division.

Early O.B.E. and M.B.E. badges carry the appropriate silver hall-mark, but some later ones may be found without the mark. Insignia of the 'Britannia' type can be worn with either the original or the modern ribbon (but most collectors show them with the original colour unless there is definite evidence that the recipient himself used the modern ribbon), but the modern badges with the heads of King George V and Queen Mary, instituted by the Statutes of 9th March 1937, *must* have the pink and grey ribbon. It should be noted that under these statutes, the sash ribbon for Dame Grand Cross, Military Division, did *not* have the grey central stripe. The reason for this is that Queen Mary (who became Grand Master after the Prince of Wales gave up that office on becoming King Edward VIII) did not wish any other Dame Grand Cross to wear a different sash ribbon from hers, which was, of course, that of the Civil Division. The central stripe was, however, restored by the Statutes of 15 May 1970.

Since the beginning of 1958, appointments to or promotions in the Order, and awards of the British Empire Medal, when granted for gallantry are so described in the announcement and are distinguished by the wearing of a silver emblem of two crossed oak leaves on the ribbon; this applies to both divisions.

The *Royal Mint Report, 1967*, indicates that the badges of the O.B.E. and M.B.E. are to have a polished instead of a matt finish, and that the M.B.E. badges and brooches are to be rhodium plated.

Early in 1972 an amendment to the statutes decreed that when a person is promoted in the order from the Military Division to a higher class in the Civil Division, or *vice versa*, the insignia of the lower class may be retained and worn together with those of the higher class on the appropriate occasions. Previously it had been usual on promotion to return the insignia of the lower class, but this created an anomaly between the Order of the British Empire and the Order of the Bath, in which a person promoted from one division to the other is entitled to retain and wear the insignia of the lower class. Members who had already returned insignia on promotion were accordingly permitted to apply for their return.

THE BRITISH EMPIRE MEDAL. (See Chapter 5)


## The Distinguished Service Order

Founded in 1886, this decoration was first issued in gold and enamel, but such examples are quite rare. Like the badges of other Orders originally in gold, later Victorian and subsequent issues are in silver-gilt, while the Royal cipher on the *rev.* changes with each reign. Copies, not always of foreign origin, are sometimes encountered, particularly of the George V issue; they are usually much flatter than the originals, which are approximately 0·535″ or 14 mm. in thickness (including the crown and cipher). There are several styles of copies, the most frequent having badly shaped arches to the crown, somewhat elongated and badly shaped letters, GR, and the red central enamel has underlying *radial* markings instead of *concentric* ones. However, a few genuine George V DSOs, made by a sub-contractor, have radial marks under the enamel, but their other details, such as

Plate 6.

Group to Sjt. William Parkinson, 23rd Ft, RWF: Crimea; Indian Mutiny; Army L.S. & G.C.; French Médaille Militaire; Turkish Medal for Crimea. (*From the author's collection*).

Medals with false bars – 1.

(*Left*) Crimea: bars in wrong order; BALACLAVA should read BALAKLAVA; compare ALMA bar with medal on Plate 6. (Kindly lent by B. A. Seaby, Ltd.)

(*Right*) Indian Mutiny: all false bars; compare the two middle bars with the medal on Plate 6. (Kindly lent by G. W. Harris, Esq.)

Plate 7.

the arches of the crown, thickness of the badge, etc., are as the normal examples. These copies often turn up at auction sales, and are usually so catalogued, whether in groups or as singles, by those firms who specialise in medal auctions, and the same generally applies to items offered for sale by reliable dealers, but collectors should beware of 'bargains', especially when they are camouflaged by being sold in an original black case which once housed a genuine example.

The D.S.O. is, of course, issued unnamed, but those of George VI, and later, usually have the year of issue engraved on the back of the suspender, with two figures on each side of the ring.

The badge is not complete without its top clasp, similar to the suspender clasp in design, and of the same metal. When the D.S.O. is mounted on a brooch with other medals, this top clasp is often detached, pierced with two small holes at each end (like the bar to the 1914 Star), and sewn at the top of the ribbon.

## The Imperial Service Order and Medal

It is important to note that the first design of the Imperial Service *Medal* – those of Edward VII and the early ones of George V – are often wrongly described in auction catalogues and other lists, as badges of the *Order*. The latter has a gold centre on a silver star for men, and on a silver wreath for ladies, but the *Medal* had a silver centre on a bronze star or wreath. Later George V medals are circular (as are subsequent issues) with either a coinage or crowned head.

There are at least two obverse dies of the George VI medal (with INDIAE IMP.). One has a rim thickness of approximately 0·118″, while the other is noticeably thicker, at 0·130″. The latter has its letters in somewhat lower relief, with smaller dots and much finer initials – PM – under the truncation of the neck. Both types have a mount which is wholly on the rim of the medal, unlike the George V types, where a similar shaped mount has two lugs, one each side, which overlap the medal and through which a rivet is fixed.

Many of the first (star) type are found unnamed, but they are often seen with engraved capitals above the central disc of the *rev*. The circular medals are usually impressed, but sometimes engraved, in small capitals, with forenames in full.

## The Royal Red Cross

A Royal Warrant of 15 December 1917 provided for a bar to the first class, for a subsequent award, consisting of a plain strip, enamelled red and edged gilt, about 1″ long and ⅛″ wide, splayed at each end; a ring soldered to the back of the bar enables the badge to hang from it (*Fig. 7*). No similar provision was made for the second class (ARRC), and it is generally believed that if an ARRC were deemed worthy of a further award, she would be promoted to the first class (RRC), thus making a bar to the second class unnecessary. (See additional note on p. 74).

FIG. 7.
Bar to Royal Red Cross.

FIG. 7a.
Bar to Order of the League of Mercy.

### The Distinguished Service Cross
Instituted in 1901 as the Conspicuous Service Cross, this naval decoration received its present name in October 1914. It is probably the plainest of all British awards, the *obv.* having only the crowned Royal cipher in a circle, while the *rev.* is completely plain.

The decoration is normally issued unnamed, but some are to be found privately engraved. Those issued for World War II, and subsequently, have the year of award engraved on the lower arm of the *rev.*, but some awards to allied personnel have the rank, name, etc., engraved in the centre of the *rev.*

Until 1954, the crosses bear the silver hall-marks on the *rev.*, having been struck by commercial firms. The dies for the early issues of Elizabeth II were cut by Spink & Son Ltd., and some forty-eight crosses were struck by them. Up to thirty-five were engraved '1952' (for the Korean War), but the dies and crosses were handed over to the Admiralty in September 1954. Since then the D.S.C. has been struck by the Royal Mint, and would thus not be hall-marked.

### The Military Cross
Copies of the George V issue exist, and are usually appreciably thinner than normal, and slightly smaller – one copy, which is quite well made, measures 1·685″ across against 1·735″ (these figures for the genuine cross vary slightly from one to another), with edge and centre thicknesses of 0·050″ and 0·115″, respectively, against 0·085″

and 0·132″ in the genuine example. Generally speaking, the copy crosses are poorly made, and it has been suggested that well made ones were, in fact, an economy measure towards the end of the war. I have never seen any evidence substantiating this, but an extremely large number of Military Crosses were certainly awarded at this time; however, the saving would have been very small, and I would require definite proof before accepting this theory as correct. Admittedly one sometimes sees them in the official purple case of issue, and the beginner should beware and always examine the contents closely.

The Military Cross is normally issued unnamed, but from about 1939 the year of award has been officially engraved on the *rev.* We understand, too, that when presented by the monarch, the crosses are named. However, the majority with names and other details on the *rev.* have all been privately named, which is quite acceptable when accompanied by the recipient's other officially named medals.

The award of the M.C. can be verified from the *Army List* or from the *London Gazette* (but the latter involves a long search, unless you know the approximate date of award), while often regimental histories list recipients of decorations, and may record the occasions on which they were won.

Bars to the Military Cross are not uncommon, certainly for the 1914–18 period, but an unnamed cross with a bar slipped over the ribbon does not justify any enhanced price beyond the value of the decoration plus about fifty pence for the bar. In a *verified* group of medals, however, whether the M.C. is named or not, it will have a value of at least double that of a similar one without bar.

### The Distinguished Flying Cross

As with the Military Cross, copies exist; several types have been noted, but all except one (well produced by a firm in the Midlands, for replacement purposes through military tailors and jewellers, and *not* to deceive collectors) are so apparent that none except the veriest beginner would imagine them to be genuine. The exception is rather dangerous unless one can compare it directly with an original. There are many minor differences in the details, but the easiest feature to note is the apex of the central 'A' (in the monogram R.A.F.); in the original the apex just touches the edge of the uppermost petal of the rose, whereas in the copy it slightly overlaps it

(*Fig. 8*); also the original usually has the initials of the designer in tiny letters on the outer rim of the central circle, while the copy (correctly) omits these. Another copy has a short crossbar to the top of the A. From recent information, it appears that some examples, believed genuine, have been seen without the initials; this is quite possible as they could have been struck from worn dies, and since the initials are never very strong, even on the early issues, they may well have disappeared after a time (*Plate 4*).

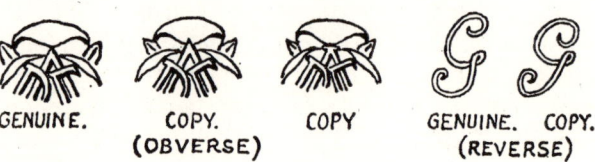

GENUINE.   COPY.   COPY   GENUINE.  COPY.
(OBVERSE)       (REVERSE)

FIG. 8. D.F.C.; some detail of original and copies: the reverse detail is of the George V type.

Recent examples of the copies have COPY impressed in small capitals on the vertical edge of the central medallion, but earlier specimens omitted this wise precaution.

The *rev.* of the D.F.C. is plain, except for a central raised circle containing the Royal cipher and 1918, the date of institution. Those issued in the reign of George V have the letters, GRI, interwoven in 'curly' script, with the tail of the R going through the upper loop of the 8 of 1918; in the copies referred to above, the right-hand down stroke of the G is sloping instead of being vertical and almost in line with the first 1 below it. Issues of George VI have two types of *rev.*, the first – issued up to 1947 – have GRI interlaced, but the letters are less flamboyant than the previous issue, and the tail of the R does not go through the 8; the later type of George VI has the cipher, G VI R, while those of the present reign have E II R in block capitals; all three of these later types have the date, 1918, in figures of the same height, but the copies have the second 1 slightly taller, and the 8 considerably taller, than the first two figures.

The D.F.C. is issued unnamed, but from 1939 the year of issue is engraved at the foot of the *rev.*

**The Air Force Cross**
Copies of the A.F.C. are much easier to detect, as, although a number

of differences in minor details of design exist, the designer's initials are much more prominent on the originals than they are on the D.F.C., being clearly shown in the 'south-east' of the central medallion. As they are absent from the copy, this can be quickly checked; I have not heard of an apparently genuine A.F.C. without the initials (as in the case of the D.F.C.), but as they were not so widely awarded as the D.F.C., it seems unlikely that the dies would have worn sufficiently for the more prominent initials to disappear. (*Pl. 4*).

As regards the *rev.*, all that has been said about the D.F.C. applies to the A.F.C., but again the copies have one peculiar feature – the original *obverse* die, with the letters, G, V, R, I, on the four arms of the cross, has been used for each subsequent reign, so that in copies, other than those of George V issues, the *obv.* and *rev.* do not tally. Recent issues also include the word, COPY, impressed on the edge.

### The Kaisar-i-Hind Medal

This decoration, originally in two classes, the first in gold and the second in silver, was instituted in 1900, and is occasionally found in groups to recipients connected with India. A third class, in bronze, was instituted by George V towards the end of his reign.

A bar could be awarded for further services, in the metal of the original medal; it is rectangular, 40mm. × 7mm., with the year of award in the centre, flanked by ornamental leaf scrolls on a grained or pitted ground, all within a narrow border (*Fig. 8a*).

The early gold and silver medals were hollow, but later issues were slightly smaller and solid.

### The Order of St John

As a point of historical interest this is now the official 'short title' of *The Grand Priory in the British Realm of the Most Venerable Order of the Hospital of St John of Jerusalem*, as provided in the Royal Charter of 15th March 1955. The original charter of 1888 gave the title as *The Grand Priory of the Order of the Hospital of Saint John of Jerusalem in England*, while the charter of 1926 altered it almost to the present style, but without the word *Most* (and the official 'short title' became *The Venerable Order of St John*).

The badges of the Order are all worn from a black watered ribbon, but Associates (who may be attached to any grade of the Order) have a black ribbon with a white central stripe one-twelfth the width of the ribbon. In a very broad definition, associates are either British or Commonwealth subjects who are not of the Christian faith, or foreigners. The sizes of the badges and widths of ribbons are as follows (the first figure being the diameter of the badge, and the second the width of the ribbon, followed by the manner of wearing):

Bailiff Grand Cross – $3\frac{1}{4}''$;             $4''$ (sash).

(*Note:* on an occasion when the badge has to be worn at the neck e.g. when wearing the sash of another Order, a ribbon of miniature width, $\frac{5}{8}''$, is used.)

Dame Grand Cross – $3\frac{1}{4}''$;            $2\frac{1}{4}''$ (sash).
Knight (of Justice or of Grace) – $2\frac{1}{4}''$; $2''$ (neck ribbon).
Dame (of Justice or of Grace) – $1\frac{3}{4}''$;      $1\frac{1}{4}''$ (bow).
Chaplain – $2\frac{1}{4}''$;                 $2''$ (neck ribbon).
Commander (Brother) – $2\frac{1}{4}''$;     $1\frac{1}{2}''$ (neck ribbon).
Commander (Sister)    – $1\frac{3}{4}''$;          $1\frac{1}{4}''$ (bow).
Officer (Brother)      – $1\frac{3}{4}''$;         $1\frac{1}{2}''$ (left breast).
Officer (Sister)        – $1\frac{1}{4}''$;          $1\frac{1}{4}''$ (bow).
Serving Brother – Circular badge, $1\frac{1}{2}''$, $1\frac{1}{2}''$ (left breast).
Serving Sister – Circular badge, $1\frac{1}{2}''$;      $1\frac{1}{4}''$ (bow).

Sisters of the Order *when in uniform* wear their insignia in the same manner as for Brothers of comparable grade, and not from a bow. Since 1947 a small silver maltese cross is worn on the plain black ribbon in undress uniform (i.e. when ribbons only are worn).

There is a further category, known as Donats, who have contributed substantially to the funds of the Order; they are not Members or Associates, and receive a badge in gold, silver, or bronze, similar to the normal badge, but with the upper arm of the cross removed and replaced by a piece of ornamental metal, elongated heart-shaped; it is worn from an Associate's ribbon, $1\frac{1}{2}''$ wide for men, and $1\frac{1}{4}''$ (in bow form) for women.

For further details of all the insignia of the order, the collector is strongly urged to buy a copy of Charles W. Tozer's authoritative book, *The Insignia and Medals of the Order of St John*, published by J. B. Hayward & Son in association with the Orders & Medals Research Society, and approved by the Order of St John. In addition to a coloured frontispiece and 11 plates (3 in colour), the book also includes details of the several railway companies' medals for their S.J.A.B. units.

## THE LIFE-SAVING MEDAL OF THE ORDER OF ST JOHN

This medal is sparingly awarded, in gold, silver, or bronze, and is consequently highly valued. This medal was instituted in 1874, in silver and bronze – the gold medal was introduced in 1907. The original medal had no lions and unicorns in the angles of the cross; when changed to the present design in 1888, a few other minor alterations were also made; the original ribbon, black with a white maltese cross woven into it, was changed at the same time to plain watered black. Since this was the same as the ribbon of the Order, it was differenced in 1950 by having red edges $\frac{1}{6}''$, separated from the 1″ black centre by white stripes, $\frac{1}{12}''$ in width. (*Plate 10*). From 1950 to 1954 there was a very narrow black line between the red and white stripes.

Apparently the medal was first worn on the right breast, but in 1904 it was worn on the left, between war medals and long service medals, while in 1911 it seems to have been placed before war medals. One writer on medals states that this was the ruling in force in the official Command Paper of June 1949, but in the 1936 Statutes of the Order, the List issued on 24th April 1936 by the Central Chancery of the Orders of Knighthood shows it as worn on the *right* breast (although listed before war medals in order of precedence).

A bar for subsequent awards was authorised on 29 November 1892, and is of the same material as the medal, $1\cdot5'' \times 0\cdot235''$, with a

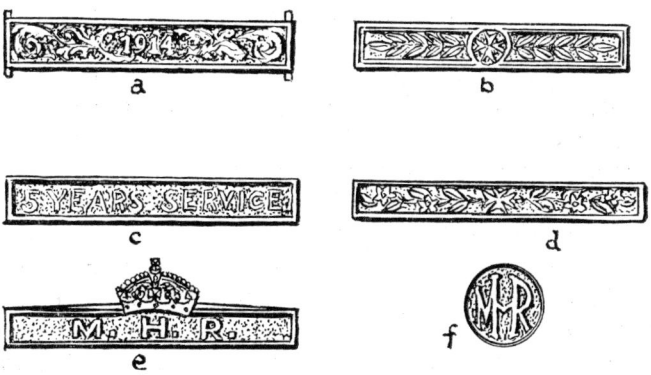

FIG 8a.
Bar to the Kaisar-i-Hind Medal.
FIGS. 8c and d.
Bars to the St. John Service Medal.
FIGS. 8e and f.
Top clasp and ribbon bar emblem for the Military Hospital Reserve (on the St. John Service Medal

FIG. 8b.
Bar to the St. John Life Saving Medal.

Maltese cross in a circle in the centre, and a spray of laurel on each side (*Fig. 8b*). When the ribbon only is worn, the bar is indicated by a $\frac{3}{8}''$ circular emblem of the same metal as the medal, on which is a white enamelled Maltese cross.

### THE SERVICE MEDAL

This medal was instituted in 1898, and retains its original style, the Queen's head on the *obv.* having been designed by H.R.H. Princess Beatrice. Originally in silver, the medal was made in bronze, silver-plated, from 1947 to 1960, then in cupro-nickel, silver-plated, from 1960 to 1966, since when, still in cupro-nickel, it has been rhodium-plated.

According to the statutes, the ribbon should be in five equal stripes, three black and two white, but while the ribbon is usually found in these proportions, it is also manufactured (and, indeed, illustrated in the statutes) with a wider centre stripe of about 0·4″.

Suspension was by a ring until about 1912-13, when it was changed to a straight bar suspender (some authorities give the date of the change as 1926, but the earliest medals which I have seen with a straight suspender have been dated 1913, while I have not seen the ring on a medal dated later than 1912). The bar to the Service Medal was authorised on 28 November 1911, and originally showed the length of additional service in words (after the initial period for which the medal was awarded, usually 15 years in the UK), but in March 1924 this was replaced by a bar with a Maltese cross in the centre and sprigs of hypericum (St John's wort) on each side (*Figs 8c* and *8d*). Since 1947, when the ribbon only is worn, the bar or bars are indicated by the same miniature maltese cross as is worn with the Order ribbon, as follows: twenty years (i.e. fifteen years to qualify for the medal, plus a further five years' efficient service) – one silver cross; for twenty-five years – two silver crosses; for thirty years – three silver crosses; for thirty-five years – one gilt cross; for forty, forty-five, and fifty years – two, three, or four gilt crosses, respectively.

It seems probable that the change from ring to straight suspender closely followed the introduction of these bars in 1911, owing to the inconvenience of fitting the bars, and those medals issued with a ring in 1911 and 1912 were probably existing stocks.

On 1 May 1907, the Military Hospitals Reserve (originally known as the Military Homes Hospital Reserve) was formed, by the Order of St John in arrangement with the War Office. This was to act as a reserve force to the RAMC, to take over the running of military hospitals at home in wartime, and to provide reinforcements for medical units of expeditionary forces overseas on mobilisation. The full strength of the reserve, 2000 in peacetime, was attained within twelve months. In 1932, with the approval of King George V, a silver brooch-bar, or top clasp, was introduced, to be worn with the St John Service Medal, for members who had attended twelve annual training courses at a military hospital (years in war service counting as double). This top clasp bore the initials, M.H.R., on a rectangular bar, surmounted by a crown (*Fig. 8e*), while when ribbons only were worn, the clasp was represented by a circular silver emblem, 11·5mm in diameter, bearing the conjoined letters, MHR (*Fig. 8f*). The Reserve was disbanded in 1946. There was also a similar clasp, lettered V.A.D., for the Voluntary Aid Detachment.

THE ST JOHN SOUTH AFRICAN WAR MEDAL

This award (reference to which is omitted from the 1955 Statutes and Regulations, presumably because it is now obsolete) is described as 'bestowed on those belonging to the Order, or to the Foundations of the Order, who served in the South African War, 1899–1902.' However, in addition to those who actually served in South Africa, it was also given to those who assisted with the dispatch of stores and medical comforts, consequently it is more highly valued by collectors when in company with the Queen's South Africa Medal.

The statutes described the ribbon as $1\frac{1}{2}''$ wide, but since the medal is fitted with a suspender bar for a $1\frac{1}{4}''$ ribbon (and the ribbons supplied by the medal dealers have apparently always been of the latter width), one must assume that the statute width is a mistake.

The medal is worn immediately after the Service Medal (if eligible; if not, then in the equivalent position, among 'Medals belonging to Orders', following long service medals and taking precedence after the Royal Victorian Medal in bronze).

For those interested in awards connected with the Order of St John, mention must be made of the three Jubilee and Coronation Medals of the 'Police' type, where special reverses exist worded for the St John Ambulance Brigade. These are Queen Victoria's Diamond Jubilee, Edward VII's Coronation, and George V's

Coronation Medals, and are adequately dealt with in Lt Col H. N. Cole's excellent little book, *Coronation and Royal Commemorative Medals, 1887 – 1977.*

### The St John Ambulance Brigade of Ireland

The S.J.A.B. of Ireland has a Service Medal, with a white ribbon, having three black stripes (the centre one wider than the side stripes) and very narrow green edges. The medal is about 1·45″ in diameter, the *obv.* showing the familiar maltese cross, with a shamrock leaf in each of the angles; in the outer circle is the legend, THE ST JOHN AMBULANCE BRIGADE OF IRELAND. The *rev.* is also simple – FOR SERVICE, within a wreath of two branches tied together.

### Order of the League of Mercy

It is not generally known that a bar can be awarded for continued services to the League. This is shown in *Fig. 7a* (*p.* 66); it is of silver, with the centre shield enamelled red.

ADDITIONAL NOTE:

### Royal Red Cross

Although the Royal Red Cross has previously been regarded as a decoration solely for women, men are in fact eligible, and the first male appointment appeared in the 1977 New Year Honours List, when Chief Medical Technician Hugh C. Gowans, RN, was appointed 'to be an Ordinary Associate of the Royal Red Cross, Second Class' (i.e. ARRC). The recipient is a State Registered Nurse, and his badge is, of course, worn from a straight ribbon in the usual way, whereas for a woman it is worn from a bow.

In the Birthday Honours List of June 1977, two further awards of the ARRC were made to men, one to a Fleet Chief Medical Technician and the other to a Flight Lieutenant, RAF.

# 5

# Gallantry in Action

THIS section of the cabinet has a great appeal to many collectors, particularly as in a large percentage of cases one can obtain details of the actions for which the medals were given. Even if the recipient's other medals are missing, the gallantry medal by itself is always worth its place in the collection – it can be replaced at a later date if a more interesting group turns up.

The medals in this section are fully described in many medal books, but some of them merit a few additional notes. Nevertheless, the collector cannot do better than to obtain a copy of *British Gallantry Awards*, by P. E. Abbott and J. M. A. Tamplin; this is an outstanding work, and essential for every serious collector of gallantry awards.

### The Medal for Distinguished Conduct in the Field (D.C.M.)

There appears to be some misunderstanding regarding the date of institution of this award, most collectors and writers believing that it was founded by the Royal Warrant of 4th December 1854, while others insist that, because there is no mention of the title, *Medal for Distinguished Conduct in the Field*, in that warrant, the Meritorious Service Medal was the appropriate award during the Crimean War and the Indian Mutiny; they contend that the D.C.M. was, in fact, instituted by the Royal Warrant of 30th September 1862.

One writer, in particular, has gone to some lengths to indicate that the later date is the correct one, but in this he has only been successful in showing that from the wording of the two Royal Warrants, *it could appear* that the medal was only instituted in 1862. If, as he asserts, the awards given in the Crimean War were M.S.Ms, then the many known Crimean D.C.Ms must either be false or retrospective issues, and if the latter, what happened to all the original M.S.Ms?

To my mind, there is absolutely no doubt that the D.C.M. was founded in December 1854, and there are many references to the medal, by that name, in military newspapers, Army Lists, and official publications (including *Queen's Regulations*, 1859) emanating from H.M.S.O. from early in 1855 onwards.

Those who have any doubts on the matter should read the excellent article by Brig. H. B. Latham, *The Origin of the Medal for 'Distinguished Conduct in the Field'*, published in the Royal United Service Institution Journal, August 1953 (from which I am able to quote by kind permission of the author and the editor of the journal).

The confusion seems to arise from the wording of the Royal Warrant of 4th December 1854, the first part of which deals with the money awards or annuities relating to the M.S.M. The second part, as Brig. Latham points out, "makes an additional grant of gratuities under similar conditions to those governing the award of the L.S. & G.C. Medal, but omitting the clause concerning the length of service required".

It is this second part that refers, for the first time, to 'gallant conduct'. Brig. Latham continues: "No mention is made of any medal till near the end of the Warrant, when rather casually the words, 'to receive a medal' are inserted. As a result, many believed that the normal annuity medal (the M.S.M.) was issued with these Crimean annuities. This was, however, far from being the case, for on 21st December (1854), the General Commanding-in-Chief wrote to . . . the Secretary at War, and asked him if this was intended or whether a new 'medal was to be struck illustrative of the gallantry exhibited'. In the resulting correspondence the General C-in-C suggested that the new medal should carry on the obverse the single word, *Crimea*, and on the reverse, *For Distinguished Conduct in the Field* (P.R.O.-W.O. 43 (89) 115083). Finally it was decided to accept the General C-in-C's suggestion for the reverse, and to retain for the obverse that common to the L.S.G.C. medal, i.e. a military trophy having in the centre the shield of the arms of Queen Victoria. A specimen copy, with the same ribbon that we know so well, was submitted to Her Majesty for approval on 29th January 1855 (Royal Archives, E.5.33)."

From the records of the Royal Mint, it appears that on 2nd February 1855, the War Office placed an order with them for 'about a thousand' D.C.Ms, and by the following 20th November some 747 had been issued.

Brig. Latham provides further proof that the D.C.M. was in existence before the Warrant of 30th September 1862, when he quotes from the Adjutant-General's *Circular Memorandum,* issued from the Horse Guards on 1st June 1859, which mentions the D.C.M., and offers some clarification of the position regarding gratuities and annuities. It is clear that the position was unsatisfactory, as the fund from which the monetary grants were made, was fully appropriated, consequently during the Indian Mutiny and later, the D.C.M. was rarely awarded except when a grant became available This caused the Duke of Cambridge to enquire if it was not time that a revised warrant was drawn up (in a letter dated 7th November 1861) so that the medal could be awarded either with or without a grant, according to circumstances. In the letter, quoted in full by Brig. Latham (under reference P.R.O.–W.O.32/76), the Duke, as General Commanding-in-Chief, draws the attention of the Secretary of State for War "to the circumstances under which medals 'For Distinguished Conduct in the Field' were last granted with annuities and gratuities under the provisions of the Royal Warrant of the 4th December 1854, such marks of distinction being then intended as rewards for service in the Crimea".

As a result of this letter, the Royal Warrant of 3rd September 1862 came into being, not to institute the D.C.M., but to widen its scope, to enable it to be awarded with or without a monetary grant, and to avoid the rather liberal award of Victoria Crosses which occurred during the Indian Mutiny – awards made, with a monetary grant, because in many cases the D.C.M. was not available owing to the full appropriation of its grants fund.

The naming of the DCM varies considerably. Those for the Crimea and Indian Mutiny were impressed in seriffed capitals, like those of the MGS Medal (*Fig. 4b*). Later ones, prior to the Boer War, 1899-1902, are usually engraved, as were some of the early Boer War awards, but these were mainly impressed in thin *sans serif* capitals (*Fig. 4t*). Similar naming appears on 1914-18 issues, although it would seem that some early ones were issued unnamed. From *British Gallantry Awards* (Abbott and Tamplin) we learn that the *London Gazette* for 17 Dec. 1914 contained a note requiring all recipients of unnamed medals listed in that gazette to send them to the D.D.O.S., Woolwich Dockyard, for *engraving.* At least one of the listed medals is known with engraved naming, but it is not known how many were in fact *engraved*, rather than impressed.

## Bars to the D.C.M.

Bars for subsequent awards of the D.C.M. were authorised in February 1881, and bore the date of the action. Nevertheless, Pte Charles Crampion of the Norfolk Regt, who won a D.C.M. in Burma, in 1889, received a second medal for his gallantry in South Africa on 29th March 1900; later, however, he must have been issued with a bar for his first D.C.M., but apparently did not return the second, as both medals (the first with a dated bar attached) are in the Royal Norfolk Regimental Museum at Norwich, together with a photograph of Crampion (in civilian dress) wearing both D.C.Ms with his two campaign medals.

Prior to 1914 ten dated bars were awarded to holders of the Victorian DCM (one of which was a second bar, and two did not show the day, with only the month and the year) and three to recipients of the Edward VII type.

These dated bars were also awarded during the early part of the Great War, up to late 1916, but only about 86 were issued (one of which was a second bar), consequently they are quite rare. With the much larger number of bars being awarded (some 481 by May 1920), the additional expense of striking individual bars was deemed to be too great, and a conventional design was adopted (and used for the Military Medal, the DSM, and other awards, none of which had had dated bars), with a laurel spray to left and right of centre; further, instead of having lugs for fitting to the suspender pin, or lower bar, like a normal campaign bar, the new type was (and is) a slip-on type, with a tight back strip, which is slid over the ribbon.

## Edward VII D.C.M. – A dangerous copy. (See *Plate 5*)

A dangerous copy of the Edward VII D.C.M. turns up from time to time, sometimes named, sometimes with a plain edge. As the originals are fairly expensive medals, care should be exercised when buying, especially from unknown vendors, and the following points should be noted:

The copies are very slightly smaller than normal, but appear to have been struck in good silver. The *obv.* seems to have been struck from a die which has been cast from an original medal (hence the slightly smaller size, due to the shrinking of the cooling metal); the tops of several of the letters of EDWARDVS VII fade away near the rim; the details of the hair of the beard and the King's medals are much rougher; the Garter sash ends in a 'cut off' line, parallel to the rim, instead of just merging into the rim; the further lapel of the coat (near the letter E) does not come down to the rim.

The *rev.* does not look at all right. The lettering is uneven, especially the D in CONDUCT, while the letter G has its horizontal serif extending only inwards, instead of on both sides. The measurements in the copy are all greater than normal, as follows, with the genuine measurements given in brackets:

(a)  From top of FOR to bottom of the oval wreath is 23·5 mm. (23 mm.).

(b)  DISTINGUISHED measures 28 mm. overall (26·5 mm.).

(c)  CONDUCT measures 16·5 mm. overall (16 mm.).

(d)  IN THE FIELD measures 25·5 mm. overall (24·5 mm.).

(e)  Wreath and points are 13·5 mm. overall (13 mm.).

The scroll suspender and claw mount are basically of the same design as the genuine, but coarser, and the sides of the claw are much flatter.

The naming is *almost* right, in the thin, close-set type normally impressed on the genuine medal (like many of the Queen's and King's South Africa Medals), but the lines of the letters are just a bit thinner, and the letters are slightly too widely spaced. One named example, which I examined, was to a South African unit, and one might have passed it, assuming (wrongly) that the naming might vary somewhat for an overseas unit.

I believe that most of the named copies are named to genuine recipients (being easier to sell if verified), and they are usually found as singles. However, one must not rule out the possibility of a genuine D.C.M. being detached from a group and sold separately, while the copy could be put in with the remaining genuine medals and thus perhaps escape detection.

Named copies have turned up in auction more than once, without being described as copies, and they have found purchasers, as genuine medals, from the ranks of both collectors and dealers.

## Conspicuous Gallantry Medal

This medal was first instituted in 1855, to reward gallantry by naval ratings in the Eastern Campaign – which we usually call, somewhat inaccurately, the Crimean War. After the war, it lapsed completely until its re-institution in 1874. So few of the original medals were given that it was not thought worth while to make a special reverse die, and Meritorious Service Medals (with the scroll suspenders) were used, with the words, *Meritorious Service* erased (leaving the original *For* untouched), and with *Conspicuous Gallantry* engraved in their place. Naturally this treatment has tempted fakers to alter Victorian M.S. Medals, and collectors should be wary of apparently genuine examples (named on the edge to known recipients), especially if they are offered at a bargain price or are "going cheaply' at an auction sale attended by dozens of experienced collectors and dealers. One such example, which appeared some years ago, had the word, *For*, also engraved.

It has been suggested that the original ten recipients (one of whom was awarded two medals) eventually had to return their medals to receive a Victoria Cross in lieu, but this does not seem to be borne out in fact. Some, but not all, certainly received a V.C., and old photographs show some of the recipients wearing both awards. The following were the recipients of the 'engraved' medals, with a note of the dates, ships, and actions, and those marked with a * later received the Victoria Cross:

Barry, David: A.B., *Cracker;* Kinburn, Black Sea; 14th October 1855.

Barry, David: A.B., *Cracker;* Sea of Azov; 4th–6th November 1855.

Belding, Geo. Ldg. Smn, *Firefly;* Gulf of Bothnia; 8th August 1855.

Hanlon, Peter: A.B., *Curlew;* Sea of Azov; 4th–6th November 1855.

*Ingouville, Geo. Capt of Mast, *Arrogant;* Tragsund Roads, Baltic; 13th July 1855.

Kerr, Thomas: Gnr R.M.A., *Vesuvius;* Sea of Azov; 4th–6th November 1855.

*Rickard, Wm. Qmr, *Weser;* Salgir R., Sea of Azov; 11th October 1855.

*Shepherd (or Sheppard), John: Bo's'n's Mate, *St Jean d'Acre* (Nav. Bde.); Sebastopol; 15th July 1855.

*Sullivan, John: Bo's'n's Mate, *Rodney* (Nav. Bde.); Sebastopol; 10th April 1855.

*Taylor, John: Capt of Fo'c'sle, *London* (Nav. Bde.); Sebastopol; 18th June 1855.

*Trewavas, Joseph: Ord,. *Agamemnon* (lent *Beagle*); Genitchi, Sea of Azov; 3rd July 1855.

Some years ago a group came up in auction, including an engraved

C.G.M., the other medals being an unnamed Crimea Medal, bars – *Inkermann, Sebastopol,* and a Legion of Honour, 5th Class. The C.G.M. was engraved on the edge: *John Taylor, Captn of the Forecastle, H.M.S. London,* but as the group had been examined by many leading collectors and dealers, and made only £4 5s., it was presumably not the same C.G.M. which was once in the W. E. Gray Collection – when that was sold, in 1920, the group included the Victoria Cross, China 1842, and I.G.S. Medal with bar, *Pegu.*

The C.G.M. of 1874 has a straight suspender, like the Naval L.S. & G.C. Medal. The $1\frac{1}{4}''$ ribbon, of equal stripes of blue, white, blue, was altered in 1921 to white with narrow dark blue edges – often described as the old Naval General Service (1793–1840) ribbon. Although very similar, the two ribbons are not identical, as contemporary pieces of the N.G.S. ribbon which are still undiscoloured, show that the blue was appreciably lighter than either that of the later manufactured N.G.S. ribbon or the present C.G.M.

In 1943 certain R.A.F. and Army personnel became eligible for the C.G.M. for gallantry in air operations against the enemy; in such cases the medal – known as the C.G.M. (Flying) – is the same as that for the Navy, but the ribbon is light blue with narrow dark blue edges.

**The George Medal**

It does not seem to be generally known that the naming on this medal is found in both impressed and engraved capitals.

**The Military Medal**

This medal does not present any difficulties for the collector, but some interesting points arise. Among awards for the Great War, particularly sought after are MMs to naval personnel, including RNVR, serving ashore with the Royal Naval Brigade in France, Gallipoli, and elsewhere, awards to the Royal Flying Corps, the RAF, and also to women. Some were awarded to allied troops (mainly French and Belgian) and these were issued unnamed.

Attention should be paid to the first type of George V (in army uniform, issued from 1916 to 1930), to see if perchance it should have a *non-swivelling* suspender. If so, while this probably means a duplicate or replacement of a Great War award (as these were not marked "(REPLACEMENT)" until George VI's reign), it *could* be a post-war award, and as such would be of much greater interest and value. To verify this, reference would have to be made to the *London Gazette*, to regimental histories or museums, or to other authoritative sources.

The second issue of George V, introduced in 1930 and used until the first George VI type appeared in 1938, is also rare, and can be distinguished by the crowned head and robed bust.

Far fewer MMs were issued in World War II than in the Great War, and usually a citation can be found in the *London Gazette*.

### Distinguished Service Medal

Instituted under Order in Council of 14th October 1914, the medals awarded during the 1914–18 War were impressed with the recipient's number, name, rating, ship (usually), location in which won, and the date (as far as space permitted), in upright serifed capitals. Some, however, in lieu of ship and location, bear SPECIAL SERVICE; it is believed that these were awarded for 'Q' Ship actions or similar operations.

A bar for further services was authorised on 27 January 1916, and most of those awarded for the Great War have the date of the action impressed in similar lettering, or engraved. They are of the same design as for the MM, with a conventional laurel spray. I have seen a bar without the date, but it may not have been the original issue. Bars for World War II are undated. During this war, NCOs and men of the RAF serving with the Fleet or in air/sea rescue were made eligible for the DSM, as were NCOs and men of the Army serving in defensively-equipped merchant ships (DEMS), and such awards are much sought after.

According to the *Royal Mint Annual Report, 1941*, the DSM was issued with a swivelling suspender up to 1941, but later issues had a fixed suspender. It seems, however, that stocks of swivelling medals were not used up until 1942.

Like the Military Medal, there was a "crowned head" type of George V, in use from 1930 until 1938, but only three were awarded, so it is extremely rare.

Medals issued during the 1939–45 period usually have the naming *engraved* in very neat letters (which at first glance look like impressed capitals), but the information is, unfortunately, often limited to number, rating, and name; a few are found impressed with small *sans serif* capitals, and some medals show the name of the ship.

## Constabulary Medal (Ireland)

Although this medal, for which a very high standard of gallantry is required and which has been obsolete since 1922, has been shown for many years in the official *Order of Wearing* (ranking between the A.F.M. and the Sea Gallantry Medal), very little has been written about it in the medal books. Some have given a brief description, without any other data, but most have omitted it altogether.

The medal is of silver, standard size; the *obv.* shows the Irish harp with a crown above, and flanked by branches of oak and shamrock (the style of the harp varies: one die has the conventional 'winged female' type, while another has the traditional Gaelic harp, similar to that on the pre-decimal Irish penny); the legend above is REWARD OF MERIT, and below, IRISH CONSTABULARY, later amended to ROYAL IRISH CONSTABULARY. The *rev.* has a wreath of laurel and shamrock, and in the plain centre, the name, rank, and number of the recipient are engraved, together with the date of the award. The precise details of the engraving probably vary over the years, as do the details of the dies used.

The medal was instituted in 1842, by Warrant, and is referred to in a Circular dated 15th April 1842, issued by the Inspector-General of Constabulary by command of the Lord Lieutenant. This Circular states that if a Head Constable, Constable, or Sub-Constable distinguishes himself by 'zealous, intelligent, and spirited conduct' he will be awarded a lace chevron to be worn on the left forearm of his uniform jacket. After winning four chevrons and becoming entitled to a fifth, he will remove the chevrons and be awarded instead 'a silver medal which he will wear suspended by a light blue ribbon on his left breast'. Para. 6 of this Circular provided that he could be awarded the medal for a single act if it be 'highly meritorious'.

In a Circular dated 10th May 1856, it was laid down that the medal should be awarded when a member qualified for the fourth chevron.

Royal Irish Constabulary Regulations of 1st January 1872, discontinued the issue of chevrons, changed the colour of the medal ribbon, and made the medal an award for gallantry; Section 1267 states, *inter alia*, "When a member of the Force in the performance of Police duty, displays pre-eminent valour and bravery, in addition to any other award he may receive, a silver medal will be conferred upon him, which is to be suspended by a light green ribbon". This Section was repeated in the last issue published of the R.I.C. Regulations, 1st December 1911. Thus, although the status of the medal changed from one of meritorious conduct to gallantry, this was not indicated on the medal, which retained its legend, *Reward of Merit*. Although the regulations describe the ribbon as 'light green', the few examples that I have seen of this scarce medal (only just over 300 were awarded, and over 250 of these were in 1919–21), all had a ribbon of mid-green, similar to that of the old Volunteer LSM.

The medal became obsolete in the disbandment of the R.I.C. on 31st May 1922, but as late as October 1959, two holders were still serving in the Royal Ulster Constabulary in Belfast, and the last retired on 20th April 1960.


## Sea Gallantry Medal

Originally known as the *Board of Trade Medal for Saving Life at Sea*, this medal has been fairly sparingly awarded, and there is always an interesting story attached to it (although this may be difficult to trace when the incident occurred in wartime, as citations and other details were suppressed). From its institution in 1855 until 1904, the medal, whether in silver or bronze, was 2·25″ in diameter, not intended to be worn (although some recipients had unofficial suspenders fitted), and was awarded in a presentation case. In 1904, however, Edward VII authorised a smaller medal, 1·27″ in diameter, so that it could be worn, with a red ribbon with narrow white side stripes (*Plate 10*). Although between 1904 and 1969 approximately the same number of silver and bronze medals were awarded – 479 and 476 respectively – the bronze ones appear to much the scarcer.

Although the practice may not have been constant, it would seem that the name of the ship to which assistance was given appears on the engraved naming, rather than that in which the recipient was serving. Thus for assisting in the rescue work at the burning of the *Volturno* in mid-Atlantic in 1913, the medal to the bosun of the *Asian* reads: DANIEL RIORDAN, 'VOLTURNO', 9 OCTOBER 1913.

Many of the awards of this medal are listed, some with details, in *Gallantry*, by Sir Arnold Wilson and Capt. J. H. F. McEwen (Oxford Univ. Press, 1939), together with much information about similar medals.

**British Empire Medal**

Since 1940 the Medal of the Order of the British Empire has become mainly an award for meritorious service, although it can still be awarded for gallantry.

There are three different phases of its history; the original issue was a small medal, about 1·1″ diameter, of frosted silver, showing Britannia within a circle bearing the motto of the Order, and, on the *rev.*, the royal cipher. This was instituted in 1917, and in 1918 it had a Military and a Civil Division, with a purple ribbon $1\frac{1}{16}$″ wide, differenced for the Military Division by a central red stripe 'about one-sixteenth of an inch'. It is reported that only about 400 of these small medals were issued but the number is believed to be very much higher; they are usually unnamed, but named examples (perhaps privately engraved) may be found.

In 1922 the small medal was replaced by two of standard size – one for gallantry and one for meritorious service. Both were awarded in the Military and Civil Divisions (and the red central strip in the ribbon of the former was now defined as 'about one-tenth of an inch'). That given for gallantry, generally known as the *Empire Gallantry Medal*, (E.G.M.), bore the words FOR GALLANTRY (described in the statutes as in the exergue, but only the second word is so placed; FOR is above the exergue, left), and had a spray of laurel leaves on the suspender. Later the ribbon was distinguished by a spray of laurel in silver.

The medal for meritorious service is similarly worded as such, and has oak leaves on the suspender. Those given in the reign of George V have a *rev.* bearing the crowned imperial cipher, GRI, in serifed capitals, with V below, within a border of six lions, while those of George VI have the cipher in script, and below, INSTITUTED BY KING GEORGE V; the border has only four lions.

With the institution of the George Cross in 1940, the Empire Gallantry Medal was abolished, and holders could have their medals exchanged for the George Cross. Although the surviving medal is designated as *For Meritorious Service*, it is sometimes awarded for gallantry, and by an Additional Statute of 6th December 1957 it was commanded that such future awards would be so stated in the announcement; they will be distinguished by the wearing of an emblem of two crossed oakleaves on the ribbon of both divisions.

Naming is both by impressed and engraved capitals. In a very broad classification, one can say that most of the George V issues are impressed, while those of George VI, and later, are engraved. Sometimes the engraved ones appear at first glance to be impressed, but careful examination shows the style of naming.

### Indian Distinguished Service Medal

This award, founded in 1907 and discontinued in 1947, is found with both impressed and engraved namings. I understand that, for many years, the medal was issued with a top brooch bar, rather similar to that seen with the D.S.O., but presumably in silver.

As with most Indian awards, verification is somewhat difficult, but from 1908 to 1922 a list of the holders was given in the Annual Supplement to the *Indian Army List*.

### Meritorious Service Medal

The M.S.M., instituted in 1845, and for many years known as *The Serjeants' Medal* or *The Medal with Annuity*, is not generally valued as highly by collectors as by recipients.

Contrary to the belief of a few writers, this was not the medal awarded for gallantry in the Crimea, as the Distinguished Conduct Medal (*q.v.*) had been instituted in December 1854. However, the M.S.M. certainly supplemented the D.C.M. and the M.M. in the latter part of the First World War. Under the order of January 1917 it could be awarded to "Warrant Officers, N.C.Os and Men who are duly recommended for the grant in respect of gallant conduct in the performance of military duty otherwise than in action against the enemy, or in saving, or attempting to save the life of an officer or soldier, or for devotion to duty in a theatre of war". This gave a fairly wide scope, particularly as many gallant acts were performed while 'at the receiving end' even if not in immediate contact with the enemy. Consequently many of these medals included in 1914–18 groups can be eventually traced as gallantry awards.

When the British Empire Medal replaced the Naval and R.A.F Meritorious Service Medals, in 1928, the Army M.S.M. was still retained, but presumably only for purely meritorious service – if the element of gallantry came into the award, then the B.E.M. could be awarded.

Up to 1917 the M.S.M. had the same ribbon as the Army L.S. &

G.C. Medal, i.e. plain crimson up to October 1916 and then, crimson with white edges up to January 1917 – and up to this date the M.S.M. displaced the Long Service Medal, as both could not be worn. In January 1917, with the change in conditions already referred to, the central white stripe was added to the ribbon, and the medal could be worn with, but after, the L.S. & G.C. Medal.

A few Army M.S.Ms were awarded to the Naval Brigade in the First World War, but they are very rare. An example in my collection shows, after the number, rating, and name, RL: NAVY, and the notification in the *London Gazette* is worded, "... in recognition of valuable services rendered with the Armies in France and Flanders".

### Naval Meritorious Service Medal

This medal was awarded from 1919–28. It is a much scarcer medal than the Army M.S.M., and is distinguished by the *obv.* portrait of the King in Admiral's uniform. This may not be apparent to the novice, but one should look out for the bullion epaulettes, which are not present on the Army medal. Also the Naval M.S.M. often has the action for which it was given, impressed on the edge (although some are only marked, SERVICES DURING WAR), whereas the Army medal has only the number, rank, name, and unit.

In 1928, the Naval M.S.M. was replaced by the B.E.M.

### Royal Air Force M.S.M.

Also awarded from 1919–28, and replaced by the B.E.M., the Royal Air Force M.S.M. has a special feature, in that it is worn *before* the L.S. & G.C. Medal.

### Colonial Forces M.S.M.

These medals, awarded between 1894–1930, are fully described in medal books, with their various distinguishing centre stripes on the ribbons, but unfortunately for collectors, many of the M.S.Ms given to Commonwealth troops during the Great War did not bear the appropriate dominion's name on the *rev.*, being the ordinary British issue. For example, in a 1914–15 Star group to a Private of the 2nd Canadian Inf. Bde. H.Q., is an ordinary British M.S.M., impressed to 7th British Columbia Regt. It seems likely that this was one given for gallantry, and thus was awarded by the C-in-C., while those given in the ordinary way, for 'routine' meritorious service, were probably local issues.

# 6

## British Campaign Medals

THIS series provides the major part of both the collection and the interest. These are the general awards given to all who participated in campaigns large and small; sometimes those who fought received the same medal and bars as those who fed, serviced, or tended them – sometimes the latter categories received only the medal without bar, or in a different metal. But the stories behind the medals, the parts played by the regiments, corps, or ships, or by individuals, form the background which makes our collection something of *personal* interest, of individuality, instead of just so many different pieces identified only by their respective labels.

Throughout these notes, little will be said about the designs of the medals, or similar data, as that is all given in the wide range of medal books, but all bars are listed, together with a note of the usual styles of namings encountered. The object here is to provide information which will assist in *collecting*, such as notes on false or unofficial bars, faked namings, etc. It must be strongly emphasised, however, that the mentioning of these should not give the beginner the impression that he will frequently be encountering 'dud' medals. There are far, far more perfectly genuine and desirable medals about than 'dud' ones, and, in point of fact, the latter are relatively infrequent and in the main are confined to the fairly expensive medals – *with one important exception:* to wit, medals which have been repaired, re-named, or fitted with unofficial bars, for the convenience of entitled recipients, and not with intent to defraud collectors. Such items include even the commonest medals, and they are usually very apparent to any careful observer, but they do occur fairly frequently among medals offered by pawnbrokers, jewellers, secondhand shops, and (sad to relate) occasionally among those still in family possession. The leading numismatic dealers invariably separate such items from their normal stock (consigning them to the melting pot, or using them for theatrical hire orders), but if they are very rare medals, then there is a demand for them at much reduced prices.

The starting point for many collectors is the Waterloo Medal, as it was to all intents the first issued to all ranks, officers and men alike, although from a date point of view we go back nominally to 1793 for the General Service Medals. I say 'nominally', as very few collectors are likely to acquire one of the seventeen Naval General Service Medals issued with a bar bearing the year 1793, and the following year, 1794, is the earliest that most of us can hope to have represented; for the Military G.S. Medal, although dated 1793–1814, the earliest bar – *Egypt* – was in respect of service in 1801.

There are, of course, the large early medals of the Honourable East India Company. Some collectors exclude them, as few of them were awarded to British troops and those that were could not be worn, except the Seringapatam Medal for which royal permission to wear was given in 1851. While, fortunately, we are free to please ourselves what we collect and what we reject, there does not seem to be any valid reason for excluding these medals from a general collection on the grounds that they are H.E.I. Co. issues (as opposed to medals issued by the British Crown), since many of our normally accepted medals, bearing the Queen's head, were issued by the H.E.I. Co. on the authority of the Crown; these include most of the medals from the Army of India, 1799–1826, to the Indian Mutiny Medal.

\*　　　\*　　　\*

In the notes which follow, all British campaign medals are listed, with their bars (if any). All medals are in silver unless otherwise stated, and all those with bars were also issued without a bar unless marked to the contrary.

### Early medals issued by the Honourable East India Company
All issued in gold and silver, except where otherwise stated.
GUZERAT & CARNATIC, 1778–84 (often called the DECCAN Medal).

MYSORE, 1790–92.

CEYLON, 1795–96.

SERINGAPATAM, 1799 (in gold, silver-gilt, silver, bronze, and tin).

JAVA, 1811.

NEPAL, 1814–16 (silver).

BURMAH, 1824–26.

COORG, 1837.

EGYPT, 1801.

RODRIGUES, BOURBON and MAURITIUS, 1809–10.

All these medals were issued unnamed, but occasionally examples may be found, with engraved naming, to British regiments, either on the edge or, more frequently, in the field. One cannot establish if the naming is contemporary, but many look genuine, and reference to the Muster Rolls in the Public Record Office may verify the entitlement. For officers, regimental records or histories may supply the answer, and for those who survived until 1840, a record of their services may be found in *Hart's Army List*.

At one period, somebody had access to the obsolete dies kept in Calcutta, and produced late strikings, albeit in good silver, but nevertheless tantamount to copies. Certain of the dies must have been cracked, deliberately or otherwise, as strikings from cracked dies are frequently found. The crack is usually an irregular one, running from the edge towards the centre of the die, and appears on the medal as an irregular ridge of metal which cannot usually be erased without damaging part of the design. I once saw a medal advertised, as if it were an unusually desirable item, as 'an attractive example from the famous cracked die'.

These re-strikes are sometimes on a thinner flan than the originals, while fakes, made from a mould taken from a genuine medal, are slightly smaller in diameter, owing to the contracting of the cooling metal, and often show pitting, sand marks, or indistinct detail. Such fakes are, of course, of no value beyond the scrap worth of the metal, while re-strikes, coming from the genuine dies, command a slightly better price; collectors should certainly not pay anything like the price of a genuine medal for a re-strike, and the only safe-guard is to buy from or through one of the leading dealers.

It must be admitted that it is often very difficult indeed to say with any certainty that a particular HEICo medal is a genuine original – one can often say that without doubt it is a restrike or forgery – and most dealers would be the first to admit that they would be uncertain.

The medal which comes up most frequently, and is the easiest to decide as to its genuiness, is that for Seringapatam, 1799. It is also the one which has most interest for collectors, as quite a number of British regiments were involved, and royal permission was given in 1851 for the medals to be worn (British officers in the HEICo forces received this permission in 1815).

There are two distinct sets of dies; those medals struck in England, at the Soho Mint, Birmingham, are 1·9″ in diameter, were struck in gold, silver-gilt, silver, bronze and tin, and have the designer's initials, C.H.K. (C. H. Küchler, who also designed the "cartwheel" 2d and 1d of 1797) in the right lower field, just above the exergue. The medals struck in Calcutta are smaller, 1·8″ diameter, in gold and silver only, and the initials are out of order, with the K inverted, thus: C.Я.H. Restrikes are often seen, the silver ones being much thinner than the original issue.

The medals were pierced for suspension, and those to Indians are often found with a ring or rings, and the medal worn round the neck from a yellow cord. Other medals, including those to officers of the HEICo regiments and those to officers and men of British regiments, usually have a loop suspender pinned or rivetted through the hole, or some other suspender, sometimes of a fancy nature. Many of the medals were worn, round the neck or on the left breast, with a yellow, pale orange, or tawny ribbon, but judging from the evidence of contemporary portraits, many officers used the Waterloo ribbon.

### Naval Gold Medals (Large and Small), 1794–1815

No bars given. Recipient's name, etc., engraved on *rev*. Medals were given for the following actions:

| | |
|---|---|
| 1st June 1794. | Capture of *Thetis*, 1808. |
| St. Vincent, 1797. | Capture of *Badere Zaffer*, 1808. |
| Camperdown, 1797. | Capture of *Furieuse*, 1809. |
| Nile, 1798. | Lissa, 1811. |
| Recapture of *Hermione*, 1799. | Banda Neira, 1811. |
| Trafalgar, 1805. | Capture of *Rivoli*, 1812. |
| 4th November 1805. | Capture of *Chesapeake*, 1813. |
| St. Domingo, 1806. | Capture of *L'Etoile*, 1814. |
| Curaçoa 1807. | *Endymion* with *President*, 1815. |

Unlike the Army Gold Medals and Crosses, possession of a Naval Gold Medal did not disbar the recipient from receiving the relative bar to the General Service Medal.

### Maida, 1806

Struck in gold only; no bars issued. Name of recipient is usually engraved on the edge, but some are known unnamed. An example in silver is alleged to have been awarded to an officer of the 4th Foot. Cast copies, easily recognised, are found, in silver-gilt or bronze-gilt.

## Army Gold Cross and Medals (Large and Small), 1808-14

Bars, not exceeding two, were added to the medals for subsequent actions; for four actions the Cross was awarded, with the actions specified on the arms of the Cross, and bars for further battles. Naming is engraved on the edge. The following are the actions concerned:

| | |
|---|---|
| Roleia, 1808. | Badajoz, 1812. |
| Vimiera, 1808. | Salamanca, 1812. |
| Sahagun, Benevente, 1808–9. | Fort Detroit, 1812.† |
| Corunna, 1809. | Vittoria, 1813. |
| Martinique, 1809. | Pyrenees, 1813. |
| Talavera, 1809. | St. Sebastian, 1813. |
| Guadaloupe, 1810. | Chateauguay, 1813. |
| Busaco, 1810. | Nivelle, 1813. |
| Barrosa, 1811.* | Chrystler's Farm, 1813. |
| Fuentes d'Onor, 1811. | Nive, 1813. |
| Albuhera, 1811. | Orthes, 1814. |
| Java, 1811. | Toulouse, 1814. |
| Ciudad Rodrigo, 1812. | |

Recipients of any of the above awards could not also have the same bar with the Military General Service Medal, consequently a number of officers who survived until 1847 did not receive the silver medal; there does not seem to be anything in the Order of 1st June 1847, instituting the medal, preventing such an award, in fact the terms of it imply that every officer, non-commissioned officer, and soldier present was to receive the medal.

## Waterloo, 1815

No bars issued; naming – see below.

As mentioned above, the Waterloo Medal is regarded by many collectors as their starting point, and certainly the possession of one was an early ambition of all beginners, but with the enormous rises in price in recent years, the realisation of this ambition has been much more difficult.

The medals were issued with a steel clip, through which passed a steel ring, about an inch in diameter; sometimes this appears as a

---

*Name of battle die struck, in raised letters, on *rev.* (on all the others, it is engraved), also the date, MDCCCXI.

†The small Gold Medal to Capt P. Latouche Chambers, 41st Foot, in the National Army Museum, is engraved DETROIT on *rev.*

'split' ring (or key-ring), but it is more likely that the original was solid. These rings rusted, and many recipients, especially officers, had them removed – not only were they detrimental to uniforms, but were very unsightly – and replaced by a variety of suspenders, sometimes with a silver clip of the same design as the steel original, with a ribbon suspender joined to the clip by a screw shackle fitting; sometimes with a silver bar, swivelling or fixed, or by various other methods. Waterloo Medals are often described as 'with original ring and clip' or 'not original suspender', but few collectors regard these points as having any serious effect on the price, especially as the ring is often a replacement, and the silver suspender usually enhances the appearance of the medals. (*See Plate 11*.)

The medals are named with large impressed serifed letters by a machine invented and constructed by two of the Mint workmen, Thomas Jerome and Charles Harrison (*Fig. 4a*); usually the blank space at each end is filled up with two or three 'stars'. If re-named, these stars were often untouched, and perhaps the regiment as well. but an *engraved* name is a certain sign of re-naming. Unofficial bars, often in the form of silver slides on the ribbon, engraved with names of actions in the Peninsular War, or just 'Peninsula', are frequently found with Waterloo medals. They were probably made for ex-soldiers, sporting their medal on their civilian clothes (the M.G.S. Medal was not given until 1848), although they may have been worn with uniform in some units, as regulations were often slack. They do not add to the value of the medal, but they are interesting.

A copy of the medal exists, well made in good silver, which may easily deceive the less experienced collector, although it was not made to deceive but as a replacement. The copy is very slightly smaller in diameter than the original, but this is only found by calliper measurement; it is also thinner. On both *obv.* and *rev.* the copy omits the name of the designer, T. Wyon, and all the lettering is slightly more 'squat'; in the exergue, the gap between JUNE and 18 is much wider than in the original. The naming is in engraved letters – capitals usually – and this, of course, immediately puts the collector on his guard, apart from the fact that the head itself, although well executed, has a 'not quite genuine' appearance.

Generally speaking, the average condition of Waterloo medals is between F and VF. They were issued early in 1816, and were proudly worn by all ranks, day in – day out (there were no ribbon strips for undress uniform at that time); they were cleaned, battered, lost, found, and always in circulation. On the other hand, the Military and Naval General Service Medals, issued in 1848 to survivors of the Napoleonic and other wars, are usually at least VF and often EF, since the majority of the recipients had long since left the services, and consequently few of the medals were actually worn.

## Military General Service Medal, 1793-1814

Twenty-nine bars issued; not issued without a bar. Naming is by impressed capitals (*Fig. 4b*).

Bars:

| | |
|---|---|
| Egypt (1801). | Java (1811). |
| Maida (1806). | Ciudad Rodrigo (1812). |
| Roleia (1808). | Badajzo (1812). |
| Vimiera (1808). | Salamanca (1812). |
| Sahagun (1808). | Fort Detroit (1813). |
| Benevente (1809). | Vittoria (1813). |
| Sahagun & Benevente (1808/9). | Pyrenees (1813). |
| Corunna (1809). | St. Sebastian (1813). |
| Martinique (1809). | Chateauguay (1813). |
| Talavera (1809). | Nivelle (1813). |
| Guadaloupe (1810). | Chrystler's Farm (1813). |
| Busaco (1810). | Nive (1813). |
| Barrosa (1811). | Orthes (1814). |
| Fuentes d'Onor (1811). | Toulouse (1814). |
| Albuhera (1811). | |

Although not the next medal in order of issue, it is convenient to deal with this, together with the Naval General Service and Army of India Medals, at this stage, as, with the Waterloo Medal, this quartet covers roughly the same period, and usually appears first in dealers' lists, auction catalogues, and many books on medals.

As some 25,000 of these medals were issued, it is not surprising that there are minor die varieties, with noticeable differences in the size of the *obv.* date figures, or the presence or absence of the designer's initials, w.w., in the *rev.* exergue. Those with the initials have them either on the far right, or divided, one on the left and one on the right. No difference in value attaches to these varieties.

The M.G.S. and N.G.S. Medals, and the Army of India Medal, were all impressed in the same style (*Fig. 4b*), in small serifed capitals, and as far as the M.G.S. is concerned, there are comparatively few snags for collectors, since the inclusion of the regiment safeguards to some extent against 'fiddling' in naming, although many cases are known of bars having been altered or added. Bars are widely spaced on many medals, when only a few appear, but large numbers of bars are usually grouped in threes per pair of rivets. Some bars have more than one die, e.g. *Salamanca* bunched or spread out; both appear to be genuine, while the majority of *Toulouse* bars have the word occupying 17 mm., but others have it measuring 15 mm Occasionally genuine medals are found with a wrong bar in comparison with those given in copies of the medal roll; in such cases either could be correct, and unless the bar on the medal is a rare one, there is no need to worry. Perhaps the most controversial bars are the rare ones, *Sahagun*, *Benevente*, and *Sahagun & Benevente*. Many of the last were given to men who should have had a single action bar (the double bar often appearing in the roll), particularly in the 7th Hussars, where only one officer and thirteen men were present at Sahagun, whereas the whole regiment were at Benevente; consequently *Benevente* should be relatively plentiful and the double bar rare, but actually many received the latter bar in error, and are shown as entitled in many copies of the roll.

Although quite a number of defective M.G.S. medals exist, they are not so dangerous as the N.G.S. and Army of India medals. Sometimes they appear with completely wrong bars, but most of the re-named ones are obvious, with *engraved* lettering. I have not kept records of many of the obviously re-named, but the following short list may be helpful:

Ace, William, 10th Hussars (*Benevente*): Renamed, but on roll.

Barks, G., Sgt. 9th Ft. (*Talavera*): Brooch marks, and has been reconstituted; on roll for two bars, *Vimiera*, *Barrosa*.

Boynton, James, 20th Regt. (*Egypt*): Officially renamed, on unclaimed medal originally named for Thos. Stiff, 18th Regt., deceased.

Cloutier, J., Canadn. Militia (*Chateauguay*): On roll, but renamed.
Dodd, John, 94th Ft. (*Fuentes d'Onor*): Apparently not on roll.

Delicott (or Delicote), Wm., 52nd Ft. (11 bars – *Tal.*, *Bus.*, *F.d'O.*, *CR.*, *Bad.*, *Sal.*, *Vitt.*, *Nlle.*, *Nive*, *O.*, *T.*): Foster's roll gives 10 bars, as above, but excluding *Tal.* and *Bus.*, and including *Pyr.* (Also had Waterloo Medal).

Greenham, S. 24th Ft. (*Egypt*): Last seven letters of surname re-engraved. Probably a perfectly genuine medal, corrected, as Samuel *Grinham* appears on the roll for the 24th Foot, with this single bar.

Hayward, James. Coldstm. Gds. (*Sal., Vitt., Tal.*): Renamed; six bars on roll.

Holmes, John. 36th Rgt. (*Salamanca*): Renamed; doubtful if on roll.

Kenny, Wolfenden, Lt. 40th Ft. (*Rol., Vim., Tal.*): Last bar unofficial; pin bar has been tampered with. On roll for first two bars only.

Lehne, William, 2nd Line Bn. K.G.L. (*Tal., Bus., F.d'O., CR., Sal., Vitt., St.Seb., Nlle., Nive*): shown on Foster's roll as *Talavera* only, but this combination of nine bars is common to the regiment.

McCasker, Dl. Cass. 96th Rgt. (*Vim., Cor., Pyr.*): Renamed; 96th had only *Guadaloupe*, and he is not on the roll for this.

McMahon, Thos., 85th Rgt. (*St.Seb., Nlle., Nive*): On roll, but bars have been re-soldered.

Maltby, S RA. Dvrs. (*Vitt, Pyr., Nive., Toul*): *Talavera* only on roll: brooch marks on *obv*. Has been re-constituted with wrong bars.

Neal, Wm. 7th Ft. (10 bars: *Mart., Bus., Alb., CR., Bad., Sal., Vitt., Pyr., St.Seb., O.*): Agrees with roll, but *Albuhera* bar sprung, and back of bars soldered. Appears to be in order, but was not fancied fetching only £22 in March 1967.

Obbert, William, Royal York Rangers, (*Mart., Guad.*): On roll, but renamed.

Piche, Pierre, Canadn. Militia (*Chry.Farm*): Unofficial bar, renamed medal. On roll.

Pickering, J., 23rd Ft. (*Mart., Alb.*): On roll, but renamed.

Reed, James. 10th Hsrs. (*Sah. & Ben., Vitt., Ort.*): On roll for last two bars only; came up for auction with his Waterloo Medal.

Schultze, C. 3rd Hsrs. K.G.L. (*Sah. & Ben.*): Renamed; not on roll.

Scott, Joseph. Qmr. 9th Ft. (*Vim., Vitt., St.Seb., Nlle., Nive*): Agrees with roll, but naming looks suspect.

Smith, Thomas. R.H.Gds. (No bar): Entitled to *Vittoria*.

Snelling, J. Serjt. 40th Ft. (12 bars: *Vim., Tal., Bus., CR, Bad., Sal., Vitt., Pyr., St.Seb., Nlle., Ort., Toul.*): on Foster's roll for four bars only – *Tal., Bad., Vitt., Nive.*

97

Swanson, D. 92nd Ft. (*Mart.*, *Alb.*, *Vitt.*, *Pyr.*, *Toul.*): Only *Egypt* on roll; 92nd did not get first two bars.

Tolleday, W. 5th Ft. (*Roleia*): On roll, but renamed.

Walker, J. 7th Lt.Dgns. (*Sah. & Ben.*): On roll, but renamed.

Walker, L/Sergt. T. 34th Foot, Good Conduct. (*Bad.*, *Sal.*, *Vitt.*, *St.Seb.*): Engraved, incl. 'Good Conduct'! 34th were not present at Badajoz, Salamanca, or St.Sebastian.

Wishe Sakahoron, Warrior (*Chry.Fm.*): Not fancied; doubtful if genuinely named, but some medals are known to Indian warriors with this type of name.

Yates, Joseph. R.H.A. (*Toulouse*): Engraved,; not on roll.

Young, Robert. 49th Ft. (*Chry.Fm.*): On roll, but renamed.

There are, of course, many others, both obviously re-named and repaired, and the serious collector is advised to try to obtain a copy of the roll (or have access to one), to use the services of a professional researcher, or to buy only from reputable vendors. Remember, too, that there are many perfectly genuine medals about which do not appear in (or agree with) some copies of the roll, and every time a medal roll is copied the risk of error increases.


### Naval General Service, 1793–1840

Not issued without a bar. Where the date of the action is not shown on the bar, it is given in brackets; the bars for *Boat Service* (shown in the list as B.S.) have the date *engraved*, at each side, thus: 1 Nov BOAT SERVICE 1809. Opinions differ as to the precise numbers issued of many bars, and the figures given after each bar must be taken as approximate only.

233 bars; 231 of these were authorised, of which nine appear to have had no claimants, and one (*Pilot 17 June 1815*), is reputed not to have been issued, although recorded against some officer recipients in Navy Lists, etc. Two bars (*B.S. 6 May 1814* and *B.S. Aug. & Sept. 1814*), are not traced as authorised, but are known to exist on apparently genuine and verified medals. Naming is by impressed capitals, as M.G.S. Medal (*Fig. 4b*). The abbreviation, *wh.*, on bars indicates *with;* thus *Amethyst wh. Thetis* is the action of H.M.S. *Amethyst* with the enemy ship, *Thetis*.

B.S. 15 March 1793 (1)
Nymphe 18 June 1793 (4)
Crescent 20 Octr. 1793 (12)
Zebra 17 March 1794 (2)
B.S. 17 Mar. 1794 (29)
Carysfort 29 May 1794 (0)
1 June 1794 (about 580)
Romney 17 June 1794 (3)
Blanche 4 Jany. 1795 (5)
Lively 13 March 1795 (3)
14 March 1795 (about 114)
Astraea 10 April 1795 (3)
Thetis 17 May 1795 (3)
Hussar 17 May 1795 (1)
Mosquito 9 June 1795 (0)
17 June 1795 (38)
23rd June 1795 (about 200)
Dido 24 June 1795 (1)
Lowestoffe 24 June 1795 (6)
Spider 25 Augt. 1795 (1)
Port Spergui 17 March 1796 (4)
Indefatigable 20 Apl. 1796 (6)
Unicorn 8 June 1796 (4)
Sta. Margaritta 8 June 1796 (3)
Southampton 9 June 1796 (4)
Dryad 13 June 1796 (8)
Terpsichore 13 Octr. 1796 (3)
Lapwing 3 Decr. 1796 (2)
Minerve 19 Decr. 1796 (4)
Blanche 19 Dec. 1796 (3)
Indefatigable 13 Jany. 1797 (8)
Amazon 13 Jany. 1797 (6)
St. Vincent (14 Feb. 1797) (364)
San Fiorenzo 8 March 1797 (7)
Nymphe 8 March 1797 (6)
B.S. 29 May 1797 (3)
Camperdown (11 Oct. 1797) (336)
Phœbe 21 Decr. 1797 (7)
Mars 21 April 1798 (26)
Isle St. Marcou 6 May 1798 (3)
Lion 15 July 1798 (21)
Nile (1 Aug. 1798) (about 350)
Espoir 7 Augt. 1798 (1)
12th October 1798 (about 77)
Fisgard 20 Octr. 1798 (9)
Sybille 28 Feby. 1799 (12)
Telegraph 18 March 1799 (0)
Acre 30 March 1799 (40)
B.S. 9 June 1799 (4)
Schiermonnikoog 12 Augt. 1799 (10)
Arrow 13 Sept. 1799 (2)
Wolverine 13 Sept. 1799 (0)
Surprise with Hermione (25 Oct. 1799) (7)
Speedy 6 Novr. 1799 (3)
Courier 22 Novr. 1799 (3)
B.S. 20 Dec. 1799 (3)
Viper 26 Decr. 1799 (1 or 2)
Fairy 5 Feby. 1800 (4)
Harpy 5 Feby. 1800 (4)

Peterel 21 March 1800 (2)
Penelope 30 March 1800 (12)
Vinceigo 30 March 1800 (2)
Capture of the Desirée (8 July 1800) (25)
B.S. 29 July 1800 (4)
Seine 20 Augt. 1800 (7)
B.S. 29 Aug. 1800 (26)
B.S. 27 Oct. 1800 (5)
Phœbe 19 Feby. 1801 (7)
Egypt (Mar.-Sept. 1801) (511)
Copenhagen 1801 (540)
Speedy 6 May 1801 (7)
Gut of Gibraltar 12 July 1801 (abt. 150)
B.S. 21 July 1801 (8)
Sylph 28 Septr. 1801 (2)
Pasley 28 Octr. 1801 (4)
B.S. 27 June 1803 (6)
B.S. 4 Nov. 1803 (2)
B.S. 4 Feb. 1804 (11)
Scorpion 31 March 1804 (4)
Beaver 31 March 1804 (0)
Centurion 18 Sept. 1804 (10)
Arrow 3 Feby. 1805 (8)
Acheron 3 Feby. 1805 (2)
San Fiorenzo 14 Feby. 1805 (12)
B.S. 4 June 1805 (10)
Phœnix 10 Augt. 1805 (22)
Trafalgar (21 Oct. 1805) (about 1650)
4 Novr. 1805 (295)
St. Domingo (6 Feb. 1806) (about 400)
London 13 March 1806 (29)
Amazon 13 March 1806 (30)
Pique 26 March 1806 (8)
Sirius 17 April 1806 (11)
B.S. 16 July 1806 (52)
Blanche 19 July 1806 (23)
Arethusa 23 Augt. 1806 (9)
Anson 23 Augt. 1806 (8)
Curaçoa 1 Jany. 1807 (67)
B.S. 2 Jan. 1807 (3)
Pickle 3 Jany. 1807 (1)
B.S. 21 Jan. 1807 (9)
B.S. 19 Apl. 1807 (1)
Hydra 6 Augt. 1807 (11)
Comus 15 Augt. 1807 (10)
Louisa 28 Octr. 1807 (1)
Carrier 14 Novr. 1807 (1)
Ann 24 Novr. 1807 (0)
B.S. 13 Feb. 1808 (3)
Sappho 2 March 1808 (5)
San Fiorenzo 8 March 1808 (16)
Emerald 13 March 1808 (12)
Childers 14 March 1808 (4)
Stately 22 March 1808 (32)
Nassau 22 March 1808 (35)
Off Rota 4 April 1808 (19)
Grasshopper 24 April 1808 (7)
Rapid 24 April 1808 (1)
Redwing 7 May 1808 (8)

Virginie 19 May 1808 (23)
Redwing 31 May 1808 (5)
Seahorse wh. Badere Zaffer (6 July
1808) (35)
B.S. 10 July 1808 (8)
Comet 11 Augt. 1808 (5)
B.S. 11 Aug. 1808 (15)
Centaur 26 Augt. 1808 (39)
Implacable 26 Augt. 1808 (45)
Cruizer 1 Novr. 1808 (4)
Amethyst wh. Thetis (10 Nov. 1808)
(34)
B.S. 28 Nov. 1808 (2)
Off the Pearl Rock 13 Decr. 1808 (16)
Onyx 1 Jany. 1809 (5)
Confiance 14 Jany. 1809 (8)
Martinique (Feb. 1809) (about 500)
Horatio 10 Feby. 1809 (16)
Superieure 10 Feby. 1809 (1)
Amethyst 5 April 1809 (28)
Basque Roads 1809 (12 Apl.) (about
550)
Pompee 17 June 1809 (22)
Castor 17 June 1809 (7)
Recruit 17 June 1809 (5)
Cyane 25-27 June 1809 (5)
L'Espoir 25-27 June 1809 (5)
Bonne Citoyenne wh. Furieuse
(6 July 1809) (12)
B.S. 7 July 1809 (about 36)
B.S. 14 July 1809 (7)
B.S. 25 July 1809 (37)
B.S. 27 July 1809 (10)
B.S. 29 July 1809 (11)
B.S. 28 Aug. 1809 (15)
Diana 11 Sept. 1809 (5)
B.S. 1 Nov. 1809 (about 115)
B.S. 13 Dec. 1809 (10 or 11)
Anse la Barque 18 Decr. 1809 (abt. 45)
Cherokee 10 Jany. 1810 (4)
Scorpion 12 Jany. 1810 (5)
Guadaloupe (Jan-Feb. 1810) (abt. 500)
Thistle 10 Feby. 1810 (0)
B.S. 13 Feb. 1810 (19)
Surly 24 April 1810 (3)
Firm 24 April 1810 (0)
Sylvia 26 April 1810 (1)
B.S. 1 May 1810 (17)
Spartan 3 May 1810 (33)
Royalist May & June 1810 (3)
B.S. 28 June 1810 (25)
Amanthea 25 July 1810 (about 30)
Banda Neira (9 Aug. 1810) (69)
Boadicea 18 Sept. 1810 (18)
Otter 18 Sept. 1810 (9)
Staunch 18 Sept. 1810 (2)
B.S. 27 Sept. 1810 (33)
Briseis 14 Octr. 1810 (2)
B.S. 4 Nov. 1810 (1 or 2)
B.S. 23 Nov. 1810 (65)

B.S. 24 Dec. 1810 (7)
Lissa (13 Mar. 1811) (abt. 130)
Anholt 27 March 1811 (46)
Arrow 6 April 1811 (0)
B.S. 4 May 1811 (11)
Off Tamatave 20 May 1811 (80)
B.S. 30 July 1811 (4)
B.S. 2 Aug. 1811 (10)
Hawke 18 Augt. 1811 (6)
Java (Aug. – Sept. 1811) (about 690)
B.S. 20 Sept. 1811 (8)
Skylark 11 Novr. 1811 (3)
Locust 11 Novr. 1811 (2)
Pelagosa 29 Novr. 1811 (67)
B.S. 4 Dec. 1811 (18)
Victorious wh. Rivoli (22 Feb. 1812)
(66)
Weasel 22 Feby. 1812 (6)
Rosario 27 March 1812 (8)
Griffon 27 March 1812 (3)
B.S. 4 Apl. 1812 (5)
Northumberland 22 May 1812 (64)
Growler 22 May 1812 (3)
Malaga 29 May 1812 (18)
Off Mardoe 6 July 1812 (50)
Sealark 21 July 1812 (4)
B.S. 1 Sept. 1812 (20)
B.S. 17 Sept. 1812 (12)
B.S. 29 Sept. 1812 (30)
(B.S. 17 Dec. 1812 – bars so dated in
error for 17 *Sept.* 1812).
Royalist 29 Decr. 1812 (5)
B.S. 6 Jany. 1813 (27)
B.S. 21 March 1813 (6)
Weasel 22 April 1813 (5)
B.S. 29 Apl. 1813 (2)
B.S. Apl. & May 1813 (some may have
had the B.S. bar dated 29 Apl. 1813)
(55)
B.S. 2 May 1813 (about 52)
Shannon wh. Chesapeake (1 June
1813 (48)
Pelican 14 Augt. 1813 (4)
St. Sebastian (Aug.-Sept. 1813) (abt.
290)
Thunder 9 Octr. 1813 (8)
Gluckstadt 5 Jany. 1814 (50)
Venerable 16 Jany. 1814 (45)
Cyane 16 Jany. 1814 (7)
Eurotas 25 Feby. 1814 (34)
Hebrus wh. L'Etoile (27 Mar. 1814)
(43)
Phœbe 28 March 1814 (28)
Cherub 28 March 1814 (10)
B.S. 8 Apl. 1814 (24)
B.S. 6 May 1814 (1) (An unpublished
bar, which exists on a medal, with
*Trafalgar*, to James Wills)
B.S. 24 May 1814 (14)
The Potomac 17 Augt. 1814 (abt.110)

B.S. Aug. & Sept. 1814 (1) (An un-published bar which exists on a verified medal to Alexr. Nesbit, Surgeon.)
B.S. 3 & 6 Sept. 1814 (1)
B.S. 14 Dec. 1814 (about 210)

Endymion wh. President (15 Jan. 1815) (63)
Pilot 17 June 1815 (probably 9)
Gaieta 24 July 1815 (about 90)
Algiers (27 Aug. 1816) (about 1360)
Navarino (20 Oct. 1827) (about 1130)
Syria (Nov. 1840) (about 7000)

This is one of the most interesting medals in the British series, covering such large actions as Copenhagen and Trafalgar, down to small cutting-out expeditions in which a few boats' crews captured enemy vessels – real swashbuckling 'Hornblower' stuff. Although the main action bars are the more popular, these small 'Boat Service' actions have a considerable appeal to collectors with nautical in-terests; and, in addition, they were well earned – such expeditions did not carry 'passengers'.

But in addition to being interesting, the N.G.S. Medal can also be a difficult medal for collectors. The many scarce bars have caused it to be frequently 'fiddled' by unscrupulous persons, particularly as the three bars, *Algiers* (over 1,300), *Navarino* (over 1,100), and *Syria* (over 7,000), include many recipients with far from unusual names which also appear in the lists for the rare bars, and in no case does the name of the ship appear on the medal. Consequently the original bar has sometimes been removed and a rare one put on in its place. The beginner must therefore be very careful before paying a large sum to an unknown vendor for a medal with a rare bar but with a common name on it (and regard a 'bargain' with more than usual suspicion). All the leading medal dealers, and many collectors, have a copy of the N.G.S. Medal Roll, and verification is not difficult. Officers' medals give their rank, and are thus less likely to be faked.

A good many years ago an unscrupulous gentleman was very clever at removing names, changing bars, and re-naming in an impressed type almost identical with the official one. The re-named medals are almost always spotted with a good pair of callipers, but there are one or two ready checks for this particular fraud, in the details of some of the letters, especially E, F, and N (*Fig. 3*).

I have seen *engraved* medals which gauge perfectly on the callipers and feel sure that they are not re-named, but duplicate issues or late issues. Examples have been seen in which the engraved naming has undoubtedly been done by the same man who engraved the 'wide suspender' LS&GC Medals. One sometimes finds that the medal has been detached from its suspender, set in a silver rim and glazed with convex glass on both sides, then re-mounted with a silver screw swivel suspender, in the style of the small Gold Medal. This, of course, lowers its value slightly, but presumably some officers wore them thus, with their name and rank engraved on the silver rim.

There were well over 20,000 Naval General Service Medals issued, and, of course, the large majority of those encountered by collectors are perfectly genuine. It is, generally speaking, only among the rarer bars that the need for caution arises.

As regards the list of medals given below, *it must be emphasised* that if a collector encounters a medal named as shown here, it does not necessarily mean that the one he is offered is a 'dud'. In the case of those medals which appear on the roll (despite several of the same name with *Syria* or *Algiers* bars), the one he encounters could just as easily be the genuine one, and he must use his own judgement after careful examination of the naming, rivets, pin bar, soldering, etc. Further, for those marked 'Not on roll', even this does not necessarily condemn the medal; it is often possible to trace officers who were present and entitled to a bar which appears on their medals, although not shown on the roll. All rolls are copies (usually re-copied several times, which increases the chance of errors and omissions), as the original Ms. rolls no longer exist, and even the Admiralty copy is by no means accurate. Spellings can vary quite a bit – a medal named to BROWN has appeared on the roll as BROME – and first names are often incorrect; even modern pairs of medals, such as QSA and KSA, or British War and Victory Medals, bear such namings as C. B. NEALE and C. R. HEALE respectively, both with the same number and regiment, and issued to the same man. Frequently the owner had the incorrect letters re-cut, so a medal marked *Name partly re-engraved* may well be genuine, but of course could also be a *Syria* one altered.

In many cases the medals mentioned below have come up for auction within the last thirty years; some have been described in the catalogues as re-named, or as 'not on the roll'; others, frequently with rare bars, have not been fancied, and have fetched a very low price after having been carefully examined by many experienced collectors and dealers. But again, I must repeat – *it does not mean that the medal you encounter is the identical one listed below.*

NOTE: Most of the medals described here as re-named are, in fact, impressed in the copy of the official style referred to earlier.

Backhouse, Joseph *(Boat Service, 4 Feb. 1804)*: On roll, but does not look right; pin bar may have been tampered with.

Baker, John *(Lissa)*: On roll, but as Midshipman – medal should show this. Name appears on *Navarino* and other rolls.

Ballard, James *(Syria)*: Unofficial bar.

Barnes, John *(Onyx, 1 Jany. 1809)*: On roll, but three of this name on *Syria* and other rolls; looks suspicious.

Bell, Geo. *(Stately 22 March 1808; Basque Roads 1809)*: This medal, noted in earlier editions as suspect, has now been established as in order. Bell served as Ord. at both actions, and 'Pte. R.M.' entry on the roll was an error, but there should be cross-entries against each bar roll to indicate a two-bar medal.

Brown, John *(Rosario 27 March 1812)*: On roll as Master, and this rank should appear on the medal. There are at least eight entries for this name on the *Syria* roll, apart from many others.

Brown, Josh. *(Trafalgar)*: On roll, but renamed.

Brown, Richard *(Dryad 13 June 1796)*: Not on roll; false bar with very small figures and letters.

Brown, William *(Banda Neira)*: On roll, but also entitled to *Trafalgar* and *Java*; seven on *Syria* roll.

Burke, James *(Traf.; Anson 23 Augt. 1806; Curaçoa 1 Jany. 1807; Mart.; Java)*: Not in agreement with roll.

Byrne, Gerald *(12 October 1798, Java)*: On roll as Pte. RM, for *Java*, but not for first bar; not fancied, but could be in order; wants checking against muster or pay rolls for the ships engaged.

Casey, D. O'B. *(Capture of the Desirée; Egypt)*: Engraved. Shown on roll as Lieut.

Chapman, John *(Nile)*: Not on roll, but is on *Syria* roll; could be genuine as a misnaming for John Chaplain, A.B. in *Minotaur*.

Collins, H., Master's Mate *(Pelagosa 29 Novr. 1811)*: Does not appear to be on the roll, but there seems to be no doubt that he was present, in HMS *Unité*, and received a medal (see Allen's *New Navy List*, 1855, and O'Byrne's *Naval Biog. Dicty.*, 1861 edn.). Was not fancied at auction in 1952, as being renamed or falsely named, but is probably quite genuine.

Cook, John *(Gut of Gibraltar 12 July 1801)*: Not on roll, but there is a John Cooke (Ord. *Pompée*), so the medal could well be in order, but there are six on the *Syria* roll.

Crawford, Jack *(Camperdown)*: Renamed (engraved); not on roll.

Davis, John (*1 June 1794; St. Vincent: St. Domingo: Martinique*): Not in accordance with roll.

Davis, John (*St. Domingo; Martinique: Algiers*): There is a two-bar medal on the roll, for first two bars, and three single *Algiers* bars, thus the medal might be in order.

Davis, Thos. (*Trafalgar*): Two on the roll, but four on the *Syria* roll; the pin bar has been tampered with.

Davis, Thos. (*Martinique; Guadaloupe*): Apparently not on the roll, but the roll is notoriously inaccurate for these two bars, with many known omissions; he *could* have been omitted from *both* rolls, but unlikely; four on *Syria* roll.

Degre (or Degee), George (*Copenhagen 1801*): Genuine, but repaired.

Dickson, W. (*B.S. 1 Novr. 1809*): On roll, but looks suspect; also appears on *Syria* roll.

Dunn, James, Purser (*Spartan 3 May* 1810): Unofficial bar; on roll.

Dutchman, H., Clerk (*Onyx 1 Jany. 1809*): On roll, but renamed.

Erring, James (*Trafalgar*): Not on roll; could be the *Syria* medal to James Errington, altered.

Filer, John (*Shannon wh. Chesapeake*): On roll, but JOHN impressed, and FILER re-engraved. Could be a genuine, but misnamed, medal, corrected by the recipient; could also be faked, using a *Syria* medal with a 5-letter surname, and changing the bar.

Ford, Wm., 1st Lt. R.M. (*Anholt 27 March 1811*): On roll, but also had *Syria* as Capt., R.M. Addition of rank suspect, and the medal should show the higher rank if originally issued with both bars. He could have had two medals (not an uncommon happening), but two others, not to officers, appear on the *Syria* roll.

Fox, Francis (*Pelican 14 Augt. 1813*): Has been mounted in ring, plugged at top and bottom; N of FRANCIS re-cut over plug. On roll, and medal quite genuine, but re-constituted, so doubtful if the bar and suspender are the original ones.

Guy, Jas. Wm. (*Java*): Renamed. Appeared in auction in 1952, with similar Army of India Medal, bar *Ava*, but he died on 23 March 1829, so was not entitled to either medal.

Hall, Geo. Sergt. R.M. (*Venerable 16 Jan. 1814*): Probably has been taken apart at one time (for a brooch?) and later re-constituted.

Harvey, Edward, Capt. in the Army (*Syria*): Suspected that the rank has been added. There *was* a Capt. Edw. Harvey, 14th Lt. Dgns., on the Staff in Syria, but the roll also shows medals to a Capt. R.M. and Pte. R.M., both Edward Harvey.

Holland, Daniel (*Trafalgar*): On roll, but engraved.

Hooper, Henry (*St. Domingo*): Cannot trace, but is on *Syria* roll.

Horn, Thomas (*Egypt*): Cannot trace, but two on *Syria* roll.

Howe, John (*Amazon 13 March 1806*): On roll, but appears 'fiddled'; two on *Syria* roll.

Hughes, John (*Martinique*): Brooch and other marks on *obv.* Cannot trace on roll, but could be genuine, despite five on *Syria* roll.

Hughes, William (*Victorious wh. Rivoli*): Unofficial bar; not on roll.

Hull, William (*Banda Neira; Java*): On roll, but the bars have bad rivets; name also appears on *Syria* roll.

Hunter, James, Midshipman (*B.S. 14 Dec. 1814*): On roll as Master's Mate, but renamed.

James, John (*B.S. 16 July 1806; Centaur 26 Aug. 1808*): Also entitled to *B.S. 4 Feb. 1804* and *Basque Roads 1809*. He *could* have been issued with two medals, with two bars each (but not likely to be split this way). Not fancied; three on *Syria* roll.

Leonard, Francis (*Copenhagen 1801; Trafalgar; Algiers*): Not on roll for first; served as Boy in *Royal Sovereign*, at Trafalgar; there is a Samuel Leonard, Boy 1st Class, in *Agamemnon*, on the Copenhagen roll, and it might be worth while checking the muster rolls and personal records of both these.

Luff, John (*Nile*): Apparently not on roll. The impressed JO is genuine, but the remainder is renamed.

Maybee, Henry (*Off Tamatave*): Small plug in exergue (ex-brooch?). On roll.

Mackey, Thos. (*Trafalgar*): Apparently not on the roll, but both medal and bar look to be perfectly in order.

Marsh, Daniel (*Nile*): Not on roll, but on *Syria* roll.

Mathews, R. B., Volr. 1st Class (*Harpy 5 Feby. 1800*): On roll, but renamed (impressed) in forged naming.

McLaughlin, Archd. (*Trafalgar; B.S. 7 July 1809*): On roll for *Trafalgar*, but the letters on the bar occupy nearly 2 mm. less than the normal 22 mm. There is some doubt whether he is on the roll for the second bar.

Mitchell, David (*Egypt*): On the roll, but renamed; the roll is marked 'Duplicate issued', and some duplicates were unclaimed medals re-issued with engraved naming.

Morris, James (*Guadaloupe*): Renamed; apparently not on roll.

Norman, William, Lieut. (*Trafalgar*): Engraved. Killed 13 Aug. 1810, so did not qualify for the medal.

Norman, Masters, Midsn. (*Egypt*): Engraved – renamed.

Page, Robt. (*Banda Neira; Java*): Not fancied, although on roll. Is also on St. Sebastian roll (which used to be regarded as a common enough bar to use the medal for 'fiddling').

Philip, John (*B.S. 29 Sept. 1812*): Not on roll, but is on *Syria* roll.

Phillips, Geo. (*Phoenix 10 Augt. 1805*): Doubtful if on roll, but appears on both *Syria* and *Algiers* rolls; not fancied.

Ratcliffe, Edwd. (*Martinique; Pompée 17 June 1809; Guadaloupe*): On the roll, but not original bars; soldered brooch marks on the medal, which is probably genuine, but re-constituted with new suspender, bars, etc., and therefore worth very much less than in original state.

Rattray, James, Lieut. (*Gut. of Gib. 12 July 1801: Trafalgar: B.S. 23 Nov. 1810*): Name partly engraved. *Boat Service* is unofficial; on roll for first two bars, but not the third, although he was serving in the area and could have been present. Allen's *New Navy List*, 1855, indicates NGS with two bars. Probably the medal and first two bars are quite genuine, and recipient may have added the third bar if he felt entitled to it. He died in 1862, as Vice-Admiral (retd.).

Reed, John (*B.S. 25 July 1809*): On roll, but also on *Syria* roll. The date on the bar is very poorly engraved, and while it could be in order, was regarded as suspect and not fancied at auction in 1949.

Reynolds, Peter (*17 June 1795; Gut. of Gib. 12 July 1801; Trafalgar*): Not in agreement with the roll, although he appears for *Trafalgar* in HMS *Victory*. Peter Reynolds may be the alias (or the correct name) of Peter Moser, who is shown for all three bars and who also served in HMS *Victory*, in which case the medal is probably quite genuine.

Riches, W. T. (*Java; Gluckstadt 5 Jany. 1814*): Renamed; on roll for *Java*, but as Midshipman; present at Gluckstadt, but not on the roll (the roll is marked 'Two disallowed').

Roberts, William (*14 March 1795; Camperdown; 12 Octr. 1798*): On the roll, but the pin bar is suspect. Could be perfectly genuine, but there are three on the *Syria* roll.

Robinson, William (*Curaçoa 1 Jany. 1807*): On the roll, but suspect as many medals with this name exist with various common bars.

Rose, James – no claw, no suspender, no bar; brooch marks on *obv*. On roll for *1 June 1794*, and another possibly for *St. Sebastian*, but any medal turning up with this name must be suspect.

Rose, Thos. (*Trafalgar; The Potomac 17 Augt. 1814*): No trace on roll, but two on *Navarino* roll, and on several other rolls. I have had two single-bar medals, *Navarino* and *Basque Roads 1809*, in this name; it is not unusual for two medals to have been issued to one man.

Schultz, G. A. (*Nassau 22 March 1806*): On roll, but medal is highly suspect. He served as Lieut (promoted in January 1806), and therefore the rank should appear on the medal.

Scougall, Alexr. (*Java; Navarino; Syria*): On *Syria* roll only.

Short, William (*Nile*): Not on roll, but on *Syria* and *Navarino* rolls.

Shreeves, Geo. (*Stately 22 March 1808*): Is on the roll as Shreeve, but the medal should also have the bar, *B.S. 25 July 1808*, and be named to Midsn, to which rank he appears to have been promoted between the two actions. The genuine medal, with correct rank and spelling of his surname, Shreeve, was offered in a leading dealer's list in February 1954.

Simpson, Benjn., Volr. (*Lively 13 March 1795*): On roll, but renamed; also entitled to *St. Vincent*.

Slade, George (*Centurion 18 Sept. 1804*): Apparently not fancied at the Dalrymple White sale in 1946, but could be perfectly genuine. On one well-known copy of the roll he is shown as '? Glade, George' (but without any rating indicated), and there does not appear to be a George Slade on any of the rolls for the common bars.

Smith, Henry (Egypt): Apparently not on roll, but eight on the rolls for *Syria* and *Navarino*.

Smith, John (*St. Vincent*): On the roll, but unofficial bar.

Smith, Thos. (*St. Vincent*): Not on the roll, but eleven on *Syria* roll.

Smith, William (*Trafalgar; Hebrus wh. L'Etoile*): The name appears on each roll, but not as a two-bar medal (but the absence of a cross reference is not necessarily important). Despite the common name, it could be in order, but was not fancied, although it appears to have been in the Sanderson and Cheylesmore collections. The William Smiths on the *Hebrus* roll should be investigated to verify this medal.

Smyth, Robt. (*St. Vincent*): Not on roll, but is on *Syria* roll.

Stewart, Charles (*Mars 21 April 1798; Trafalgar*): On the roll, but was not fancied, so presumably the naming must have looked suspicious; the name does not appear on any of the rolls for the common bars.

Sullivan, Dennis (*B.S. 1 Nov. 1809*): A perfectly satisfactory medal, with this single bar, exists, named to Dennis Sullivan, who served as Ord. in *HMS Topaze*. Also a suspect medal exists, probably the *Syria* medal with the bar altered; the first name may be Denis or Dennis (no record). Thirdly, a genuine 3-bar medal exists, to Dennis Sullivan, with this bar, also *Lissa* and *Pelagosa 29 Nov. 1811*, who served as Pte., RM, in HMS *Active*, but it was in error, as he was entitled only to the last two bars.

Sweeny, Edward (*1 June 1794*): Not on the roll, but is on the *Syria* roll.

Teed, Richard M., Volr. (*Copenhagen 1801*): "Seed" on roll; correct name is Teed (Lieut., 1809, Commdr. retd. 1848). R has been plugged and re-cut, so medal has probably been dismembered for a brooch at some time, and re-constituted.

Thompson, William (*Emerald 13 March 1808*): On roll, but also entitled to *Basque Roads* 1809): there are several on the *Syria* roll, and this medal, with only the one bar, was not fancied.

Thompson, William (*Trafalgar; Basque Roads 1809; Algiers*): Not in agreement with the roll.

Urwin, Geo. (*The Potomac 17 Aug. 1814*): Crude bar, soldered on. There is a Geo. Unwin on the roll, which could be a copying error for Urwin (or *vice versa*).

Walke, John (*B.S. 16 July 1806*): Not on the roll, but is on *Syria* roll.

Wedlock, Thomas (*Gluckstadt 5 Jany. 1814*): Not on roll, but two on *Syria* roll.

White, Thos. (*Martinique; Guadaloupe*): Apparently not on the roll, but the rolls for these two bars are known to be incomplete; five on *Syria* roll.

Williams, John (*Acre 30 May 1799*): On the roll, but also entitled to *Egypt;* as this latter bar was not authorised until 1850, it is possible that the recipient, having had his claim allowed (as shown by his name appearing on the roll), never had the bar added to his medal. However, the medal was not fancied, no doubt because there are some fourteen on the *Syria* roll.

Wilson, James (*Trafalgar; Martinique; Java*): In agreement with the roll, but since the bars are in poor condition on a VF medal, and the name is a common one, appearing on *Syria*, *Navarino* and elsewhere, the medal is suspect.

Wood, David (*Copenhagen 1801*): Not on the roll, but is on the *Syria* roll.

Wright, Robert (*The Potomac 17 Augt. 1814*): On the roll as Lieut, RMA, and the medal should have the rank on it. The name (not as an officer) appears on the *Syria* and other rolls.

*      *      *

**Sultan of Turkey's Medals (The Order of the Crescent)**
The long succession of Turkish awards to British personnel started with the Sultan's Gold, or Silver, Medal, also known as the Order of the Crescent (but apparently regarded by the Admiralty as a medal and not an order), in 1801. The sizes quoted in most medal books are, for the gold medals, 2·1″, 1·9″, 1·7″, and 1·4″ diameter, and 1·4″ for the silver medals (for NCOs), but some discrepancies occur in individual specimens, the workmanship being generally rather poor. Since these medals are unnamed, it is difficult to identify the army and navy recipients, but when one is found in company with the NGS Medal with *Egypt* bar, reference to *Haultain's Navy List* will show if the recipient was entitled to the gold medal. At one time I had a pair consisting of the NGS Medal with bar, *1 June 1794*, and the Gold Medal; reference showed that he was entitled to both, and would have had the *Egypt* as well, had he lived until 1850, when that bar was authorised (See *Plate* 15).

**Turkish Medal for Acre, 1840**
The Turkish medals for St. Jean d'Acre, 1840, were issued in 1842 to the crews of 31 of the 32 ships which later received the NGS Medal

109

with *Syria* bar – according to the Admiralty Notice of 26 March 1842. The ship omitted from the list is HMS *Dido*, Capt. Lewis Davies, and one wonders if this was omitted in error, since some 66 of the crew received the NGS Medal, and the ship appears to have received the battle honour, *Syria*, in common with the others present. As far as we can trace, the ship did not play an important part in the operations, and this may be the reason for the omission; on the other hand, it might well be that the crew received the Turkish medal. In addition to *Dido*, Major Gordon, in *British Battles & Medals*, also quotes *Fury* and *Lady Franklin* as ships whose crews did not receive this medal, but since it would appear that no names for crew members of either of these ships are shown on the *Syria* medal roll, it is not surprising that they did not get the Turkish medal; certainly *Fury* did not get the battle honour, and I cannot trace any reference to either of these two ships in connection with the Syrian operations, but they could well have been in the neighbourhood.

The medals were awarded in gold (to commanders and higher), silver (to quarter-deck and warrant officers), and copper (to working petty officers, seamen, marines, and boys). They were issued unnamed, although privately named ones are found. There was no issue of copper-gilt, silver-gilt, or copper-silvered medals, and all such examples have been privately 'embellished'. Several dies appear to have existed, and since some of the medals are of much better workmanship than others, it seems likely that these may have been made in the UK, to replace the rather crude originals (as was done for the Turkish Crimea Medal, *q.v.*).

The ribbon for all three grades is the same – a deep cherry red with narrow white edges, although a number of writers and ribbon collectors seem to allocate different shades of red and pink to each medal. The modern ribbon, as now supplied by dealers, is usually pink and watered, but this almost certainly originated through a manufacturer copying the very faded red of an old piece of ribbon. It has also been made in varying widths to go with the various types of unofficial suspenders. The original medals were pierced and fitted with one or two rings (some illustrations show only one ring, but then the ribbon sits unnaturally); some medals have a single ring soldered on, while others have been fitted with a plain or ornate bar suspender, with or without a swivelling screw.

Although a rather humble medal, especially in copper, yet for some five or six years it was the only campaign medal which thousands of our seamen had to show for their years of active service up to that date.

## Army of India, 1799-1826

Not issued without a bar; bars read downwards, the earliest action being shown on the top bar. Naming to British troops is generally in impressed capitals of the same type as the M.G.S. and N.G.S. Medals (*Fig. 4b*), but engraved examples are found, almost certainly issued from Calcutta to recipients who were living or serving in India when they applied for their medals.

Medals to Indian recipients are usually engraved in running script, and are not easy to verify. There are also occasional examples found impressed to natives, in lighter and slightly irregular letters (compared with the British style), both in full capitals and otherwise: they may be regimentally named, but no evidence exists on this point.

21 bars issued, as follows:

| | |
|---|---|
| Allighur (4 Sept. 1803) | Kirkee (5 Nov. 1817) |
| Battle of Delhi (11 Sept. 1803) | Poona (Nov. 1817) |
| Assye (23 Sept. 1803) | Kirkee and Poona |
| Asseerghur (21 Oct. 1803) | Seetabuldee (26-27 Nov. 1817) |
| Laswaree (1 Nov. 1803) | Nagpore (16 Dec. 1817) |
| Argaum (29 Nov. 1803) | Seetabuldee & Nagpore |
| Gawilghur (15 Dec. 1803) | Maheidpoor (21 Dec. 1817) |
| Defence of Delhi (Oct. 1804) | Corygaum (1 Jan. 1818) |
| Battle of Deig (13 Nov. 1804) | Ava (1824–26) |
| Capture of Deig (Dec. 1804) | Bhurtpoor (17–18. Jan. 1826) |
| Nepaul (Oct. 1814–March 1816) | |

There are two dies of this medal, one struck at the Royal Mint, with a short hyphen between the dates and with the designer's initials, w.w., in the *rev.* exergue; the other, which may or may not have been struck at the Calcutta Mint, but appears to have been issued by them, has a much longer hyphen and no initials.

There are believed to be many spuriously named examples of this medal, especially among the engraved medals to natives, but I have a note of only a few. In some instances the original name has been removed, and the rim 'bumped up' to give the appearance of the original rim, before the new name has been impressed or engraved;

this device can, of course, be detected by callipers against a known genuine medal, but is usually visible to the eye. Several of these cases are on medals with rare bars, originally named to natives, but renamed in impressed lettering to British recipients, to whom the bars are far rarer.

As with the N.G.S. Medal, it must be stressed that the genuine medals may also be on the market, so if any of the following are encountered, they are not necessarily the 'dud' ones.

Boscawen, Lieut. H. A. 2nd Infantry Battn. (*Ava*); renamed (impressed).

Bradford, Lieut. Chas. 28th N.I. (*Ava*): renamed.

Clayton, Corporal J. Regt. of Arty. (*Gawilghur; Argaum*): engraved; apparently not on roll.

Farrell, M. 11th Lt. Dragns. (*Bhurtpoor*): Looks genuine, but gauges loosely on the callipers.

Gordon, Capt. C. 94th Ft. (*Asseerghur; Argaum; Garwilghur*): Impressed, but possibly renamed.

Guy, Jas. Wm., Jnr. Capt., Bombay Marine (*Ava*): Renamed. Died 23 March 1829, thus not entitled. Came up for auction with NGS (*Java*), also renamed.

Hartnell, Gunner Maurice, H. Arty. (*Assye; Argaum; Gawilghur*): Last bar defective; on the roll for *Bhurtpoor* only.

Jones, Evan David. Horse Arty. (*Bhurtpoor*): Unofficial bar; impressed small capitals.

Kelly, Ptk. 45th Foot. (*Ava*): re-engraved.

Reed, Thomas, P.O., R.N. (*Ava*): Renamed; came up for auction in a group with China 1842 and LS&GC Medal (wide suspender).

Ross, Sgt. H. Volr.L.C. (*Assye*): Not fancied.

It is difficult to verify many of the medals to native troops, but the following have not been fancied, some frequently, and some have been withdrawn from sales although listed in the catalogue. All the following are engraved, unless marked as impressed:

1 bar, *Nagpore* (Sepoy Rodo Eradut, M.N.I.B.): impressed, but doubtful.

1 bar, *Maheidpoor* (Sepoy Schaick Hoosain Bux, 14th N.I.): suspect.

1 bar, *Maheidpoor* (Shaik Moideen, 2d. 3rd Light Infy.).

1 bar, *Nepaul* (Sepoy Tallyar Khan, 1st Battn. 8th N.I.): renamed.

1 bar, *Kirkee* (Sepoy Nadir Rai, 12th Bombay N.I.).

Medals with false bars – 2.

(*Left*) India General Service, 1895, with genuine MALAKAND 1897 bar.

(*Right*) With false MALAKAND 1897 bar (Kindly lent by G. W. Harris, Esq.)

Plate 8.

Medals with false bars – 3.

(*Above*) Queen's South Africa Medals with genuine bars, NATAL
and DEFENCE OF MAFEKING.

(Below) With false bars, NATAL and DEFENCE OF MAFEKING;
the CAPE COLONY bar is genuine; note the rods joining the bars
instead of rivets. (Kindly lent by G. W. Harris, Esq.)

Plate 9.

1 bar, *Seetabuldee* (Hutty Mohurs, V.M.N.I.).

1 bar, *Allighur* (Sepoy Gunness Singh, S.N.I.).

1 bar, *Gawilghur* (Mahomed Gharti Khan, B.N.I.).

1 bar, *Argaum* (Bhagul Singh, Artillery); renamed.

2 bars, *Poona; Corygaum* (Sepoy Kasseram Rana, 2nd Rgt. N.I.): renamed and 'bumped up'.

2 bars, *Assye; Nagpore* (Sepoy Kabad Rama, 2nd Regt. N.I.).

2 bars, *Allighur; Bhurtpore* (Seid Hussein, 31st N.I.): impressed, but not fancied.

3 bars, *Battle of Delhi; Laswarree; Capture of Deig* (Sepoy Kedar Nath, 30th Regt. N.I.).

3 bars, *Assye; Argaum; Gawilghur* (Havilr. Eshwar, Arty.).

\*          \*          \*

**Ceylon Medal, 1818.** Issued by the Government of Ceylon; no bars. Name engraved on the *rev.*

**Burma Medal, 1846-26**

Although issued by the H.E.I. Co., the Waterloo (or British military) ribbon was used –1½″ wide, crimson with blue edges. There were no bars, and the medal (about 750 in gold, for officers, and about 24,000 in silver, for native troops and seamen) was issued unnamed. British forces present did not receive this medal, but later the survivors were awarded the Army of India Medal with the bar, *Ava*.

**Capture of Ghuznee, 1839**

No bars issued. This medal was issued unnamed, but many were named either in the field of the *rev.*, or on the edge, engraved in various styles. Since quite a number exist in each of several styles, it seems likely that each regiment had a batch of medals named by a silversmith at one time. Generally speaking, collectors seem to prefer those named in the *rev.* field.

**Candahar, 1842.**\* No bars issued.

**Cabul, 1842.**\* No bars issued.

**Ghuznee, Cabul, 1842.**\* No bars issued.

**Candahar, Ghuznee, Cabul, 1842.\*** No bars issued.

**Jellalabad, 1842** (1st type: *obv.* Mural crown; *rev.* date.)

**Jellalabad, 1842\*** (2nd type: *obv.* head of Queen Victoria; *rev.* winged figure of Victory, flying). No bars issued.

**Defence of Kelat-I-Ghilzie, 1842.** No bars issued.

All these medals for the First Afghan War appear to have been issued unnamed, except the 2nd ('Flying Victory') type for Jellalabad, as the omission of the naming of the first issue was the subject of a reprimand from the Secretary of War, and was speedily corrected.

Many of the medals are found engraved, and often those to a particular regiment are lettered in the same style – e.g. those for Cabul 1842 to the 9th Foot are usually engraved as in *Fig. 4c.* Some are impressed, in various styles, while those for Kelat-I-Ghilzie, if named, are usually engraved in running script.

There is a rare variety of the Cabul 1842 Medal, lettered CABVL on the *rev.* The five medals marked with an asterisk (above) can all be found with the *obv.* inscription, VICTORIA REGINA, instead of the normal VICTORIA VINDEX; they are almost certainly late issues, for which the later *obv.* die of the Sutlej (or similar) Medal was used. I have examined a number of the Cabul REGINA medals, to the 9th Foot, and not only are they all named (engraved, and some impressed) in a different style from the ordinary VINDEX medals, but most of them have a wide scroll suspender which appears to be an original fitting; all the VINDEX medals which I have seen with a scroll suspender, have obviously had this substituted for the original clip (*See Plate 11*), as the top of the rim shows the marks where the steel clip bit into the silver; these marks are absent on the REGINA medals.

As regards the 'Flying Victory' Jellalabad medals, it is reported on official correspondence that only five out of the 780 men of the 13th P.A.L.I. applied for the new medal; consequently one might assume that there were either some 775 unnamed medals left over, or a similar number of named but unclaimed specimens. Whether any of these were melted down by the Royal Mint is not known, but several collectors report that they have seen many more than five of these medals named to the 13th Regt., and recent research has produced a list of a further forty-five exchanges; no doubt many more cases will eventually be proved.

The medal for the Defence of Kelat-I-Ghilzie is among the rarest campaign medals, especially when named to a verified recipient. Unnamed examples are, of course, much cheaper, but the best that most of us can hope for is one of the copies sometimes available; these are impressed COPY or SPECIMEN on the edge.

### China, 1842

No bars issued originally. Naming is impressed in large capitals, as for the Waterloo Medal (*Fig. 4a*).

### China, 1857-60

Six bars issued, the first being awarded to recipients of the China 1842 Medal, and apparently intended to be affixed to that medal, together with any other bars to which the recipient was entitled.

Bars: China 1842; Fatshan 1857; Canton 1857; Taku Forts 1858; Taku Forts 1860; Pekin 1860.

Medals to the Roval Navy were issued unnamed, but are often found privately engraved; some to the Royal Marines and Indian Marine, and those to the Army, were impressed in small capitals, rather similar to the M.G.S. Medal (*Fig. 4b*).

It is convenient to deal with these two rather similar medals together, in view of the results of research on the *China 1842* bar, undertaken by Sqdn. Ldr. F. E. Rymills, and, to a lesser extent, by the author.

The China 1842 Medal, as originally issued, presents no difficulties. As regards the naming in the style of the Waterloo Medal, it would appear that, during the issue, new punches were made for the naming machine, as many of the China medals show cleaner cut letters not so heavily impressed as those of the Waterloo and early Army L.S. & G.C. Medals.

As with many other medals, the matrices, punches, and dies are in the museum of the Royal Mint, and it is significant (as will appear later) that the Museum catalogue (1910 edition) records the mount or suspender of this medal as 'plain straight bar, also scroll bar', while the ribbon, red with yellow borders, is shown as 1·25″ wide, instead of the accepted 1·5″.

The China 1857–60 Medal is almost identical with that for 1852, except that the exergue of the *rev.* has no date below CHINA, while the suspender is the same as that for the Indian Mutiny medal, officially described as 'cusped'. The last five bars listed above were certainly issued with the medal; other books on medals usually indicate that the bar, *China 1842*, was also issued with the later medal, but recent research seems to make it clear that this bar (together with any later bars to which the recipient was entitled) was awarded *without the 1857–60 medal* to those already in possession of the China 1842 Medal, provided they complied with regulations and admitted possession of the earlier medal when applying for the later awards. This is clearly shown in the Naval rolls, which are in two parts – the medal roll, and the clasp (or bar) roll. Where the claimant did not have the 1842 medal (or did not admit to having it) the rolls show that the 1857–60 medal was issued, with or without bars for that campaign, but *never* with the *China 1842* bar. If he admitted possession of the 1842 medal, the 1857–60 *medal* roll is marked "No, already has 1842 medal" (or a variation of words to that effect), and in every such case there is a tick in the column for the *China 1842* bar (and others, if applicable). While it has not been possible to check all the ratings' entries, it has emerged that at least five officers, who held the 1842 medal, did not report this in their claim, and in each case the roll shows that the 1857–60 medal was issued to them, each with one bar, but none received the *China 1842* bar. Undoubtedly there must have been many ratings in the same category, and thus quite a number of persons must have received both medals, *originally* without the *China 1842* bar, but we have no means of telling how many of them obtained this bar from somewhere and added it to the others on their 1857–60 medal.

As regards those who admitted possession of the 1842 medal, and received a bar or bars, it is at present a matter of conjecture how they fixed these bars. Obviously they could not be fixed in the normal way, to the wide suspender, neither could bars, made for a ribbon $1\frac{1}{4}''$ wide be conveniently slipped over a $1\frac{1}{2}''$ ribbon. I have a China 1842 Medal to a man who also served in 1857–60, and the medal has a *China 1842* bar slipped over and stitched to a ribbon $1\frac{3}{8}''$ wide – an unofficial width, no doubt, but it *can* be used with the bar, and reasonably fits the wide suspender. But to make a neat job, it would seem desirable to alter the suspender, and this is where the scroll suspender, referred to in the Royal Mint Museum catalogue, may have originated. If, after issuing the bars, the authorities realised that they could not be fitted to the earlier medal, it seems reasonable to suppose that a narrower suspender could have been substituted, Some recipients probably did this on their own initiative, as evidenced by photographs of two admirals, Vice-Admiral W. R. Rolland, CB., and Admiral of the Fleet Sir Henry Keppel, GCB. Both are wearing what is obviously the China 1842 Medal, the first with one bar and the second with two, and both have a straight suspender of the N.G.S. pattern, with $1\frac{1}{4}''$ ribbon. Keppel admitted having the 1842 medal, and was awarded just the bars *China 1842* and *Fatshan 1857*, while Rolland, who did not report having the earlier medal, received the 1857–60 medal with bar, *Fatshan 1857;* from the photograph it is clear that he did not wear both medals, but transferred his bar to his 1842 medal, altering the suspender and ribbon, but did not add the *China 1842* bar to which he was certainly entitled.

It has been suggested that in view of the situation, the authorities later revised the regulations, and issued the later medal to all who had served in both campaigns, and if any evidence can be found of this it will be warmly welcomed.

Collectors should beware of paying a fancy price for 5-bar medals. Major Gordon, in *British Battles & Medals*, records that only one genuine 5-bar medal was issued – to Thomas Cole, R.M.A., and it is known that this medal has impressed naming. However, many 5-bar medals exist, either as 'specimens' or made up by some opportunist.

According to the 1893 edition of *War Medals of the British Army*, by Carter and Long (footnote to p. 279), the medal was originally issued with a ribbon in five equal stripes of blue, yellow, red, white and green – and this statement has been copied by many later writers – but there does not seem to be any authority for this. Not only does the notice from the Secretary of State for India to the Governor-General, No. 106 – Military, dated 28 Feb. 1861 (see Mayo, p. 261), clearly indicate that the ribbon for the medal then to be prepared is to be of the same width and pattern as that worn with the China 1842 Medal (although we know that in fact it was $1\frac{1}{4}''$ wide, and of a darker red and slightly narrower yellow edges), but we understand that a document exists, initialled by Queen Victoria, approving the submitted design of the medal, with a specimen of this ribbon attached, and no mention of any other ribbon. However, there is no doubt that the five-striped ribbon was manufactured, and until fairly recently was obtainable from several of the leading medal dealers. It was of a rather soft silk, not watered but with something of a sheen, and with an extremely narrow corded edge of red silk, less than 1 mm. wide.

**Meeanee, 1843.**   No bars issued.

**Hyderabad, 1843.**   No bars issued.

**Meeanee – Hyderabad, 1843.**   No bars issued.
These three medals are often found unnamed, but many are named – impressed in small capitals, or engraved in capitals or running script.

**Punniar Star, 1843.**   No bars issued.

**Maharajpoor Star, 1843.**   No bars issued.
These two medals, issued for the Gwalior Campaign, are often referred to as the GWALIOR STARS, and are of bronze, with a silver centrepiece superimposed. A higher value attaches to examples with the original brass hook at the back (for fixing in the tunic, apparently without ribbon). Stars exist with a brass hook which is not genuine, having been substituted for a suspender which itself replaced the original hook. The latter was of rather heavy brass strip, wider and thicker than most of the false ones, with the outer surface somewhat rounded (*Fig. 9*). Stars with hooks often have the ribbon through a ring, with the hook flattened down to prevent the ring coming off. Many fancy unofficial fittings exist, with oriental swords and a crown, down to a plain suspender bar similar to the Afghan 1842 medals.

Naming is engraved in running script, on the *rev.*, and some unnamed native stars have been engraved with British names and regiments: the style follows the genuine naming, but is often more

FIG. 9.
Brass hooks on
Gwalior Stars

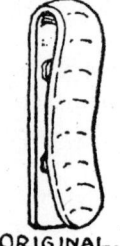 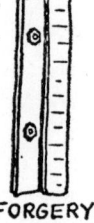

ORIGINAL.          FORGERY.

lightly incised, and is frequently found on a medal with an imitation 'original hook'.

## Sutlej, 1845–46

Four different *revs.*, with the recipient's first action in the exergue; bars (reading upwards) were issued, in respect of the second and subsequent actions, for the first three medals.

> Exergues: MOODKEE 1845; FEROZESHUHUR 1845; ALI-
> WAL 1846; SOBRAON 1846.
>
> Bars: Ferozeshuhur; Aliwal; Sobraon.

Naming is by impressed tall capitals (*Fig. 4d*) for British units; some Indian units have a similar style of impressing, but very irregular (and a Z set sideways has been used for N), and some have been seen engraved in script.

Examples of this medal have been seen on a thicker flan than usual; it is probable that these are late issues or replacements.

## Punjab, 1848–49

Three bars issued; bars usually read downwards.

> Bars: Mooltan; Chilianwala; Goojerat.

Naming is similar to the M.G.S., impressed capitals (*Fig. 4b*). There are no three-bar medals, and none with both *Mooltan* and *Chilianwala*. It is not uncommon to find genuine medals with two bars, where the bars read upwards instead of downwards.

## New Zealand, 1845–47; 1860–66

No bars issued. The centre of the *rev.* may be undated, or may contain either a single year or a pair of dates (i.e. 1846 TO 1847) relating to either the first or the second period. No medals are known to have been issued with dates covering both periods, but 'specimens' in silver or bronze are known, usually but not always without suspender, dated '1846 TO 1865'.

Naming to U.K. units is by impressed capitals (*Fig. 4b*), while those to N.Z. units are usually engraved. Engraved medals to U.K. personnel, if they gauge perfectly in the callipers, are probably late or duplicate issues, but if they fit loosely they are certainly re-named.

The medal does not present much difficulty to collectors, except perhaps, in the multiplicity of *rev.* date dies. At one time it was thought that two *obv.* dies existed – with and without the designers' names on the truncation of the bust – but it seems certain that the normal wearing of the die caused the gradual disappearance of the rather faint letters under the bust.

The various dates on the *rev.* were produced by engraved steel cylinders or plugs, fitted into the die. These are at the Royal Mint, but in their Museum catalogue they list several date dies which do not appear on known medals, viz., 1845, 1846 to 1865, 1861 to 1867, and 1862 to 1864, and they omit several which are known, namely, 1861, 1863, 1866, 1860 to 1863, 1860 to 1866, 1861 to 1863, 1861 to 1864, 1862 to 1866, and 1864 to 1865; these latter may, of course, have been mislaid or destroyed owing to deterioration.

It is quite possible that medals with dates at present unknown may eventually come to light; in some cases only one or two examples of certain dates are known. Most medals with a single date are rare, although 1866 is encountered more often than the others.

The medals with no date are fairly common. They are usually awarded to the army, both to units present during 1845–47, or during 1860–66. Since medals to the army with any of the 1845–47 dates are almost unknown, it has been concluded that undated medals were issued for this period, but as many of the undated medals have proved to have been earned only during the later period (for which *dated* medals to the army are usual), it follows that undated ones could relate to either or both periods – certainly those who served in both periods received an undated medal. The undated medals usually make a lower price than the dated ones, unless to scarce units, or proved to be for the 1845–47 period.

### South Africa, 1834–53

Issued for the three campaigns against the Kaffirs, 1834–35, 1846–47 and 1850–53. Dated 1853 in the exergue. No bars issued, but according to regulations, recipients who qualified for the South Africa 1877–79 Medal, should receive only their date bars for that medal, to be added to their earlier medal; these regulations do not appear to make provision for recipients of the 1853 medal who qualified for the later medal without bar.

Naming is by impressed capitals, as for the M.G.S. Medal (*Fig. 4b*).

It is often stated that the Zulu War Medal, 1877–79, should have the *bright yellow-orange* ribbon, with blue stripes, while the Kaffir War Medal should have a paler one, usually supplied in a biscuit shade. I am convinced that *both* medals should, in fact, have the bright ribbon; in the first place, the illustration in Carter's *Medals of the British Army*, published in 1861, nearly twenty years before the

Zulu War, shows the 1853 medal with the bright yellow-orange ribbon (and the colours in this book are generally very good): secondly, the modern bright ribbon fades to *exactly* that biscuit shade if exposed to the light for some years. I have seen an Army Sealed Pattern of the 1853 ribbon, dating from about 1885, in this biscuit shade, and it seems certain that a piece of faded ribbon was used at some time as a pattern for the manufacturers, which has been copied ever since.

### India General Service, 1854 (1849–1895)

Not issued without a bar. Issued in silver only for the first nine bars, but in silver and bronze for the last fourteen bars; the bronze medals were issued to non-combatants, such as native bearers, sweepers, drivers, and other camp followers.

Twenty-three bars:

| | |
|---|---|
| Pegu (1852–53) | Burma 1885–7 |
| Persia (1856–57) | Sikkim 1888 |
| North West Frontier (1849–68) | Hazara 1888 |
| Umbeyla (1863) | Burma 1887-89 (also Burma |
| Bhootan (1864–66) | 1887–9) |
| Looshai (1871–72) | Chin Lushai 1889–90 |
| Perak (1875–76) | Samana 1891 |
| Jowaki 1877–8 | Hazara 1891 |
| Naga 1879–80 | N.E. Frontier 1891 |
| Hunza 1891 | Chin Hills 1892–93 |
| Burma 1889–92 | Kachin Hills 1892–93 |
| Lushai 1889–92 | Waziristan 1894–95 |

The medal is usually designated '1854' as this was the date of its institution, although it covers a period from 1849 to 1895; even its geographical title is not wholly accurate, as it covers locations from Persia to Malaya. Two bars have a final single date figure, while the others show the last two figures. The bar, *Burma 1887–89*, is also found as *Burma 1887–9*, and enquiries made by Capt. W. R. Morgan show that the bar die at the Calcutta Mint is the former, while the Royal Mint hold a die with the latter dates.

Generally speaking, the bars are supposed to read upwards, but often the first bar awarded is at the top if the sidepieces had been cut off flush, leaving no pierced lugs (or 'ears') for subsequent bars to be riveted; sometimes these flush sides have been pierced, and then the second bar is correctly placed if untidily affixed. In many cases later bars were secured by rings, wire, or even straight soldering – such medals are not necessarily faked, but have merely had the later bars added by a local craftsman in the village where the regiment was then stationed.

There are many styles of naming, varying according to the original bar; in some cases more than one style exists, but the following is an approximate guide:

*Pegu:* impressed in small upright capitals, smaller than M.G.S.

*Persia:* impressed as above, also as M.G.S. (*Fig. 4b*).

*North West Frontier:* impressed in tall capitals (*Fig. 4d*), also as M.G.S., for British units; engraved in running script (*Fig. 4g*) for Indian units.

*Umbeyla:* impressed in small capitals, similar to M.G.S.

*Bhootan:* impressed as *Fig. 4b*, also tall capitals, as *Fig. 4d*. Medals to 80th Foot, for instance, appear in both styles.

*Looshai:* engraved in running script (*Fig. 4g*).

*Perak:* engraved in large sloping capitals (*Fig. 4e*).

*Jowaki 1877–8:* impressed in tall capitals (*Fig. 4f*).

*Naga 1878–80*, and subsequent bars (except *Lushai 1889–92*): engraved in running script (*Fig. 4g*).

*Lushai 1889–92:* impressed in larger capitals, as *Fig. 4f*, also engraved in running script.

*Burma 1885–7*: to Navy and Royal Marines, impressed in tall upright capitals (*Fig. 4p*).

Some bars are found with varieties of letters and figures larger than normal, e.g. *Hazara 1888*, *Hazara 1891*, *Samana 1891*, etc It has been suggested that they are unofficial, but there does not appear to be any evidence for this; it seems more likely that as some bars were struck both in England and Calcutta, slight differences in the dies existed. Certainly both types have been seen on medals which are undoubtedly genuine, and since the bars are common ones, it is unlikely that there has been any intent to deceive.

*Chin Hills 1892–93* bar to the Norfolks: medals with the single bar, *Chin Hills 1892–93* should all be engraved (in running script) to the 1st Battn., whereas those with two bars, *Burma 1887–89* and *Chin Hills 1892–93*, should be similarly engraved to the 2nd Battn. After serving in the Burma Campaign, the 2nd Battn. were returning home, when they met the 1st Battn. just arriving in India. About one hundred men transferred to the 1st Battn., and some of these were among the two hundred or so who served in the Chin Hills action.

The bars were not issued until 1903, and were thus added to the medals, named to the 2nd Battn., already received for Burma.

As regards the 1st Battn. medals, the I.G.S. Medal 1895 had already been in issue for some eight years by the time the *Chin Hills* bar was authorised, and it is believed that for most of the recipients, unclaimed medals were used (probably with *Burma* bars), with the name erased, the bar removed, and the Norfolkmen's names officially re-engraved, in the same running script, with the *Chin Hills* bar substituted. Quite a number of medals are found thus, in agreement with the roll, and as they have never been out of family or regimental possession, there is every reason to believe that they are perfectly genuine as issued, although officially re-named. Although no authority can be quoted for this particular re-naming of medals, there is a precedent, in the Order of 1864 (quoted in Mayo, p. lxxxiv) when unclaimed Indian campaign medals were melted down, except for a few retained for re-issue.

### Baltic, 1854–55

No bars issued. Like the Crimea Medal, this was issued unnamed, although about a hundred, all to the Royal Sappers and Miners, were officially impressed, in the same style as the M.G.S. (*Fig. 4b*).

Collectors are warned to be very wary in purchasing these medals, as not only have some unnamed Baltic Medals been 'named' by the same faker who re-named the N.G.S. Medals (*q.v.*), using the same punches (see *Fig. 3*), but in 1976 it was discovered that some had recently been named on a naming machine purchased from an engineering firm in the north of England, These are very dangerous forgeries (the medals themselves are, of course, perfectly genuine), but one point to note is that the left serif on the right leg of the A is missing, while the ampersand (&) is not quite right. Consequently medals impressed to the Royal Sappers & Miners should only be bought from a dealer who is prepared fully to guarantee the medal, or from some other absolutely reliable source. These medals, genuinely impressed, command a far, far higher price than those *engraved* to naval recipients.

The original (or contemporary) ribbon is distinctive, having a corded edge, as did the first Arctic Medal (rather like modern U.S.A. ribbons); it was slightly watered, in a rather thick weave; it was also very slightly wider, 1·3″, than most modern makes of Baltic ribbon, which do not adequately fill the suspender pin.

## Crimea, 1854–56

Five bars issued, but not more than four on any medal. Bars read upwards, but occasionally may be found out of order.

Alma (20th Sept. 1854) Inkermann (5th Nov. 1854) Azoff (1885) Balaklava (25th Oct. 1854) Sebastopol (1854–55)

(Medals issued to French personnel may also be found with bars, *Traktir, Malakof, Mer d'Azoff*, and *Kinnburn*.)

The medal was issued unnamed, but could be returned for official naming. Those officially impressed, in the M.G.S. style, are more highly prized (and priced) than those engraved, as they carry the stamp of authenticity. In many regiments a fair proportion were so impressed, but one often sees officers' medals engraved (perhaps entrusted to military tailors or jewellers, as the same style is often found throughout one regiment), while in some units one frequently finds a consistent style of irregular punching or impressing, known as 'regimentally or depot named'; notable examples of these are some of the medals to the 93rd Highlanders ('The Thin Red Line'), 23rd R.W.F., and the Guards, all of which, however, also turn up officially impressed and privately engraved. Be very wary of medals to Light Brigade regiments, unless impressed and verified, although undoubtedly many genuine engraved medals exist, and provided they verify and 'look right', they still command a good price but lower than the impressed medals.

Falsely impressed medals exist, discovered in 1976, similar to those described above, under the Baltic Medal. These would appear to be mainly to known participants in the Charge of the Light Brigade, members of the Heavy Brigade, and the 93rd Highlanders, but others may exist. Those falsely named to the Light Brigade seem to be ones which were not known to have appeared previously on the market, but one cannot be sure that they are limited to these. The naming is so very like the officially impressed style that it is extremely dangerous, so before paying a high price for one of these medals (or, indeed, any expensive medal), not only make sure that the vendor is prepared fully to refund your money if it should prove to falsely named, but also if otherwise 'fiddled', i.e. with bars added to which the recipient was not entitled, or re-constituted having had the suspender and bars removed to make the circular medal into a brooch and later another suspender and bars replaced to make the medal look genuinely 'as issued'.

Continental copies of the medal exist; these do not 'look quite right' and do not have Wyon's name on the truncation of the bust.

*There is no official roll of the 'Charge of the Light Brigade'*, as such, but from the Muster Rolls in the Public Record Office (which are the pay rolls for the week in question), and from such regimental records as exist, it has been possible to compile a fairly accurate roll, particularly of those killed, wounded, taken prisoner, decorated, etc.; also certain men can be eliminated, as the Muster Roll shows them on detached duty, sick, or elsewhere. Collectors are strongly urged to obtain a copy of *Honour the Light Brigade*, by Canon W. M. Lummis and K. G. Wynn (J. B. Havward & Son, 1973), which gives full details of participants (and others) and considerable 'medal' information. Another most useful book from the same publisher, is the sumptuous *Casualty Roll for the Crimea, 1854–1855*, by F. & A. Cook (1976). Although it may appear expensive, it is a 'must' for the serious collector of Crimea Medals. Medals to men of late drafts of participating regiments, with the *Sebastopol* bar, have frequently had *Balaklava* (and others) added, so rivets must be watched for signs of tampering. Unofficial bars also exist, usually thicker and clumsier than the originals, and one has *Inkerman* instead of *Inkermann*, another has *Balaclava* instead of *Balaklava* (*Plate 7*).

*Medal Brooches.* About this time a number of individual ornamental medal brooches made their appearance, usually in silver.

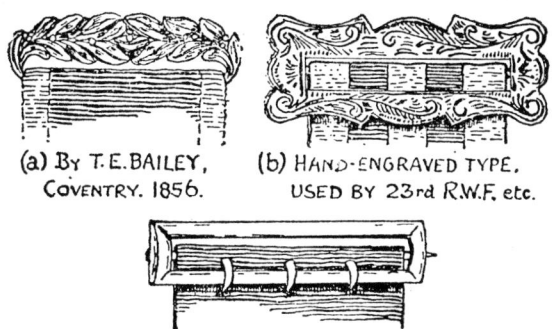

(a) By T. E. BAILEY, COVENTRY. 1856.

(b) HAND-ENGRAVED TYPE, USED BY 23rd R.W.F. etc.

FIG. 10.
Some mid-19th century Medal Brooches.

They are, of course, unofficial, but as medals were pinned to the uniform singly, their neat appearance certainly enhanced the style, and apparently they were tolerated for some years (*Fig. 10*). They must not, however, be confused with those of the later Royal

Humane Society's medals, the gold buckle of the old C.B., or the top brooches of the D.S.O., T.D., and some other decorations, without which these would not be complete.

### Turkish Medal for the Crimea

The Sultan of Turkey awarded this medal to all serving personnel of the three countries who 'assisted' him in the war against Russia – Britain, France and Sardinia – with slight differences for each country, in that the basic design showed the four national flags, but with the Turkish flag crossing, in the centre, the flag of the respective country to whom the medal was awarded, and with the other two flags on the outside. In this arrangement, the flag of the country concerned is generally described as 'to the fore'. The ship bringing part of the consignment of medals to Britain, with the red ensign to the fore, was apparently wrecked, consequently many British recipients were given medals with either the Sardinian or (more rarely) the French flag to the fore.

The medals are in poorer silver than ours – 80% against 95% (according to the Royal Mint, war medals were struck in silver of 950 fineness until 1875, when a change was made to standard silver of 925 fineness) – and, like the Acre Medal, were issued pierced at the top and fitted with a single ring. Through this was threaded the five-eighths inch wide ribbon of cherry red with green edges. Not only was the single ring, at right angles to the medal, unsuitable for a neat seating of the ribbon, but the narrow width was different from our standard ribbon, consequently ribbon of the same design was made in $1\frac{1}{4}''$, and most of the medals were fitted with either a second ring or a suspender – plain, scroll, ornamental, or as the recipient desired.

The medals were issued unnamed, and all named medals are either regimentally or privately named; if the former, they are frequently found with the lettering, engraved or punched, identical with regimentally named Queen's medals.

There are also British-made copies of this medal, in sterling silver (92·5%), in higher relief, supplied by military tailors at the request of some officers who disliked the rather crude originals. There are at least three dies, all of which have the Sardinian flag to the fore, and there may also be dies for the other types. The chief differences in these copies are most noticeable on the *rev.*, i.e. the side depicting the flags, cannon, etc. (usually, but incorrectly, called the *obv.* in most medal books). Two of the dies have the initials, J.B., in the right corner of the exergue, while the third has no initials but has a 'stepped' rim with the outer one grained. All are slightly larger in diameter than the originals, and they usually have a scroll suspender, or some other fancy design. From the collector's angle, they should not be worth as much as an original medal, but since this is not valued very highly, there is, in fact, very little difference. They *are* copies, and unofficial, but they were certainly worn by the men who earned them, and I, for one, would not detach them from an otherwise desirable group.

### Indian Mutiny, 1857–58

Five bars issued:

| | |
|---|---|
| Delhi (May-Sept. 1857) | Relief of Lucknow (Nov. 1857) |
| Defence of Lucknow | Lucknow (Nov. 1857-Mar. 1858) |
| (June-Sept. 1857) | Central India (Jan.-June 1858) |

Bars should read downwards. The medal is impressed in the M.G.S. style (*Fig. 4b*); Privates had their name and regiment only shown, but official re-issues (often on a thicker flan) were impressed in taller, thinner capitals, with number and rank.

Some medals to Indian troops are to be found engraved in running script, or impressed in somewhat irregular alignment.

Medals named to H.M.P.V. *Calcutta*, refer to H.M. Pendant Vessel, and not H.M. Patrol Vessel as frequently quoted in some books and catalogues.

Note the false bars shown on Plate 7.

### China, 1857–60 – *See under* CHINA, 1842.

### Canada General Service, 1866–70

Not issued without a bar; three bars issued:

| | | |
|---|---|---|
| Fenian Raid 1866 | Fenian Raid 1870 | Red River 1870 |

Naming is usually impressed in either square *sans serif* capitals, or in upper and lower case roman type (*Fig. 4j* and *k*).

### Abyssinia, 1867–68

No bars issued. Naming is in the centre of the *rev.*, and the medal shows a feature not present on any other British medal – the naming is in raised lettering (apart from most of those issued to Indian troops, which were engraved). There has been some uncertainty as to how this was actually achieved, and I am indebted to the late Mr W. P. Dawson for permission to quote the results of his research into this question, in which he received considerable assistance from officials of the Royal Mint. It appears that the Mint, having entrusted the engraving of the original dies to Messrs. J. S. & A. B. Wyon, medallists in Regent Street, London, sought tenders for mounting and naming the medals. They were struck at the Mint, with a blank-centre *rev.*, and the contractor was to supply and fix a small silver plate to each medal, on which the naming was to be in relief. In submitting their tender, Wyons suggested an alternative method using composite dies with detachable centres (presumably like those used for the various dates on the New Zealand Medal), (*q.v.*). But the Mint accepted the tender of G. Austin, who also suggested an alternative, but unrecorded, method, in place of the superimposed centre plates. In the event his alternative method was adopted, and appears to have consisted of individual centre dies, probably cylinders of mild steel, punched with ordinary letter punches. The die was hammered onto the blank centre of the *rev.*, but it seems that the process was not wholly satisfactory, as some medals show, on close examination, a flattening on the *obv.*, of the beads around the head, and the coronet, top of the head, or the truncation sometimes appear double or blurred. If the medals had been more firmly held in place, in an obverse matrix, when the naming was done, the damage could have been minimised. In addition, the mounting style adopted was weak, and a number of medals were returned to the Mint for attention.

A few medals to British personnel have been found engraved, and while these could be original issues, it is more likely that they are either replacements or re-named medals. Some Indian units received medals named in relief, but the majority are engraved, as mentioned above.

When buying this medal, care should be taken to see that the mount below the crown has not been damaged, as many examples exist in which the crown has been soldered to repair a break.

### Ashantee, 1873–74
One bar: Coomassie. Recipients who also qualified for the EAST

Some Medals for Gallantry in Life-saving.

(*Above*) *Left* – Life-saving Medal of the Order of St John (2nd type).

*Right* – Liverpool Shipwreck & Humane Society (*circa* 1871–72).

(*Below*) *Left* – Gold Medal of the Royal Natl. Instn. for the Preservation of Life from Shipwreck (now the R.N.L.I.).

*Right* – The Sea Gallantry Medal (*reverse*).

Plate 10.

Some Medal Mountings.

(*Above*) *Left* – Waterloo, 1815; original clip and ring.

*Right* – Cabul, 1842; original clip and steel bar suspender.

(*Below*) *Left* – Army & R.A.F. General Service, with fixed mount and suspender;

*Right* – with swivelling suspender

Plate 11.

& WEST AFRICA Medal (1887-1900), (*q.v.*), were supposed to receive only the later bar or bars, to be attached to the Ashantee Medal; in some cases both medals were awarded and worn.

Naming is by engraved roman capitals, rather squat and heavy in style, and blackened in, with the dates, 1873–4 or '73–'74, at the end (*Fig. 4l*).

Examples of this medal with the later bars should be verified before purchase, as they are very scarce; it is difficult to obtain verification of those to native regiments, but they are the ones most often encountered, and many are perfectly genuine, despite the poor looking local rivets used to affix the bars. If, however, the unit to whom the Ashantee Medal was issued also participated in the actions of the later bars, the medal is probably in order.

### South Africa, 1877–79

Six bars: 1877; 1877–8; 1877–8–9; 1878; 1878–9; 1879.

At one time there was some doubt whether the bar, 1877, was authentic, and Mayo, in the Corrigenda to *Medals and Decorations of the British Army* (p. 604) deletes it from his list of bars, as "no authority from the War Office for this clasp exists, and there is no die of it at the Mint". However, the Royal Mint Museum catalogue lists it, with the note, "In the Army Order no mention is made of a clasp dated '1877'. But this clasp was issued from the Mint on the demand of the War Office in 1880."

Several examples are known, believed to be genuine, but there are several medals about with an unofficial bar.

Naming is usually engraved, in sloping or upright capitals, both styles appearing in medals to the same regiment (*Fig. 4h* and *i*).

Of the same basic design as the medal for the Kaffir Wars of 1834–53, the Zulu War medal can be distinguished at once by the shield and assegai in the *rev.* exergue (the earlier medal has the date, 1853); if the naming is impressed in the M.G.S. style, it is certainly the earlier, while if it has a bar, it is almost certainly the later medal. It is just possible that some Kaffir War medals exist with a Zulu War bar, as the Army Order of 1880 states that the recipients of the earlier medal would receive only the date bar in respect of later operations. Although I have never seen a *genuine* example of this, Dr F. K. Mitchell, of Cape Town, has found in the medal rolls the names of two members of the Cape Mounted Riflemen who were so entitled. He has not, however, seen either of the medals, and it is not known whether they did in fact receive the bar only, as recorded in the medal rolls, or a further medal. In the Tombs Sale, in 1918, there was a pair of medals to P. McCarthy: South Africa 1853, to Pte., 2nd Foot, and South Africa 1877–79, with bar, 1877–8, to the same man in King William's Town Veteran Volrs.

Officially there should not be more than *one* date bar (some recipients did not qualify for a bar), covering one, two, or all three years, but at least two medals exist with the two bars, 1877–8 and 1879. One of these is to Asst. Commissary J. L. Dalton, V.C. (of Rorke's Drift), and was on show at the Victoria Cross Exhibition in 1956. Nevertheless, any such medals encountered should be regarded with the highest suspicion until it can be verified that the recipient was entitled and also (if possible) that the medal was issued with one bar and the claim to the second bar admitted at a later date.

Unofficial bars, ULUNDI, have been noted, including one formed from the original 1879 bar, with the date erased and ULUNDI engraved, with raised letters, in its place (17th Lancers).

### Afghanistan, 1878–80

Six bars:

| | |
|---|---|
| Ali Musjid (21st Nov. 1878) | Kabul (10th–23rd Dec. 1879) |
| Peiwar Kotal (2nd Dec. 1878 | Ahmed Khel (19th Apl. 1880) |
| Charasia (6th Oct. 1879) | Kandahar (1st Sept. 1880) |

Several styles of naming are used, the most usual being engraved upright square capitals or sloping capitals (*Fig. 4m* and *n*); a few are found with impressed capitals, while some to Indian units are engraved in running script.

Unofficial or copy bars exist, presumably made as replacements. I have seen only one, *Kabul*, with large letters, occupying 20 mm., but no doubt others exist in similar style.

### Kabul to Kandahar Star, 1880

Struck in bronze; no bars issued. Naming is by impressed *sans serif* capitals, on the *rev.*, surrounding the central depression; some stars issued to Indian troops are engraved in similar letters, and quite a number of unnamed examples may be found – these last may be surplus stock – and some of these have been falsely named to British regiments. 'Specimens' are sometimes seen, impressed in the usual style, with the name of the makers – H. JENKINS & SONS, BIRMINGHAM – but they are of little value to collectors.

The star should be accompanied by the Queen's Medal for Afghanistan, with the bar, *Kandahar* (but not necessarily with the *Kabul* bar, as the bar related to the action of December 1879, and not to the 'Kabul' part of Lord Roberts' march from Kabul to Kandahar).

### Cape of Good Hope General Service, 1880–97
Three bars issued; not issued without a bar:
Transkei (Sept. 1880–May 1881) Basutoland (Sept. 1880–Apl. 1881)
Bechuanaland (Dec. 1886–July 1897)

These medals are usually engraved in light, square capitals, but I have seen some impressed in narrow capitals, similar to the Queen's South Africa Medal (*Fig. 4t*).

### Egypt, 1882–89
Two types of *rev.*, the first dated 1882, with which the first two bars were issued; the second *rev.* is undated, and the later bars are normally found on this type, although they are frequently found on the dated medal when this was originally awarded without bar, and (of course) added to a dated medal with early bars.

Alexandria 11th July (1882)  Abu Klea (17 Jan. 1885)
Tel-el-Kebir (13 Sept. 1882)  Kirbekan (10 Feb. 1885)
El-Teb (29 Feb. 1884)  Suakin 1885 (1 Mar.–14 May)
Tamaai (13 Mar. 1884)  Tofrek (22 Mar. 1885)
El-Teb-Tamaai  Gemaizah 1888 (20 Dec.)
Suakin 1884 (Feb.–Mar.)  Toski 1889 (3 Aug.)
The Nile 1884–85

Several types of naming are found, both engraved and impressed (*Fig. 4 o* and *p*); the latter is often on medals to the Royal Navy and Royal Marines, although those with the dated *rev.* are engraved. Medals to Indian units may be found engraved in script, and those to Egyptian troops may be unnamed or engraved in arabic.

Apart from exercising some care in verifying those with the bars, *Kirbekan, Tofrek, Gemaizah 1888*, and *Toski 1889*, the collector should not have any trouble with this medal, but I have come across a re-named medal with unofficial bars. This was evidently a replacement, not made to deceive collectors, as the bars were common ones, wider than usual with much larger lettering and poor rivets (*Fig. 11*).

FIG. 11.
Bars on the Egypt Medal. Left, genuine bars, right false bars.

Other unofficial bars exist, in several styles. One had ABU-KLEA (with a hyphen) in very large letters, occupying 24 mm., while another, with round pointed tops to the As (but no hyphen), has the words measuring 21·5 mm., and the background, which should be granulated or pitted, has diagonally crossed lines. A similar bar, *The Nile 1884–85*, also has the crossed lines background. The medal with these last two bars also has two other unofficial bars, *El-Teb – Tamaai* and *Suakin 1884*, both with pointed tops to the As instead of the flat top of the narrow A of the official bars, also wide instead of narrow 8s (*Fig. 11a*); these two bars both have a granulated background, but slightly different from normal, and the letters are all the wrong shape. These differences cannot always be described, and it is

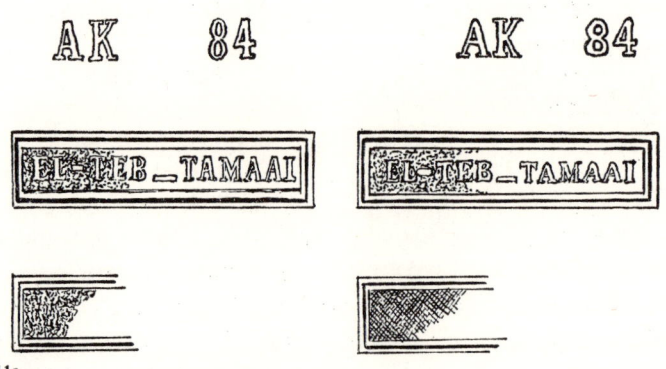

FIG. 11a
Further genuine (left) and false (right) bar details for the Egypt Medal. Some false bars exist with a crossed-hatched background (bottom right).

132

essential for the collector to learn to recognise the correct shape and spacing of the letters on all the various bars.

## Khedive's Stars, 1882–91

The Khedive's Bronze Stars exist in four varieties, three bearing the respective dates, 1882, 1884, 1884-6, and the fourth is undated. The first three are very common, but the undated one is scarcer.

The star dated 1882 should accompany the Queen's Medal bearing the same date on the *rev.*, while the others should accompany the undated Queen's Medal. Frequently pairs of medals are found with the wrong star. While this could have been due to an incorrect issue, it is more often the result of a collector or dealer adding the first available star to a 'lonely' Queen's Medal.

Although issued unnamed, a few regiments, including the Guards, had these stars punched on the *rev.* Often this shows only the man's number and regiment (abbreviated), but others have the name as well. A Queen's Medal to one of the Guards regiments, with an unnamed star, is likely to have had the star 'added'.

The bar, *Tokar 1308* (in Arabic; the date, A.H., corresponds to A.D. 1891), was given with an undated star, while officers and men of HMS *Dolphin* and *Sandfly* received the undated star without the bar, and no Queen's Medal; there are, however, some British naval officers and others who, having already received a dated Khedive's Star, also qualified for the *Tokar* bar, which was then added to the dated star.

## North-West Canada, 1885

One bar: Saskatchewan. Issued unnamed, but often found engraved in capitals. The bars, *Fish Creek* and *Batoche*, sometimes found on this medal, are unofficial.

## Royal Niger Company's Medal, 1886–97

Issued in silver to white officers, with bar, *Nigeria 1886–1897*, and in bronze to natives with bar, *Nigeria*. Not issued without a bar.

The silver medals are usually described as impressed in capitals, but some, at least, are engraved; the bronze medals are impressed only with a number – presumably the recipient's.

The original medals had SPINK & SON, LOND. below the bust of Queen Victoria. The *obv.* die was renewed in 1933, and the naming below the bust was altered to SPINK & SON, LTD. It is believed that the specimens struck from this 1933 die were all appreciably thicker than the originals, and thus easily distinguishable. Since about 1955, the specimens struck have all been of the original thickness, but the s of "SON" below the bust, has been erased; in addition the rim has been impressed, COPY or SPECIMEN.

## East and West Africa, 1887–1900

Usually found in silver, but a few were issued in bronze. Not issued without a bar, except for the M'wele operations, when the edge is impressed MWELE on one side of the claw, and 1895 or 1895–6 on the other: some medals, issued earlier, have it *engraved*.

Twenty-one bars were issued, and some writers include two more, 1896–97 and 1896–99, of which no official records appear to exist, but they could well be genuine; the 21 bars are:

| | | |
|---|---|---|
| 1887–8 | Lake Nyassa 1893 | Benin 1897 |
| Witu 1890 | 1893–94 | Dawkita 1897 |
| 1891–2 | Gambia 1894 | 1897–98 |
| 1892 | Benin River 1894 | 1898 |
| Liwondi 1893 | Brass River 1895 | Sierra Leone 1898–99 |
| Witu August 1893 | 1896–98 | 1899 |
| Juba River 1893 | Niger 1897 | 1900 |

Naming varies considerably; the most usual style is by impressed tall serifed capitals, similar to *Fig. 4p*, while some of the later ones have narrow capitals as *Fig. 4t*, or square capitals as *Fig. 4j*. Some medals to officers are engraved in sloping capitals, while some to Indian and colonial regiments are in running script.

The medal is identical with that for Ashantee, 1873–74, but is struck on a thinner flan. Those with MWELE 1895 (or 1895–6) impressed on the edge, are often found with bars such as *Brass River 1895* or *Benin 1897*.

Some years ago Mr F. Pridmore, serving in the District Pay Office, Aden, sent for my inspection an interesting variety of the M'wele medal. With no bar, it was issued to a sepoy of the 126th Baluchistan Infantry, and is impressed in the narrow *sans serif* capitals used on the Africa G.S. Medal; "MWELE", however, is *engraved* in sloping serifed capitals, and double inverted commas, without date, but the medal looks authentic. It was accompanied by a China 1900 Medal, with bar, *Relief of Pekin*, to the same man and named in exactly the same style. They are probably late issues or replacements, although the China Medal might be the original, with the M'wele Medal issued at the same time.

False bars have been noted for the three rare ones, *Liwondi*

*1893, Lake Nyassa 1893,* and *Dawkita 1897,* but no details are available. Since only these very rare bars have been noticed, it would seem that they were made to deceive and not for replacements, but it may well be that copies of the other bars also exist; at the time these false bars were made, the others were regarded as common, so possibly it was not worth while falsifying them.

### British South Africa Company's Medals, 1890–97

There are four types of *rev.,* lettered respectively:
(i) Matabeleland 1893; (ii) Rhodesia 1896; (iii) Mashonaland 1897; (iv) without place or date, authorised in 1926, for the Mashonaland campaign of 1890.

Four bars: Mashonaland 1890; Matabeleland 1893; Rhodesia 1896; Mashonaland 1897.

Naming is usually by heavy, engraved narrow capitals *(Fig. 4s),* but sloping capitals may be found, also impressed capitals.

It should be noted that the bars, *Mashonaland 1890, Matabeleland 1893,* and *Mashonaland 1897,* all have the date below the place name, while that for *Rhodesia 1896* has the date alongside. Unofficial bars exist for these medals, and some of the first three have the date in line with the place name. It has been suggested, however, that bars with the date in line are not necessarily unofficial, as some of these medals bearing such bars have been verified and there is no reason to believe that the bars are other than 'as issued', perhaps belatedly.

### Central Africa, 1891–98

One bar: Central Africa 1894–98. Usually found in silver, but a few were issued in bronze.

Impressed naming is usually by square *sans serif* capitals *(Fig. 4j),* but some are engraved in script, while others are found unnamed.

When issued without bar, the medal has a swivelling ring suspension, but those with the bar have a plain straight suspender, as for the East & West Africa Medal, with which it is identical except for its distinctive black, white, and pinkish-brown ribbon. The medal with bar is rare, and should be purchased with caution; those to the B.C.A. Rifles and impressed in square capitals, are usually regarded as the safest. As regards the medal without bar, beware of the ordinary East & West Africa Medal with the suspender removed and a ring suspension fitted in place.

135

In 1948 a medal came up for auction, with a ring suspender and with MWELE 1895-6 impressed on the edge. It was engraved to a sepoy of the 24th Bombay Infantry. There is considerable doubt as to its genuineness, and it is almost certainly the ordinary M'wele Medal with the straight suspender removed and replaced by a ring and claw. There is no doubt that the 24th Bombay Infantry were at M'wele, but they do not seem to have qualified for the Central Africa Medal in 1891-94. The 24th *Bengal* Infantry received it, but they did not get *Mwele*, and since it is somewhat unlikely that a sepoy of the Bombay Infantry would transfer to the Bengal Infantry, it is felt that this medal, with its ring suspender, is extremely suspect.

### India General Service Medal, 1895–1902
Issued in silver and bronze; not issued without a bar. Medals with the last bar only, have the head of Edward VII, and the date (1895) does not appear on the *rev*. Seven bars issued.:

| | |
|---|---|
| Defence of Chitral 1895 | Samana 1897 |
| Relief of Chitral 1895 | Tirah 1897–98 |
| Punjab Frontier 1897–98 | Waziristan 1901–2 |
| Malakand 1897 | |

Naming is usually in rather heavy running script (*Fig. 4q*), but exceptions can be found; I have one with bar, *Relief of Chitral* 1895, impressed in slightly irregular square capitals to a muleteer of the Commissariat Transport Dept, while medals to the D.C.L.I. are usually engraved in a crude, almost childish, running script – so crude that not infrequently they have been refused by both collectors and dealers as re-named; medals to the 2nd H.L.I. are often found engraved in smallish upright *sans serif* capitals, not very deeply incised, while many late issues and official re-issues are impressed in the thin, narrow capitals often seen on the Queen's South Africa and Africa General Service Medals.

The medal does not present any real difficulties to the collector, but as many of the later bars were issued to recipients while still serving in India, they have been added to the medal by native craftsmen, whose ideas of riveting vary from a neat job, through rough riveting, down to links or pieces of silver (or white metal) wire; in many cases the first bar had no upper lugs for fitting later bars, and it is not unusual to find the side members pierced, with the later bar either riveted to it direct, or a small distance piece inserted to hold the second bar at a suitable distance; alternatively, the first bar is sometimes removed and replaced at the top.

An unofficial *Malakand 1897* bar has been noted, with very small letters, and with the date underneath, whereas the genuine bar has large letters and the date is in line with the name. I have only seen this unofficial bar in silver, but it also exists in bronze (See *Plate 8*).

The last issue of the medal, with the head of Edward VII and with the date on the *rev.* removed, is on a much thinner flan than the Victorian ones.

### Ashanti Star, 1896

Struck in bronze; no bars issued. The star was unnamed, but those to the 2nd Bn. West Yorkshire Regt., were named at the expense of the colonel.

Copies of the star exist, thinner than the originals, and with cruder detail, especially the crown.

### Sudan, 1896–97

Issued in silver and bronze; no bars issued. Naming varies, the most usual being by engraved sloping capitals (*Fig. 4r*), but other styles may be found, including impressed, while arabic engraving and unnamed examples are not uncommon. An unofficial bar has been noted, DONGOLA. The original ribbon had a corded edge.

### Khedive's Sudan Medal, 1896–1908

Issued in silver and bronze, the latter are much scarcer than the former. Naming varies; those to British troops are engraved, either in rather large upright square capitals or sloping capitals, although some unnamed medals are found paired with named Queen's Medals, but it is possible that these may not be originals; others have an impressed naming in very small letters, and these may have been regimentally named; naming for Indian troops is usually engraved in running script, while those for Egyptian and Sudanese troops are named in Arabic – it is usually possible to recognise at least the recipient's number and the number of his regiment. According to Gordon, most of the later issues were unnamed.

In most cases the medal was issued with at least one bar, except to personnel who did not take part in any actions, but it can also be found without bar to the crews of H.M.S. *Melita* and H.M.S. *Scout*, who took part in the Dongola Expedition of 1896 (for which the army received the bars, *Firket* and *Hafir*.

Unofficial bars are sometimes found, so similar in style to the official ones that they could easily be mistaken for genuine bars; one is lettered OMDURMAN, with the Arabic equivalent on the right, but the official bar for this battle is, of course, *Khartoum*. There are also unofficial copies of authorised bars, such as *The Atbara*, with much smaller letters than the genuine ones.

### East and Central Africa, 1897–99

Issued in silver and bronze; four bars issued:

| | |
|---|---|
| Lubwa's (Sept. 1897–Feb. 1898) | 1898 |
| Uganda 1897–98 | Uganda 1899 |

The silver medals do not appear to have been issued without a bar, but bronze ones without bar have been seen; one was recently offered in a dealer's list, to the 27th Bombay Infantry, which was at all four actions, but it is possible that some of its camp followers were entitled to the bronze medal without bar. Naming is usually by engraved sloping or upright capitals, but running script to Indian regiments has been noted.

### British North Borneo Company's Medals, 1897–1937

(1) *Medal for Punitive Expeditions:* issued in silver and bronze; not issued without a bar. Three bars were issued:

Punitive Expedition (1897); Punitive Expeditions (1897–98); Rundum (1915–16). The medal with bar *Rundum* was issued in silver only.

(2) *Medal for Tambunan*, 1899–1900: issued in silver and bronze, with one bar, Tambunan; not issued without a bar.

(3) *General Service Medal, 1937:* no bars issued.

All these medals were issued unnamed, but some were privately engraved. Owing to their great rarity, Spink & Son, Ltd., (who struck the originals), struck a number of specimens so that collectors can have them represented in their collections; all have COPY or SPECIMEN impressed on the rim, and in addition all those struck since 1955 have the s of SON obliterated, where the maker's name appears on the medal.

### Queen's South Africa, 1899–1902

Three types of *rev.* exist, the first having the dates, 1899–1900, in the right upper field, and Britannia's wreath points to R of AFRICA;

this type is rare, and was used for medals to Strathcona's Horse and a few other early issues; when it was discovered that the war had not, in fact, ended in 1900, the dates were removed from the *rev.*, thus forming the second type. On many of the medals the dates are still faintly visible, particularly if the medal has acquired some toning; on cleaning, the figures disappear, and do not return for some months. Although the first type is rare, those of the second type, with the date faintly visible, have no additional value and are worth the same as those of type 3. The third type is from a new die, without any trace of the dates, and the wreath points to F of AFRICA; this die was also used for the King's Medal.

The Queen's Medal was issued in silver, with and without bars, and in bronze without bar. Twenty-six bars were issued, but neither of the dated bars is usually found on the Queen's Medal if the recipient was also entitled to the King's Medal. The twenty-six bars are:

| | | |
|---|---|---|
| Cape Colony | Belmont | Wepener |
| Natal | Modder River | Defence of Mafeking |
| Rhodesia | Tugela Heights | Transvaal |
| Relief of Mafeking | Relief of Kimberley | Johannesburg |
| Defence of Kimberley | Paardeberg | Laing's Nek |
| Talana | Orange Free State | Diamond Hill |
| Elandslaagte | Relief of Ladysmith | Wittebergen |
| Defence of Ladysmith | Driefontein | Belfast |
| South Africa 1901 | | South Africa 1902 |

### King's South Africa, 1901–02

Two bars: South Africa 1901; South Africa 1902.

Normally both these bars are always on the medal, except for about six hundred, issued without bars to nursing sisters. In a few instances the medal was issued with the *South Africa 1902* bar only, when the Queen's Medal had been issued earlier with the *South Africa 1901* bar (see below).

Various types of naming are found for these two medals, both impressed and engraved, the most usual being as in *Fig. 4t, u* and *v*.

Although perhaps the cheapest of our campaign medals bearing battle bars, the Queen's South Africa Medal is one which can give the collector much of interest in its background reading, and provides a wonderful scope for those seeking medals to unusual or little-known units. Apart from the two rare bars, *Wepener* and *Defence of Mafeking*, and the somewhat scarce bar, *Rhodesia*, all the others should be within the price range of most collectors.

Three types of bars are to be found – official, unofficial copies of genuine bars, and unofficial fictitious bars. The medal is so common that the style of the official bars should be known to all collectors, but medals may be encountered with what the navy might call 'tiddley' bars; these usually have slightly different letters, the recessed portion of the field is sometimes frosted, and the high reliefs of the letters and frame are highly polished. Since these are seen often on officers' medals, it is probable that they were supplied by military tailors to 'improve' the appearance of both this and the King's Medal.

Occasionally bars may be found on the Q.S.A. Medal with the letters spaced differently from normal – some wider, some very tightly grouped – while others have letters of slightly different appearance from usual. It had generally been thought that these were unofficial bars, and some credence can be given to this because some of these bars have proved to be ones to which the recipient was not entitled. On the other hand, such a large number of bars were required that it is known that the Royal Mint put the making of them out to contract by several firms. It is more than probable that some variation in style must have resulted from this, and consequently it is likely that some of these 'different' bars might well be genuine, especially if it can be shown that the recipient was entitled to them. It is known that in many cases additional bars were issued after the award of the medal (which accounts for rivets of slightly different types appearing on the same medal), and it could well be the case that the extra bar was one of the 'different' type. This is borne out to some extent by the fact that in many such examples the 'different' bars are not those next to the medal, although some are found with all bars of what has previously been called an unofficial type. It must be admitted that opinion is divided on these bars, and although at one time I would have rejected a medal carrying them (and, indeed, have done so), I would now feel inclined to accept it provided that the entitlement was confirmed – unless the style of lettering clearly shows that it is obviously an unofficial bar. On the bottom medal in plate 9, the top two bars are definitely unofficial, as are several of the *Wepener* bars with the word very bunched, and in small letters.

In the fictitious class I have seen three examples, but believe that

others exist; one reads *Orange River Colony*, and is clearly a manu-
facturer's mistake due to the change in the title of the Orange Free
State after our occupation in 1900; the others are *Pretoria* and
*Standerton;* they are well made and look quite official, but the
*Transvaal* bar accompanying the last had very bunched lettering,
and was obviously an unofficial copy. See also *Plate 9.*

When checking bars against a particular regiment's fighting record
you may come across a medal with a totally different selection from
those usually awarded; these are often to Mounted Infantry units,
drawn from various county regiments, but the medal might or
might not have M.I. after the name of the regiment. Late drafts, too,
often gained different bars from the main body of their regiment, as
they were sometimes attached to other units as necessity required.

The bar, *Defence of Mafeking*, wants watching, as quite a number
of false ones exist. Medals impressed to the Mafeking Town Guard
are the safest, while those to such units as the Bechuanaland Rifles,
Protectorate Regiment, or South African Light Horse, etc., should
be verified, as although quite a number of members of each were
present, there were many others who were not.

Examples of both the Queen's and King's Medals are known with
fixed (i.e. non-swivelling) mounts. These are either very late issues or
official replacements, struck or assembled in the 'economy' period
following the 1914–18 War, in the manner of the British War Medal
and others of that time.

It is generally accepted that, apart from the medals without bars
issued to nursing sisters, the King's Medal always has the two bars,
*South Africa 1901* and *South Africa 1902;* the conditions governing
its award preclude its being issued with only one bar. This is techni-
cally correct, and it would seem that those with only the 1901 bar
*must* have had the 1902 bar removed, but perfectly genuine medals
have been issued bearing only the 1902 bar. They are certainly very
rare, but are worthless unless their authenticity can be proved. In my
own collection is a pair of Boer War medals, of which the Queen's
Medal, to 9625 Pte. C. Browne, 45th Coy., Imperial Yeomanry, has
four bars – *Cape Colony, Orange Free State, Transvaal,* and *South
Africa 1901* – the last bar being fixed by different (but official) rivets,
as if added later. The King's Medal has but one bar, *South Africa
1902,* and is impressed in the usual style to Agent C. Browne, F.I.D.
Thanks to the kind co-operation of the Public Record Office, I find
that the recipient served in the Imperial Yeomanry and the Jo'burg

Mounted Rifles until September 1901 and in the Field Intelligence Dept. from October 1901 to 31st January 1902. The medal rolls show that he was issued with the Queen's Medal with the first three clasps, on 27th August 1901, while the *South Africa 1901* was issued to him on 8th January 1904 (hence the different rivets). The medal rolls of the F.I.D. show that he was issued, on 15th May 1907, with the King's Medal with clasp, *South Africa 1902* only.

### Mediterranean Medal, 1899–1902
No bars issued; naming as for the Queen's South Africa, of which it is, in effect, a variety.

### China, 1900
Issued in silver and bronze; three bars:
Taku Forts; Defence of Legations: Relief of Pekin.

Naming may be impressed or engraved, in any of the three styles of *Fig. 4t, u* and *v*, while some medals to the Royal Field Artillery, Royal Garrison Artillery, some Indian units, and others, may be found engraved in running script as *Fig. 4q:* most medals to the navy and marines are impressed in square serifed capitals, similar to *Fig. 4p*. Medals with the bar, *Defence of Legations* (which is extremely rare, and of which unofficial copies exist), should not be bought without a very careful check to see that the recipient shown on the medal was entitled to that bar. Another unofficial bar, *Relief of Pekin*, has also been seen, with larger, squarer letters than normal.

Bronze medals were issued without bar, and with bar, *Relief of Pekin;* I have no records of the other bars in bronze, but they may exist.

### Transport Medal, 1899–1902
Not issued without a bar; two bars:
South Africa 1899–1902          China 1900

Naming is usually impressed in square capitals; rank is not usually shown, but names of Masters are followed by IN COMMAND.

### Ashanti, 1900
Issued in silver and bronze; one bar: Kumassi.

Naming is usually by impressed thin upright letters (*Fig. 4t*), but engraved running script is also found. There are two dies of the medal, one with the details in high relief and the other in low relief.

## Africa General Service, 1902–

Usually found in silver, but very occasionally in bronze; not normally issued without a bar but a very few bronze medals have been seen without a bar. This medal appears with the head of Edward VII, George V, or Elizabeth II, and forty-five bars have been issued so far. Being current over such a long period, there are obviously differences in naming; generally speaking, medals to the army and R.A.F. are impressed in thin tall capitals, while those to the navy are in square serifed capitals, although my *Aro 1901–1902* example, to H.M.S. *Thrush*, has the former naming, while an officer's medal with *Gambia* bar is engraved in sloping capitals. The *Kenya* bar medals to the army are impressed in the usual modern small square capitals.

Forty-five Bars:

| | | |
|---|---|---|
| N. Nigeria (1900–01) | East Africa 1902 | Aro 1901–1902 |
| N. Nigeria 1902 | East Africa 1904 | Lango 1901 |
| N. Nigeria 1903 | East Africa 1905 | Kissi 1905 |
| N. Nigeria 1903–04 | East Africa 1906 | Nandi 1905–06 |
| N. Nigeria 1904 | West Africa 1906 | Shimber Berris 1914–15 |
| N. Nigeria 1906 | West Africa 1908 | Nyasaland 1915 |
| S. Nigeria (1901) | West Africa 1909–10 | East Africa 1913 |
| S. Nigeria 1902 | Somaliland 1901 | East Africa 1914 |
| S. Nigeria 1902–03 | Somaliland 1902–04 | East Africa 1913–14 |
| S. Nigeria 1903 | Jidballi (Jan. 1904) | East Africa 1915 |
| S. Nigeria 1903–04 | Somaliland 1908–10 | Jubaland 1917–18 |
| S. Nigeria 1904 | Uganda 1900 | East Africa 1918 |
| S. Nigeria 1904–05 | B.C.A. 1899–1900 | Nigeria 1918 |
| S. Nigeria 1905 | Jubaland (1900–01) | Somaliland 1920 |
| S. Nigeria 1905–06 | Gambia (1901) | Kenya (1952–56) |

(The above bars are not in order of being awarded, but are grouped for convenience.)

## Tibet, 1903–04

Issued in silver and bronze; one bar: Gyantse. Naming is in engraved script, as in *Fig. 4q*.

Unofficial bars exist with smaller, more compact letters; there is also a bar with slightly larger letters than normal, but it is not known whether this is unofficial or whether it may be from a Calcutta Mint die.

### Natal, 1906 (Zulu Rising)

One bar: 1906. Naming is usually by impressed thin square capitals, rather like *Fig. 4y*, but often very faint; some have been seen with engraved script, and occasionally unnamed examples are found.

Medals without bar, if verified, are appreciably scarcer than those with the bar, but beware of medals from which the bar has been removed; examine the pin carefully to see if it shows any sign of having been removed and replaced. There were approximately four medals issued with bar to every one without bar.

The original ribbon had a corded edge.

### India General Service, 1908–35

Issued in silver, and also, with the first two bars, in bronze. Twelve bars have been issued, the first with the medal bearing the head of Edward VII, the next seven with the head of George V with title, KAISAR-I-HIND, and the last four also with the head of George V, but with titles, D.G. BRITT. OMN. REX ET INDIAE IMP. Not issued without a bar.

Twelve bars:

| | |
|---|---|
| North West Frontier 1908 | Waziristan 1921–24 |
| Abor 1911–12 | Waziristan 1925 |
| Afghanistan N.W.F. 1919 | North West Frontier 1930–31 |
| Mahsud 1919–20 | Burma 1930–32 |
| Waziristan 1919–21 | Mohmand 1933 |
| Malabar 1921–22 | North West Frontier 1935 |

Naming varies, and is usually engraved in running script for the first two bars, and impressed in thin small capitals for most of the later ones. The rivets are often poor, especially when the recipient was still serving in India when the later bars were issued.

Two types of mount may be found, the rather ugly claw on medals from the Calcutta Mint, and the neater type on those from the Royal Mint (*Fig. 12*).

The bar, *Waziristan 1925*, was awarded only to the R.A.F., and is very rare.

FIG. 12.
Mounts on the India General Service Medals – George V and George VI issues. Left: Struck at the Royal Mint. Right: Struck at the Calcutta Mint.

## Naval General Service, 1915–64

Not issued without a bar. This medal bears the head of successive sovereigns from George V to Elizabeth II (except Edward VIII), and medals with bar, *Malaya* were issued first with the head of George VI, and later, Elizabeth II.

Fifteen bars issued; there has been some confusion regarding the exact number and wording of these bars, and the following list has been kindly supplied and verified by the Royal Mint:

| | |
|---|---|
| Persian Gulf 1909–1914 | Bomb & Mine Clearance 1945–53 |
| Iraq 1919–1920 | Malaya |
| N.W. Persia 1920* | B & M Clearance Mediterranean |
| Palestine 1936–1939 | Cyprus |
| S.E. Asia 1945–46 | Near East |
| Minesweeping 1945–51 | Arabian Peninsula |
| Palestine 1945–48 | Brunei |
| Yangtze 1949 | |

(*Originally N.W. Persia 1919–1920, but later withdrawn and replaced as above.)

The naming of medals with the first bar is by impressed large capitals, similar to *Fig. 4p;* I have never seen medals with the second and third bars (although one with *Iraq 1919–1920* has been on the market), so cannot quote the style of naming; subsequent medals are impressed in small capitals similar to *Fig. 4w*.

The *Royal Mint Report for 1957* quoted a new bar, *Bomb and Mine Clearance, 1945–56*. As the same bar to the General Service Medal (Army & RAF), 1918–64, was awarded only to the Australian Army, it would appear that only the Royal Australian Navy would have received it with the N.G.S. Medal.

## MEDALS OF THE FIRST WORLD WAR

### 1914 Star:

Bronze; one bar; 5th Aug.–22nd Nov. 1914.

### 1914–15 Star:

Bronze; no bars.

Naming is impressed on the *rev.* in either small or square *sans serif* capitals, as *Fig. 4w, x, y*. 1914 Stars to the Royal Naval Division (R.N., R.N.R., R.N.V.R., and R.M.) are impressed in large square serifed capitals (*Fig. 4p*).

**British War Medal,** 1914–20 (dated 1914–1918)
Issued in silver and bronze; no bars authorised. Naming is impressed
in several sizes, as *Fig. 4w, x,* or *y.*

**Mercantile Marine War Medal, 1914–18**
Bronze; no bars. Naming is by impressed capitals (*Fig. 4z*); no rank
is given, and usually the first name is in full. (See additional note on
p. 155).

**Victory Medal, 1914–19**
Bronze; no bars. Naming as for British War Medal.

**Territorial Force War Medal, 1914–18 (dated 1914–1919)**
Bronze; no bars. Naming as for British War Medal, except that
officers' medals usually show the regiment.

*　　*　　*

For those who collect with more than a passing interest in the
recipient or the unit, there is quite a story to be found in many of
these common medals.

Groups with the 1914 Star and bar to units of the "Old Contemptibles" earn their place in the cabinet; for many of our Territorial
regiments these were the first campaign medals issued impressed
with the regiment's name (those who, as members of the old Volunteer Force, took part in the Boer War, received mainly medals named
to the units with which they served – either the parent regiment
(although some were marked "Volr. Battn.") or Imperial Yeomanry,
C.I.V., etc.). Also of interest are groups to some of the lesser known
units, such as the Army Cyclist Corps or the Ceylon Planters Rifles
Corps.

Unfortunately the British War Medal and Victory Medal to
officers do not normally give the unit (although R.N. and R.A.F. are
indicated), but this information can be found from the *Army List.*
The Quarterly List gives only regular officers, while the Monthly
List gives these and holders of temporary commissions; also at
intervals awards of the M.C. and other decorations are listed. If an
officer qualified for the 1914 Star or 1914–15 Star *after* being commissioned, his unit is shown thereon, but if, as happened in thousands
of cases, he gained the Star while in the ranks and was commissioned
later, then the unit shown on the Star is frequently different from
that to which he was posted as an officer.

146

Medals to the Royal Navy normally show the number and rating, or the rank, of the recipient, and the branch, such as R.N., R.N.R., R.N.V.R., M.F.A. (Mercantile Fleet Auxiliary), etc., but no ship's name – often a man served in several ships – but I have a 1914–15 trio, all officially named to a rating, R.N.R., H.M.S. *Philomel*. This ship was lent to the Royal New Zealand Navy throughout the war, and served with the Royal Naval Australian Squadron. From the national, archives at Wellington, I learn that the recipient, whose service number starts with the initials, NZ., was a qualified stoker in the R.N.V.R. A similar group is known with the number starting with N.S.W., also named to H.M.S. Philomel on all three medals, and he is verified as an Australian seaman in the R.N.R.

### 1914 Star and 1914–15 Star

It is not always realised that the ribbons for these two stars are *absolutely* identical unless the recipient of the 1914 Star was also entitled to the dated bar, through having been "under the fire of the enemy in France or Belgium", when a silver rose is superimposed on the ribbon when the star itself is not worn. Thousands did not qualify for the bar – the proportions are, approximately, for every five entitled to the bar, seven were not, and something like 378,000 stars were issued – but a large number of those not entitled incorrectly wore the silver rose on their ribbon strip (and even on the medal ribbon itself), under the impression that it indicated the earlier star.

Another point, not always known, is that the 1914 Star was awarded only for service in France or Belgium (naval personnel qualifying only if landed for shore service in these countries), whereas the 1914–15 Star was given to those who served in widespread theatres of war between August 1914 and 31st December 1915.

The collector will often come across groups including a 1914 Star, but with no ribbons; it is then difficult to know if the recipient was entitled to the bar, unless he had a gallantry award won before 22nd November 1914, or is known to have been killed, wounded, or taken prisoner before that date.

It need hardly be mentioned that the recipient of either of these Stars must also have both the British War Medal and the Victory Medal.

### British War Medal, 1914–20

Although this medal bears the dates, "1914, 1918", it was also awarded for naval service during 1919–20, covering mine clearance at sea, also service in North and South Russia, the Baltic, Siberia, and in the Caspian and Black Seas.

In the majority of cases the B.W.M. is accompanied by the Victory Medal, but in certain instances it can be found alone (and if not eligible for the Victory Medal, the recipient will certainly not have had either the 1914 Star or the 1914–15 Star). Such recipients are usually either naval personnel, often re-called reservists, who served in depot ships, boom defence vessels, etc., or in the post-1918 period, or army personnel serving overseas but not in an area included in the eligibility for the Victory Medal, such as certain parts of India. It must also be remembered that one sometimes finds a group containing, say, a D.C.M., British War Medal, and a Long Service Medal – all silver medals, but no bronze ones. While it *could* be complete, it almost certainly has the Victory Medal (and possibly a Star) missing, and the most likely explanation is that the medals have been pawned or sold only for their silver value, the bronze medals having been refused and detached.

One sometimes finds this medal impressed with the recipient's name (but no rank or rating) and SERVICE WITH THE ROYAL NAVY. It has been suggested that these medals were awarded to the crews of 'Q' ships (armed merchant ships disguised as unarmed vessels), but there does not seem to be any evidence to support this, especially as several groups, containing an award for gallantry known to have been earned in 'Q' ships, have the B.W.M. named in the ordinary way. A much more likely explanation is that such medals were awarded to civilians, such as canteen staffs who served in a ship of war at sea (which is an eligible category), or perhaps to civilian technicians or tradesmen who performed repair or maintenance work at sea.

Considerable numbers of the B.W.M. were struck at the Calcutta Mint, but there do not appear to be any die differences; there are, however, differences in size; compared with the average diameter of 1·428″ of some thirty British issues (and these vary by several thousandths of an inch), the Calcutta ones are approximately 0·011″–0·014″ (eleven to fourteen thousandths) larger. There is also a slight difference in the naming, some being impressed in letters which are very slightly wider spaced and not so evenly indented.

The B.W.M. was also issued in bronze, and is much scarcer than in silver. It was given to all British subjects who were enrolled in native labour corps units and who served in theatres of war. These are usually found to Maltese, but some were awarded to the Indian Labour Corps and to Chinese from British possessions. I have never seen the bronze medal accompanied by a Victory Medal, and it would appear that recipients would not have been eligible for the latter. (See additional note on p. 155).

### Mercantile Marine War Medal

This medal is worn immediately after the British War Medal, and before the Victory Medal (if entitled). Basically recipients (details of whose eligibility are given in Taprell Dorling's *Ribbons & Medals*) were also entitled to the B.W.M. In addition, Mercantile Marine officers and men who served under special Naval Engagements (Form T124 and its variants, including T299) in H.M. Ships of War and Commissioned Fleet Auxiliaries, also received the Victory Medal.

The ribbon, typifying the green and red of a ship's starboard and port lights, with the white of the masthead light in the centre, is worn with the green nearest the centre of the chest, i.e. on the left as you look at the medal in your collection.

### Allied Victory Medal, 1914–19

Although the period of service qualifying for this medal ended, in the main, in November 1918, in at least two instances service up to midnight, 13–14th January 1919, was eligible – namely in Hedjaz and in operations conducted by the Aden Field Force. Thus the dates appearing on the medal, though often criticised, are justified.

This medal and its conditions of award, have been fully covered in the various editions of Taprell Dorling's *Ribbons and Medals* (particularly in the smaller format editions appearing between 1920 and 1946).

One occasionally finds this medal in a dull, somewhat brownish brass, with rather a 'dusty' finish. Various explanations have been given, including the story that they are early issues to officers. It seems more likely that they may be the result of an experimental finish, or that a batch was made from a slightly different mixture of metals, which has reacted differently to the atmosphere.

Although the Victory Medals issued by the other allies all have the figure of Victory, and use the same ribbon, they are all different in design. The British type was also issued to all eligible Commonwealth troops, but for South Africa the *rev.* has the inscription in both English and Afrikaans, the *obv.* remaining the same as ours.

### Territorial Force War Medal, 1914–18

Although it bears the dates 1914–1919, the qualifying period for this medal ended on 11th November 1918. It is not common, as so many of those who would otherwise have been eligible did, in fact, serve overseas in time to qualify for either the 1914 Star or the 1914–15 Star. Instances have been recorded where the Territorial Force War Medal was actually awarded to men who received one of the stars, although contrary to regulations. Occasionally one finds the B.W.M. and T.F.W.M., but no Victory Medal; the latter may have become detached, but it has been suggested that the recipient might have served in some parts of India which did not qualify for the Victory Medal.

### General Service Medal (Army and R.A.F.), 1918–64

Not issued without a bar.

Naming is usually by impressed thin capitals, but later medals to the R.A.F. are engraved; some of the R.A.F. medals of Elizabeth II are so neatly engraved that at first glance they appear to be impressed.

Sixteen bars issued; there has been some confusion, as with the Naval General Service Medal, 1915, regarding the exact number and wording of these bars, and the following list has been kindly supplied and verified by the Royal Mint:

| | |
|---|---|
| S. Persia | Bomb & Mine Clearance 1945–49 |
| Kurdistan | Bomb & Mine Clearance 1945–56* |
| Iraq | Palestine 1945–48 |
| N.W. Persia | Malaya |
| Southern Desert, Iraq | Cyprus |
| Northern Kurdistan | Near East |
| Palestine | Arabian Peninsula |
| S.E. Asia 1945–46 | Brunei |

(*According to the Royal Mint records, this bar was issued only to the Australian Army.)

The first five bars appear on medals with the coinage head of George V; the second issue, with the crowned head of George V, and the bar, *Northern Kurdistan*, is very rare, and was awarded only to the R.A.F. and Iraq Levies. The third and fourth types bear the crowned head of George VI and are, respectively, with and (after early 1949) without the title, INDIAE IMP.

So far all issues have non-swelling mounts, but some late issues and official replacements of both George VI types have swivelling mounts.

The bars relating to the third type are *Palestine, S.E. Asia 1945–46*, and *Palestine 1945–48*, while those for the fourth type are *Bomb & Mine Clearance 1945–49* and *Malaya*. It must be mentioned, however, that *Palestine 1945–48* can be found on both third and fourth issues, as no doubt can some of the other bars.

There are two dies for the *Malaya* bar; on one, probably the earlier, the letters occupy 19 mm., while on the other they occupy 20 mm.

The fifth and sixth issues have the crowned head of Elizabeth II, the fifth carrying the *obv.* legend: ELIZABETH II D:G:BR:OMN:REGINA F:D:, while the sixth type follows the change in our coinage legend, introduced in 1954, reading: ELIZABETH II DEI GRATIA REGINA F.D. The bar, *Malaya*, also appears in this reign, mainly with the fifth type medal, but has also been seen on the sixth type.

The Royal Mint has been issuing this medal with the swivel mount (or suspender) since 1954. For details regarding the change see Chapter 9.

It is not unusual to find this medal in fairly recent issues, with the second (or subsequent) bar either loose on the ribbon or fixed in an apparently irregular manner. Subsequent bars were issued to the R.A.F. with rivets for fixing, but often the rivets were lost, and recipients either slipped the bars over the ribbon or had them fixed to the lower bar by local craftsmen. Complaints were lodged by the army regarding the issue of loose bars, and it was decided to issue pins (similar to that in the suspender) so that the bars could easily be fixed from outer rivet hole to outer rivet hole, thus avoiding the need to supply easily lost rivets.

### India General Service, 1936–39

Not issued without a bar. Two bars:

North West Frontier 1936–37    North West Frontier 1937–39

Naming is by impressed thin capitals. The two strikings of this medal have the respective mounts as described for the George V issues of the India General Service Medal, 1908 (*Fig. 12*), and differences in the *rev.* dies, etc., are adequately described by Major

Gordon, in his *British Battles & Medals;* there is one further point –
on all the Calcutta strikings I have seen, the designer's initials
P.M., are omitted below the King's head (although the ligate initials,
HWP, appear on the *rev.* of both issues).

## MEDALS FOR WORLD WAR II, 1939–45

The campaign stars were struck in copper-zinc alloy; not more than
five stars can be worn by one individual, and not more than one bar
on each star.

**1939–45 Star**
One bar: Battle of Britain (10th July–31st Oct. 1940).

**Atlantic Star**
Two bars: France and Germany; Air Crew Europe.

**Air Crew Europe Star**
Two bars; France and Germany; **Atlantic.**

**Africa Star**
Three bars: 8th Army; 1st Army; **North Africa 1942–43.**

**Pacific Star**
One bar: Burma.

**Burma Star**
One bar: Pacific.

**Italy Star**
No bars.

**France and Germany Star**
One bar: Atlantic.

**Defence Medal, 1939–45**
Cupro-nickel (Canadian issues in silver). No bars issued.

**War Medal, 1939–45**
Cupro-nickel (Canadian issues in silver). No bars issued.

None of the stars or medals for the second World War, listed above, issued to British personnel, was named, but many have been privately impressed or engraved; awards to some Commonwealth troops were, however, named before issue.

There is little to worry the collector in this uninspiring series, except to note that copies of the stars and medals have been produced commercially, for sale as replacements. These differ slightly from the official issues, but the only one likely to cause concern is the copy of the Air Crew Europe Star, owing to the high price commanded by an original.

The following notes will enable collectors to recognise these copies; the details probably apply also to the other stars, but so far I have not encountered any.

One copy appears, at first glance, to be a fairly good production, but rather too well finished by polishing. The following differences are noted: (1) the letters VI (of the roman six) are joined at the top in the original, whereas in this copy they are separate; (2) in the copy the crown is in lower relief and the centre arch has only three pearls against five on the original (although the top and bottom ones are only partly showing), also the orb at the top is poorly struck; (3) this copy is thinner than the original.

Another copy appears to be *cast* instead of struck, and although the VI are joined, the base of the V is cut off square instead of being pointed as on the original. The whole production is rough, and should not deceive anybody, especially if compared with any other star.

In addition to these copies one can also find *faked* Air Crew Europe Stars, which should not be difficult to recognise. Genuine common stars were used, with the wording surrounding the royal cipher removed, and a thin struck band, lettered THE AIR CREW EUROPE STAR, superimposed. This can easily be spotted by the slight gap at either end and at the top and bottom of the inserted band.

The copies of the Defence Medal are easy to recognise, as the design is generally much cruder than the original. The copy is thinner, approximately 0·103″ against 0·133″, while the diameter is approximately 1·442″ against 1·428″ of the original. On the *obv.* there are no designer's initials below the truncation of the bust, and there are differences in the shape of the letters in the legend, particularly in the M, where the centre point comes low on the genuine medal, but high on the copy, while the copy X is much wider than the original. On the *rev.* there are many differences, but one will enable the copy to be recognised – while the original medal has three pearls on the centre arch of the crown, the copy has only two; also the designer's initials are absent in the copy, but can be seen – HWP, ligate – between the left and centre roots of the oak tree on the genuine medal.

The Defence and War Medals issued by Canada are of *silver*, unnamed, and are thinner but heavier than the British cupro-nickel ones.

### Korea, 1950–53

Cupro-nickel; no bars issued. Naming is by impressed capitals, small and thin.

The same medal was awarded by Australia and New Zealand, but Canada issued a *silver* medal (with the same ribbon), very similar in design, but with shorter royal titles and with CANADA below the Queen's head.

### United Nations Medal for Korea

Bronze; bar, Korea, integrated with the non-swivelling suspender; issued unnamed.

This medal, which was awarded to personnel of land, sea and air forces of all the nations serving in Korea or adjacent areas, on behalf of the United Nations, has the spelling of Korea on the bar, and the *rev.* inscription, in the language of the country of the recipient; those given to French-Canadian troops have them in French. While the Queen's medal for Korea is always accompanied by the UN medal, British recipients are not infrequently seen with only the UN medal. This is because the latter could be awarded for service (even for one day!) in "adjacent areas" (as mentioned above), including Japan.

Examples of this medal with inscriptions in English, but with a corded edge to the ribbon, were awarded to USA personnel, but some were also given to British recipients.

### General Service Medal, 1962–

Not issued without a bar; bars issued, up to time of writing, are:
Borneo (24th Dec. 1962–     )
Radfan (25th Apl.–31st July 1964)

South Vietnam (For Australian and N.Z. troops; 24th Dec. 1962–
  28th May 1964)
South Arabia (1st Aug. 1964–    )
Malay Peninsula (17th Aug. 1964–11th Aug. 1966)
Dhofar (1st Oct. 1969–    )
Northern Ireland (14th Aug. 1969–    )

This medal replaces the two previous General Service Medals,
i.e. the Naval G.S.M., and the Army & R.A.F. G.S.M., and is
common to all three services. The *obv.* shows the crowned head of
Queen Elizabeth II, with titles, while the rather plain *rev.* has a
crown and FOR/CAMPAIGN/SERVICE, in an oak wreath. The ribbon is
violet with narrow green edges.

ADDITIONAL NOTES:

**Mercantile Marine War Medal, 1914-18** (See pp. 146, 149).
Medals awarded to personnel of the Australian Mercantile Marine
are impressed in small capitals (*Fig. 4w*), with the recipient's *initials*
and surname, followed by AUSTRALIA and his MM number, thus: G.
GEE. AUSTRALIA 2715. The word, AUSTRALIA, comes in the centre of
the edge, immediately below the point of the truncation. Falsely
named examples have been noted, using a UK recipient's medal (with
first name in full), with AUSTRALIA and a number added further round
the edge.

**British War Medal, 1914-20** (See pp. 149).
Examples in silver have been impressed in thin *sans serif* capitals
(*Figs. 4w, 4x*), with number and unit only – no name – thus: 7274.
ARTILLERY E. A. Another has 1114. TRANSPORT C.E.A., while a third has
6325. 6-BN.E.A. These were all found in Cairo, and apparently the
E.A. stands for Egyptian Army. Another example has no number but
an Egyptian name followed by M.W.D.E.A., which would seem to
indicate Military Works Dept., Egyptian Army.

# 7

# Polar Medals

BRITISH medals awarded for arctic and antarctic exploration are, apart from the first type, all in the category of rare or very rare. They have a story behind them equal to that of any campaign medal – they are medals which have really been earned by men fighting a much more relentless foe than any human one. In qualifying for these white-ribboned awards, generations of men have pitted their wits and their strength against the mighty forces of nature, and more often than not nature has been the victor.

### Arctic Medal, 1818–55
This octagonal silver medal, with the North Star surmounting the claw clasp, was authorised in 1857, and the *London Gazette* of 5th May 1857 specified some twenty-two ships whose officers and crews were entitled to the award, although seven others appear to have been eligible and their personnel are known to have received the medal.

Unfortunately the medal was issued unnamed, although quite a number are to be found engraved (privately, of course) with recipient's name and ship, and sometimes with the date as well. Until 1968 verification was difficult, but Neville W. Poulson's book, *The White Ribbon*, includes a roll of all recipients. Officers' records can be verified from *The Arctic Navy List*, by C. R. Markham, published in 1875 (see page 224); this gives a list of officers (and a few others), in many cases with details of services, participating in polar expeditions from 1773–1875.

Accounts of many of the expeditions have been written, often by the leaders, but while some give a list of the officers, few include full crew lists of ratings. When attempting to verify a medal to a rating, however, it is worth scanning these accounts (which can often be obtained on loan through public libraries), as more than once I have been able to trace the entitlement from the mention of the recipient's name in lists of sledge parties or other details of events.

The unofficial Navy Lists and O'Byrne's *Naval Biographical Dictionary* often include, in the services of officers, reference to participation in an arctic expedition, while those who rose to high rank are often shown in naval magazines, wearing the medal.

There is one interesting point regarding the range of dates; although this expedition took place in 1857–59, later than the 'closing date', it is apparent that Capt. (later Admiral Sir Leopold) McClintock's crew, of the screw yacht, *Fox*, received the medal. This is borne out by the record in his book, describing the presentation of the medals on his return, when he brought home the first proofs of the fate of Sir John Franklin. Since many of the expeditions, qualifying for the medal, were unsuccessfully made with the same object, it would seem that McClintock's success brought the award of the medal to those of his crew who had not previously qualified. The award was sanctioned by Admiralty Order No. 5022, of 22nd September 1859. Several examples are known, engraved with names of members of his crew; one of these, to G. Carey, describes the ship as ARCTIC YATCH (*sic*) 'FOX'.

The mount of this medal is very vulnerable, like that of the Abyssinia, 1867–68, Medal, and when buying, care should be exercised to see that there has been no fracture and re-soldering above or below the star; if there has been a repair, and the medal is part of a verified group, it is still acceptable but at a reduced price; if, however, it is an unnamed single, most collectors would prefer to let it pass.

Unlike the $1\frac{1}{4}''$ ribbon of later polar medals, the first medal had a *watered* ribbon, $1\frac{1}{2}''$ wide, the original issue having a corded edge, like that of the Baltic Medal.

An interesting pattern of this medal exists, and specimens are sometimes offered for sale. It is $1\cdot3''$ in diameter, but circular instead of octagonal, and appreciably thicker than the issued medal. The design of both medals is the same, except for the beaded inner rim of the octagonal one. The two examples were submitted to Queen Victoria, who chose the octagonal medal.

In view of the fact that many of the named medals give the ship but not the date of the expedition, the following list may be helpful to collectors in placing the background of their medals. Ships' names given in *italics* made only summer cruises; those in *ITALIC CAPITALS* wintered, while those marked with an * asterisk were abandoned or lost.

*Alexander.* 1818. Lieut (later R-Adml Sir Edward) Parry, with Commdr Ross (*Isabella*).

*ASSISTANCE.** 1850–51. Capt. (later Adml Sir Erasmus) Ommanney. Franklin search with Austin (*RESOLUTE*).

1852–54. Capt. (later Adml) Sir Edward Belcher, commanding an expedition of search for Franklin, also for Collinson and McClure. Abandoned, 1854.

*Blossom.* 1825–28. Commdr (later Adml) F. W. Beechey. Two summer cruises in Behring Strait, intended to act in concert with Parry and Franklin.

*Breadalbane.** 1853. Master W. H. Fawckner. Transport, crushed by ice off Beechey Island, 1853. Not listed in the *London Gazette,* but the crew certainly received the medal.

*Dorothea.* 1818. Capt. David Buchan's attempt to reach the North Pole *via* Spitzbergen.

*ENTERPRISE.* 1848–49. Capt. (later R-Adml) Sir James Clark Ross. Franklin search.

1850–54. Capt. (later Vice-Adml) R. Collinson. Franklin search.

*EREBUS.** 1845–48. Capt. Sir John Franklin. To discover the N.W. Passage; abandoned, 22nd April 1848.

*FELIX.* 1850–51. Capt. (later R-Adml) Sir John Ross. Franklin search. Not listed in *London Gazette,* but apparently entitled.

*FOX.* 1857–59. Capt. F. L. McClintock, Screw yacht. Was the first to bring back proofs of the fate of Sir John Franklin. Not listed in the *London Gazette,* being outside the specified dates, but the medal was awarded to the crew (Admiralty Order No. 5022, of 22nd September 1859).

*FURY.** 1821–23. Commdr Parry, commanding an expedition to discover the N.W. Passage.

1824–25. Capt. H. P. Hoppner, with Parry (*HECLA*). Wrecked and abandoned, August 1825.

*GRIPER.* 1819–20. Lieut Matthew Liddon, with Parry (*HECLA*).

*Griper.* 1823. Commdr D. C. Clavering. Summer voyage to Spitzbergen and Greenland.

1824. Capt. G. F. Lyon. A disastrous attempt to reach Repulse Bay.

*HECLA.* 1819–20. Lieut E. Parry, commanding an expedition to discover the N.W. Passage.

1821–23. Commdr G. F. Lyon, with Parry (in *FURY*).

1824–25. Capt. E. Parry. Wintered at Port Bowen.

*Hecla.* 1827. Capt. Parry. Summer cruise to Spitzbergen, in an attempt to reach the Pole.

*Herald.* 1848–51. Capt. (later Vice-Adml Sir Henry) Kellett. Summer voyages up the Behring Strait.

*INTREPID.** 1850–51. Lieut J. B. Cator. Part of Austin's expedition, but not listed in *London Gazette.* The crew received the medal. 1852–54. Commdr F. L. McClintock. With Belcher (in *ASSISTANCE*) in Franklin search. Abandoned, 1854. Not listed in *London Gazette,* but obviously eligible.

*INVESTIGATOR.** 1848–49. Capt. E. J. Bird. Franklin search, with Ross (in *ENTERPRISE*). 1850–53. Capt. (later Vice-Adml Sir Robt) McClure. Franklin search, with Collinson. Abandoned, 1853.

*Isabel.* 1852. Commdr (later Adml Sir Edward) Inglefield. Summer cruise in Baffin's Land. Not listed in the *London Gazette,* but the crew received the medal.

*Isabella.* 1818. Commander John Ross' first expedition. A summer cruise to explore Baffin's Bay.

*LADY FRANKLIN.* 1850–51. Franklin search, under the command of a whaling captain, William Penney.

*Nancy Dawson.* 1849. Robert A. Sheddon (a former Mate, R.N.). A private searcher for Franklin's expedition, in Behring Strait. Not listed in the *London Gazette,* but the crew received the medal.

*NORTH STAR.* 1849–50. Master Jas. Saunders. Store ship, Franklin search. 1852–54. Commdr W. J. S. Pullen, with Belcher (*ASSISTANCE*).

*Phoenix.* 1853. Commdr (later Adml Sir Edward) Inglefield. Summer search for Franklin. 1854. Capt. E. A. Inglefield. Summer search for Franklin.

*PIONEER.** 1850–51. Lieut (later R-Adml) S. Osborn, with Austin (*RESOLUTE*); not listed in *London Gazette.* 1852–54. Commdr S. Osborn, with Belcher (in *ASSISTANCE*). Abandoned, 1854. Not listed in *London Gazette,* but apparently eligible in respect of both voyages.

*PLOVER.* 1848–52. Commdr (later R-Adml) T. E. L. Moore, Franklin search. (Not listed for her 1852–54 commission, Commdr R. Maguire, but the crew received the medal).

*Prince Albert.* 1850. Commdr C. C. Forsyth. Summer search for Franklin. Not listed in *London Gazette,* but the crew received the medal.

159

*PRINCE ALBERT.* 1851–52. Commdr Wm. Kennedy. Franklin search. Not listed in *London Gazette*, but eligible, as previous.

*RATTLESNAKE.* 1853. Commdr H. Trollope. Took up supplies to Commdr R. Maguire (*PLOVER*), in Behring Strait. It seems strange that this ship should be listed as eligible, as the 1852–54 voyage of *PLOVER* is not listed, neither are three other ships which took supplies up to her in these years.

*RESOLUTE.** 1850–51. Capt. (later Vice-Adml Sir Horatio) Austin, commanding a Franklin search expedition.

1852–54. Capt. H. Kellett, with Belcher (*ASSISTANCE*). Abandoned, May, 1854.

*SOPHIA.* 1850–51. J. Stewart. Franklin search, with Penney (in *LADY FRANKLIN*). Brig.

*Talbot.* 1854. Commdr R. Jenkins. Came out, with *Phoenix*, to bring home part of Belcher's Expedition. Not listed in *London Gazette*, but appears to be eligible.

*TERROR.** 1836–37. Capt. (later Adml Sir Geo.) Back. Voyage to Frozen Strait.

1845–48. Capt. F. R. M. Crozier, with Franklin. Ship abandoned with *EREBUS*, 22nd April 1848.

*Trent.* 1818. Lieut (later R-Adml Sir John) Franklin, with Buchan (in *Dorothea*).

*VICTORY.** 1829–33. Capt. John Ross. Paddle-wheel steamer. Search for N.W. Passage; abandoned 1832.

In addition to the crews of the above-named ships, the medal was also awarded to members of various land expeditions, foreign expeditions, and those organised by the Hudson's Bay Company.

**Arctic Medal, 1875–76**

This medal was given to the crews of H.M.S. *Alert* (Capt. G. S. Nares) and H.M.S. *Discovery* (Capt. H. F. Stephenson), for the Arctic Expedition under the command of Capt. (later Vice-Adml Sir George) Nares, also to the crew of the steam yacht, *Pandora* (Capt. Allen Young), which made two polar voyages during the same period and, according to W. H. Long (*Medals of the British Navy*), "rendered valuable assistance to H.M. Ships, while in the Polar Seas". The medal must be classed as rare, as although about 170 were issued, only a small percentage of these appear to have found their way into the collector's market.

The naming is engraved, usually blacked in, in serifed capitals

160

France: Legion of Honour.
*Left – Chevalier*, 2nd Empire (Crimean War period);
*Right – Officier*, 3rd Republic

Plate 12.

Italy
Sardinian Medal for Military Valour, 1855–56,
awarded to Richd. Rowe, Gunner, RN

War Cross, 1918

Plate 13.

(not unlike the Ashantee Medal, 1873-74), sometimes with the dates included. Occasionally unnamed examples are encountered, and it is not known if any were issued thus or not. Some of these unnamed medals have been 'named', both with names of known recipients and with false names, but the style of naming is usually lighter and thinner than the originals. Consequently, as this is an expensive medal, it is as well to obtain expert advice before buying from an unknown vendor.

## Polar Medal, 1904

Reverting to the octagonal shape, this medal has been retained up to the present time, with the interesting *rev.* design (in low relief) of Scott's *Discovery* and a sledging party. The *obv.* has varied, of course, with the changes of sovereign, and in the later issues of George V, the 'Admiral' type is replaced by the coinage head (silver medal, bar: *Arctic 1930-31*, authorised in 1932,) or the crowned and robed bust (bronze medal, bars: *Antarctic 1929-30*, *1929-31*, or *1930-31*, authorised in 1934).

A considerable number of bars have been issued (all listed, with brief details, in Neville W. Poulsom's book, *The White Ribbon*), many of them merely date variations for the same expedition. Some of the latest bars, in the present reign, are engraved instead of being struck, and are very poor in appearance.

Naming includes both impressed and engraved styles, but all the medals are rare, and I have seen only relatively few of them. I can say, however, that those in my own collection show the naming as follows: *Antarctic 1910-13* (Scott's last expedition) – two examples, both impressed; *Antarctic 1912-14* (Mawson's Australian Expedition) – impressed; *Antarctic 1929–30* (Mawson's B.A.N.Z.A.R. Expedition: bronze medal, crowned head) – engraved.

The original issue of the medal was for Scott's first expedition, and the landing party received it in silver, with bar, *Antarctic 1902–04*, while the supply ships' party received it in bronze *without bar*. The only other instance of the medal being issued without bar, which I can trace, was for the Aurora Relief Expedition of 1916–17, where a number of bronze medals were issued thus, but those already in possession of a bronze medal received the bar. *Antarctic 1917.*

For some expeditions both silver and bronze medals were given (bars only, to holders of previous medals), while for others only silver or only bronze medals or bars were awarded. Those who have received both a silver and a bronze medal are entitled to wear both (and two adjacent white ribbons when ribbons only are worn), while those who receive subsequent bars can wear a rosette of the appropriate metal (similar to that worn on the ribbon of the 1914 Star and Bar), to indicate participation in two or more expeditions.

The bronze medal is no longer awarded, the last being those authorised in 1941 for the various Antarctic voyages between 1925 and 1939, by *Discovery II* and *William Scoresby*.

There are several examples of the Polar Medal about, stamped SPECIMEN, usually on the bottom straight edge; some have a single bar, while others have an impossible combination of bars all relating to the same expedition. Reputable dealers do their best to ensure that these medals do not fall into the wrong hands, but they are in large demand as representative medals and consequently command quite a high price. Although I have never seen one of these specimen medals which has been 'fiddled', I have heard on good authority that at least one is known with SPECIMEN removed, and the medal falsely engraved with a name and a ship.

**An Unofficial Award**

In November 1950 an interesting group of medals came up for auction, consisting of the first Arctic Medal, 1818–55, the Crimea Medal with bar, *Sebastopol*, the Turkish Crimea Medal (these last two unnamed), and a silver medal of standard size, with the Wyon young head of Queen Victoria on the *obv.* (probably a Baltic Medal was used), while the *rev.* had been erased smooth, and engraved: ARCTIC EXPEDITION, 1850–54, encircled by FOR EXCEPTIONAL BRAVERY AND INTREPIDITY. The medals were awarded to Colr Sgt John Woon, R.M., of H.M.S. *Investigator*. The medal for bravery has a normal scroll suspender, and was presumably given, unofficially, by the leader of the expedition. The expedition referred to is obviously that of the *Investigator*, 1850–54 (although the ship herself was abandoned in 1853), under Commdr R. J. L. McClure. Although primarily engaged in the search for Sir John Franklin, McClure achieved what many explorers had sought for centuries – the discovery of a North-West Passage. For this he was promoted to Captain and knighted; also, he and his officers and crew were granted the reward of £10,000 for being the first to pass from the Pacific to the Atlantic by the Arctic Sea (had I known all this in 1950, I would have bid for the group up to quite a high price).

**Royal Geographical Society's Medals**

These large medallions, although outside the scope of 'worn' medals, are of considerable interest to collectors of polar medals, and they really form part of the group since they were given only to those who had participated in certain expeditions, men who had also received the official medal.

The medal for Capt R. F. Scott's first Antarctic Expedition, 1902–04, is 70 mm. in diameter, showing a three-quarter bust of the explorer in a naval cap, with laurel sprays below, and inscribed on either side of the head, *January 2, 1902. March 5 1904.* Around is the legend: *To Captain Robert Falcon Scott, R.N., C.V.O., F.R.G.S., Commander of the Expedition.* The *rev.* shows Scott in polar dress, standing in front of a sledge, with a sledge party in the distance and *Discovery* in the ice in the background. The surrounding legend reads: *Presented by the Royal Geographical Society for Antarctic Discovery.*

A similar medal was given for Shackleton's Antarctic Expedition, 1907–09, also 70 mm. in diameter. The *obv.* shows a three-quarter bust of Shackleton, with the surrounding legend: *Ernest Shackleton, M.V.O., F.R.G.S., Commander of the Expedition.* On the *rev.* is a sledge drawn by two ponies, with mountains in the distance. The *rev.* legend is the same as for the previous medal.

Both these medals were struck in silver, and, presumably, in bronze as well.

The medals for Scott's last expedition, 1910–13, were struck in silver for officers and in bronze for petty officers and ratings, and are almost 55 mm. in diameter. The *obv.* has a three-quarter bust of Scott, bare-headed, and wearing his C.V.O. and the polar ribbon. The surrounding legend is: *British Antarctic Expedition, 1910-13. Captain R. F. Scott, C.V.O., R.N. Commander.* The *rev.* shows the five who reached the Pole and died on the return journey, in polar kit with skis and sledge, with the legend, *Presented by the Royal Geographical Society;* below the group, in incised letters, is: *For Antarctic Discovery 1913.*

The society also struck medals for Dr (now Sir) Vivian Fuchs and the members of his party who made the first complete crossing of the Antarctic continent, 1955–58. The medal is approximately 64 mm. in diameter, struck by Spink & Son Ltd, and was given in gold to Dr Fuchs, while thirty-six were struck in bronze for the other members of the party.

The *obv.* shows the bare-headed bust of the explorer in polar dress, left, with the inscription: *Vivian Ernest Fuchs.* On the *rev.* is a map of the Antarctic continent, with the route marked from the Weddell Sea to the Ross Sea, and the legend: *Presented by the Royal Geographical Society. Trans-Antarctic Expedition. 1955–1958.*

# 8

## Commemorative Medals
## and Long Service Medals

**Commemorative Medals**

IT IS unfortunate that, apart from some of the medals awarded to the police and other public services, most of the Jubilee, Coronation, and Durbar Medals are issued unnamed. Consequently for those who collect groups, these items are frequently difficult to verify. Sometimes a reference in *Who's Who,* or similar works, confirms the award, while photographs of recipients may show them wearing these medals. In the case of 'other ranks' back numbers of the regimental magazine or the personal recollections of members of the Old Comrades' Association, may supply the evidence. Frequently one finds the medals privately named, and this can be accepted as a reasonable indication that the recipients were so entitled, particularly if the group, mounted as worn (and perhaps accompanied by miniatures) has come from the family of the recipient. For those who collect only single medals, the lack of naming does not matter, as the medal is then shown 'unnamed as issued'.

Coronation and similar commemorative medals have been struck in this country for some four hundred years, but all the early ones (and many of the modern ones) are of the non-wearable type. These do not come within the interests of most medal collectors, who start in this field with Queen Victoria's Jubilee Medals, 1887. From this date these medals are all very adequately described by Lt Col Howard N. Cole, O.B.E., T.D., in his book, *Coronation and Royal Commemorative Medals, 1887–1977* (J. B. Hayward & Son, 1977). There is, however, one earlier medal which has a variety intended to be worn and is, furthermore, found named on the edge, so we will consider this first.

GEORGE IV's CORONATION MEDAL, 1821
This medal was designed by Pistrucci (whose initials, B.P., appear

on the truncation of the laureated bust), with the *rev.* showing the king seated, being crowned by a winged figure; on the left are three helmeted figures, representing England, Scotland, and Ireland. In the exergue is INAUGURATUS DIE JULII XIX ANNO MDCCCXXI. It was struck in gold and silver, diameter 1·38″, and the matrices, punches, and dies are in the Royal Mint Museum. It was not intended to be worn, so has no mount or suspender, and is often found in its small circular leather box of issue.

A *copy* of this medal is frequently seen, usually in silver, of rather poor workmanship, somewhat thinner and very slightly smaller than the original, and the initials, B.P., are missing; also the lettering in the exergue is particularly poorly executed.

The medal is usually pierced for a two-ring suspension, and the edge is engraved in serifed capitals, with the name of the recipient and his unit, either 1st or 2nd Reg. B.Y.C.H.

These copies were struck for issue to members of the Buckinghamshire Yeomanry Cavalry Hussars, who were on duty at the coronation, albeit in a very minor capacity, lining some outlying part of the route. I have seen original Pistrucci medals so named and similarly pierced, and would think that some of the recipients (perhaps the officers) preferred to substitute the better official medal for their inferior copies. The medal is referred to in several well-known medal books, with mention of its issue to the B.Y.C.H., but so far I have found only one – *Descriptive Particulars of English Coronation Medals, etc.*, by William Till – which correctly describes it as a copy, and a poor one, of the official Pistrucci medal.

It does not seem possible to discover which is the correct ribbon as worn by the B.Y.C.H. Several medals have what looks like a contemporary dark red ribbon, similar to the old Army L.S. & G.C. Medal, and a few have a black ribbon. One in my collection, accompanied by the M.G.S. and Waterloo Medals (both to 1st or Royal Dragoons), came with an old piece of M.G.S. type ribbon in the unusual width of 1·4″, thus showing a group of three medals all with the same design ribbon, but in three different widths.

### ORDER OF PRECEDENCE OF JUBILEE AND CORONATION MEDALS

*Queen's Regulations & Admiralty Instructions* of 10 October 1891 stated that Queen Victoria's Jubilee Medal, 1887, was to be given precedence over all other medals (thus coming immediately after orders and decorations), and in *Dress Regulations, 1911* (the last before the Great War), the Jubilee and Diamond Jubilee Medals, and the Coronation Medals of King Edward VII and King George V took precedence over campaign medals. In an official list dated 5 July 1918, jubilee and coronation medals were to be worn before gallantry and war medals, but this was quickly countermanded by another list, on 6 November 1918, in which they were placed *after* campaign medals. This appears to have meant after war medals, polar medals, Constabulary Medal (Ireland), and a few others, including the Edward Medal and the King's Police Medal.

When displaying groups of medals in one's collection, any jubilee or coronation medals should be placed in the position in which they would have been worn on the latest occasion. However, if a group is acquired "mounted as worn", with a jubilee or coronation medal before the campaign medals, it could be kept thus, on the assumption that the recipient did not wear them again after the change in regulations; it would be wrong, however, to display them in this order if the group included any campaign medals awarded after November 1918 (and this includes the medals for the Great War).

QUEEN VICTORIA'S JUBILEE MEDAL, 1887
QUEEN VICTORIA'S DIAMOND JUBILEE MEDAL, 1897
Both medals were issued unnamed, and those awarded to civilians had the colours of the ribbon reversed; i.e., for military recipients, mid-blue with wide pale blue side stripes; for civilians, pale blue with wide mid-blue side stripes (it has been suggested that the pale blue is intended to be white, but the cross-weave threads of mid-blue have given the white the effect of pale blue).

Recipients of the 1887 medal who were again honoured in 1897 received a bar, dated 1897 with a crown above, to be sewn onto the ribbon (*Fig. 12a*).

The rare 1897 medals in gold (14 issued) for Lord Mayors and Lord Provosts, and in silver (512 issued) for Mayors and Provosts, with the civilian ribbon as above, were diamond shaped, incorporating the small (shilling size) official coronation medallion with the veiled coinage head of the Queen on the *obv.*, and the Wyon young head on the *rev.*

The police type Jubilee Medals for 1887 and 1897 are stated by many writers to have been struck in silver and bronze, although the Royal Mint Museum Catalogue (1910) records them only in bronze. While *silvered* bronze medals have been seen, factual evidence of genuine silver medals would be welcomed. The 1887 issue has four types of *rev.*, for the City of London Police, Metropolitan Police, Police Ambulance Service, and London County Council Metropolitan Fire Brigade. For the 1897 medal a fifth type was issued, for the St. John Ambulance Brigade. The medals are usually named, engraved in upright or sloping capitals. A plain rectangular bar with the date, 1897, was awarded to recipients who already had one of the four types of the 1887 medal.

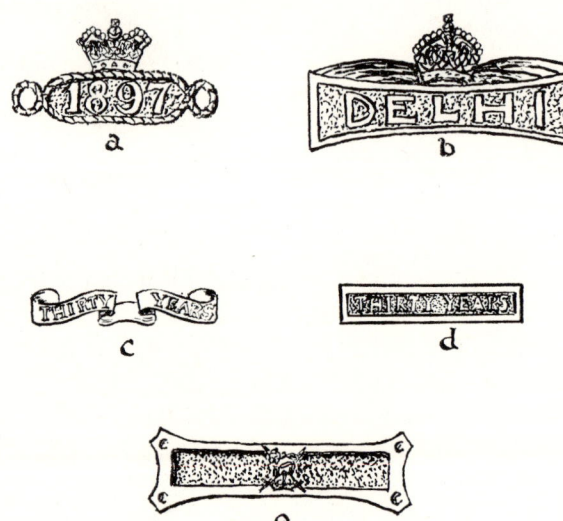

FIG. 12a.
1897 Bar to the 1887 Jubilee Medal.
FIG. 12b.
Bar for the 1911 Delhi Durbar for holders of the 1911 Coronation Medal.
FIGS. 12c and d.
Bars for the Royal Household Long & Faithful Service Medal.
FIG. 12e.
Bar to the Military Long Service & Good Conduct Medal (from Aug. 1944).

## EDWARD VII's CORONATION MEDALS, 1902

The normal coronation medal, in silver or bronze, as awarded to prominent civilians and selected members of H.M. Forces (including one seaman or marine of 'very good' character in each of the ships present at the Naval Review at Spithead), cannot be named on the edge, owing to the rounded ornamentation, but examples are sometimes found (usually in bronze and to army 'other ranks' or naval ratings) engraved in the *rev.* field.

As on the occasion of Queen Victoria's Diamond Jubilee, a medal of different design was awarded to provincial mayors, Scottish provosts, and other civic dignitaries who took part in the Coronation celebrations. Unlike the normal medal, where the two heads look to the left, on this medal they look to the right. The *rev.* is rather similar, with the crowned royal cypher and the date, but within a border of rose, thistle and shamrock sprays; there is no crown; above the medal.

The medals for the police, etc., have six different reverses; for the City of London Police, Metropolitan Police, County & Borough Police, L.C.C. Metropolitan Fire Brigade (lettered L.C.C.M.F.B.), St. John Ambulance Brigade, and the Police Ambulance Service.

### EDWARD VII's DURBAR MEDAL, 1903
It will be noted that the wording on the medal is DELHI DARBAR, not DURBAR.

Unofficial copies of this medal may be found, without the designer's initials, and rather crude in detail on both *obv.* and *rev.*

### GEORGE V's CORONATION MEDALS, 1911
Unofficial copies may be found, without the designer's initials, B.M., on the riband at the bottom of the *obv.*, slightly to right of centre. More than one type of copy exists, including a very well made one and a very poor production.

The medal was issued unnamed, but many service recipients (and, no doubt, some civilians) had them engraved.

The police medals are only in silver, with ten reverses, as follows: City of London Police, Metropolitan Police, County & Borough Police, Scottish Police, Royal Irish Constabulary, London Fire Brigade, St. John Ambulance Brigade, St. Andrew's Ambulance, Police Ambulance Service, and Royal Parks.

### KING's VISIT COMMEMORATION MEDAL (IRELAND), 1911
Although this medal, which was awarded to the Dublin Metropolitan Police, the Royal Irish Constabulary, and some leading civic officials, has its own special ribbon of green with narrow red side stripes, it is often confused with the police Coronation Medals, especially if the ribbon is missing, owing to its very similar design. The only difference is the *rev.* inscription, which has CORONATION 1911 in the top portion of the outer circle, and the dates of the royal visit, JULY 7-12, in the lower arc.

## GEORGE V's DURBAR MEDAL, 1911

Copies exist, with slight die differences from the genuine medal (which itself has minor differences in the *obv*. die from the smaller Coronation Medal, and I have not seen one with B.M. on the riband). Like the Coronation Medal, it was issued unnamed, but many regiments had them engraved for their personnel. An eye-witness has stated that in one regiment, the nominated recipients filed past a table on which was a box of medals, marked 'DO NOT TAKE MORE THAN ONE'.

The Durbar Medal was not awarded to persons who had already received the Coronation Medal, but by the King-Emperor's command, they were given a clasp or bar, bearing the word, DELHI (*Fig. 12b*). This was rather badly made, no doubt locally, and probably at short notice. Some 200 Indian officers and other ranks received the bar, and it is probable that most of them were members of the Indian Contingent at the U.K. coronation ceremonies.

## ELIZABETH II's CORONATION MEDAL, 1953

Over 129,000 of the official medals were issued, all unnamed, including thirty-seven which were specially lettered on the edge, MOUNT EVEREST EXPEDITION, in *sans serif* capitals. These last were presented to members and Sherpas of the successful British Mount Everest Expedition.

An unofficial copy of this medal exists, without the designer's initials, C.T., near the rim (at the 'five-o'clock' position). Even in the original, however, the initials are faint and very near the edge, in fact the T is only partially visible. But there are also other differences by which the copy can be recognised; the Collar of the Order of the Garter is very rough in detail; there does not appear to be a central cross piece to the bow on the right shoulder, and the pearls on the centre arch of the crown are missing. On the *rev*. there are no markings on the body of the orb of the crown, and the lettering is crude compared with an original.

Beware of these copies being offered for sale in an official red box which once contained a genuine medal.

## THE QUEEN'S SILVER JUBILEE MEDAL

This is the official title of the silver medal, struck in 1977 to commemorate the 25th anniversary of Queen Elizabeth II's accession to the Throne. It was designed by David Wynne, and the *obv*. shows a new version of the crowned effigy of the Queen. The appropriate *rev.* inscription is within an unusual wreath of silver birch foliage and catkins. Suspension is by a ring, and the watered ribbon, $1\frac{1}{4}''$ wide, is white, with a $\frac{1}{16}''$ central stripe of cardinal red flanked by $\frac{1}{8}''$ of Garter blue, and with $\frac{1}{16}''$ edges of cardinal red.

## Long Service Medals

There is a tendency among collectors to regard the Long Service Medal without much enthusiasm, except perhaps those who have themselves served the necessary number of years and have striven to maintain the standard of conduct required to qualify. There is no doubt that it adds interest to a group of medals, and sometimes provides evidence of a further step up the ladder of promotion, or of transfer to another regiment or arm of the services. Furthermore, the whole field of long service awards – and there are well over a hundred major varieties – offers a fascinating study, with most of the medals within the financial range of all collectors. In the main, they are straightforward enough, and the only trouble encountered is the occasional re-named medal – not usually re-named to deceive the collector, but as a replacement.

There are very many single Long Service Medals on the market, and, as far as regular service personnel are concerned, many of the recipients must have earned campaign medals during their many years of service. Consequently the collector would do well to keep a note of the number, name, and unit of the recipients of his Long Service Medals, particularly if he specialises in certain units, in case the campaign medals are found at a later date; similarly, of course, the recipients of one's campaign medals may also have had L.S.Ms, and it is as well to 'know your medals', assisted by a record in your medal notebook. Sometimes the search will be fruitless, as many an old campaigner has put in the 'long service', but has fallen down badly on the 'good conduct' qualification.

### GEORGE V'S LONG AND FAITHFUL SERVICE MEDAL

In the current order of precedence of wearing Long Service Medals, the Royal Household awards come before those of the forces. The dates of service covering the original award are *engraved* on the suspender bar, on each side of the crown. There are two types of bars for subsequent awards; the earlier ones have a double scroll, while the later ones have a straight rectangular bar (*Figs. 12c* and *12d*).

One point needs clearing up as regards the ribbon; more than one publication has represented it, in its diagonal stripes of red and blue, *with the addition of a horizontal blue stripe*. This is due to a manufacturer's error in making the ribbon, and the roll of incorrect ribbon was, in fact, used. The horizontal stripe occurred only at intervals, and the ribbon can be adjusted so that it does not show. It has been suggested that the stripe was introduced to indicate the length of ribbon to be used for each medal, but enquiries in the trade would indicate that it was purely a weaving mistake which was not at first noticed, but was corrected when subsequent rolls were made.

The same ribbon was used for the medal given by King George VI, but turned back to front so that the stripes run from top right to bottom left.

### Army Long Service and Good Conduct Medal, 1830
### Military Long Service and Good Conduct Medal, 1930

Although the Royal Navy is the senior service, and its officers take precedence of Army officers of equivalent rank, the Army L.S. & G.C. Medal comes before the naval one in the official order of precedence of wearing medals. One suggested reason is that Queen Victoria is alleged to have favoured the Army rather than the Navy.

*First Issue, 1830*
Designed and engraved by B. Pistrucci (best known, perhaps, for his 'St George and Dragon'), the first issue of this medal depicted the royal arms with the small shield, or inescutcheon, of Hanover in the centre, and surrounded by the familiar trophy of military arms. The lettering on the *rev.* is large, and the first few to be issued had a steel clip with a ring, and a plain crimson ribbon, one inch in width. Very shortly afterwards, a rectangular steel suspender was used, with a 'U' in the lower bar to support the steel clip (*Fig. 13*), and the ribbon became $1\frac{1}{4}''$ wide. The naming was impressed by the same machine which named the Waterloo Medal, and the year of issue was included (*Fig. 4a*).

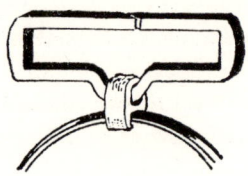

FIG. 13.
Army L.S. & G.C. Medal: early steel clip and suspender.

*Victorian Issues*

With the accession of Queen Victoria in 1837, the shield of Hanover disappeared from the royal arms, and new dies were prepared for this medal, but they do not appear to have been ready until early in 1839. The steel clip and steel suspender were still used, and medals fitted with these had, at first, the same impressed naming as before, including the date, but later, probably about 1850, engraved naming was used, with or without the date (*Fig. 4bb*).

The exact date of the introduction of the silver scroll suspender and claw mount, replacing the ugly steel fittings, is not known. Some writers suggest as early as 1846, while others give 1850 or 1851. In my own collection is a medal with steel clip and suspender, with engraved naming and the date, 1851, while another collector has one to the 23rd R.W.F., dated 1855. There may have been a period during which both types were in use. On 5th February 1850, a Memorandum was issued at the Horse Guards, providing that in future the necessary engraving should be done at the relative Regiment or Depot. This order would seem to apply to the 'steel suspender' medals which had been previously named by the 'Waterloo' machine, and certainly later issues of these were engraved. The medals with the silver scroll suspenders were, however, impressed at the Mint, in small capitals as for the M.G.S. Medal (*Fig. 4b*); this type of naming, the medals of which had much smaller letters on the *rev.*, continued for many years. Many collectors accept a date of about 1874 as the change back from impressed to engraved naming (usually as *Fig. 4cc*), but it may well be that both methods were in use concurrently. Certainly the impressed naming was in use later, as a very few medals are found impressed in this style with the 1881 regimental titles. For example, I have one so impressed, to 2ND BN. ESSEX R. This could not have been issued before 1881, and quite possibly later.

Some medals are found regimentally (or *Depot*) impressed, usually in thin serifed capitals, or capitals and lower case, often somewhat irregular both in spacing and alignment (*Fig. 4dd*). These may be very early issues, before the second impressed style came into use. The later engraved naming appears in several styles, the most usual being in sloping capitals, but upright capitals and running script are also found, the last usually on medals issued to men serving in India.

There are several minor varieties of *rev.* lettering. The early issues (steel clip) have large letters, but the 'scroll suspender' medals have

173

smaller letters. The latter have several varieties, including the over-all length of, and spacing between, the lines, but these are not of importance to the collector, as they are merely due to the recurring need to re-cut the dies over a long period of years.

## Twentieth Century Issues

The royal arms disappeared from both the L.S. & G.C. and Dis-tinguished Conduct Medals with the accession of Edward VII, since when they have borne the sovereign's head on the *obv*.

The first issue of George V appears with the normal swivelling suspender, but later issues, from about 1920, have the fixed mount, like most medals of that period.

In September 1930, the medal became known as the MILITARY LONG SERVICE AND GOOD CONDUCT MEDAL, and the style of the medal was changed, having a rectangular suspender bar, lettered REGU-LAR ARMY, also there were several changes in the conditions of award.

A holder of the Army L.S. & G.C. Medal who, after 1930 com-pleted a further period of eighteen years' service, was eligible for a second medal, i.e. the Military L.S. & G.C. Medal, but a holder of the latter medal received a bar (slip-on-type; authorised in August 1944) for further qualifying service. The bar bears the Army insignia of the lion and crown over crossed swords; there is a circular 'punch mark' at each corner, but these are not pierced through (*Fig. 12e*). Under certain conditions officers are eligible for the present medal, and women became eligible in 1955.

The change of ribbon in 1916, adding white edges to the plain crimson ribbon, means that a group containing the medal (including the George V issue) to a recipient who died before 1916, should show the plain ribbon, while groups containing a Victorian or Edward VII issue, should have the modern ribbon if the recipient wore his medals after that date.

## NAVAL LONG SERVICE AND GOOD CONDUCT MEDAL

Instituted by William IV in 1830 (in the past the date of 1831 has been quoted, but this is now known to be incorrect), the first issue (anchor type) was somewhat smaller than later types, and was pierced for a two-rings suspension, but sometimes a bar suspender was privately fitted. On many medals a curious die flaw, or crack, is noticeable in lesser or greater degree, from a short irregular ridge of metal (from the edge, between E and R of SERVICE, extending to just beyond the row of dots), to a series of such die-cracks, including a wavy line in the south-west sector (from NG of LONG to T of CONDUCT) and a line through the base of FOR, with branches to the rim and through the circle of dots. Medals also exist with the *rev.* inverted, and some of these also show the same flaws.

Naming is engraved, in the centre of the *rev.* Although some variations exist, the following is the usual style: recipient's name, in block capitals, is curved parallel to the circle of dots, and J is often engraved as I; the rating is in italics, in one or two straight lines, frequently with a flourish in the small space above; the name of the ship (or depot) is in two lines of capitals (H.M.S. in double lining); the length of service is below, in italic figures, and *Years* in sloping script, but sometimes in italics. So far, the last known date of award of the Anchor type medal is 27th November 1847, when two awards were made.

### Victorian Issues

Several research workers have tried to establish when the first issue of Queen Victoria, with the wide suspender (designated WS) for a ribbon of $1\frac{1}{2}''$, was instituted. But Capt. K. J. Douglas-Morris, RN., has confirmed 1847 as the date. In an authoritative article,* he shows, from official records, that after the two awards of the Anchor type medal, in Nov. 1847, the first known award of the second type – Queen's head *obv.*, and wide suspender – was made on 8 December 1847.

In April 1849 a batch of 100 WS medals was supplied to the Admiralty by the Royal Mint, with 1848 below the Queen's head, and it now seems certain that this was in error, using the *obv.* die of the Naval General Service Medal, 1793–1840, although at one time it was thought that these might have been the first striking of the WS type. Of these 100 medals, Captain Douglas-Morris has been able to trace only fourteen in private hands or museums, and while no doubt others will eventually come to light, they are certainly very rare. Capt. Douglas-Morris has recorded three *rev.* die types of the WS medal, the earliest having both the undated *obv.* die – used for medals awarded between Dec. 1847 and May 1849, also between May 1851 and Nov. 1862 – and the dated *obv.* die – used for medals awarded between June 1849 and Nov. 1850. Undoubtedly further

*Hayward's Gazette*, No. 8, March 1977, pp. 5–17, J. B. Hayward & Son.

research will extend these periods slightly, but it certainly seems to prove that the dated *obv.* was *not* the prototype, and therefore was undoubtedly an error.

The naming on these medals is engraved in block capitals, blackened, with the number of years' service at the end (*Fig. 4aa*). Sometimes the word *Yrs.* is in sloping script, sometimes in upright capitals, no doubt depending on which engraver named the medal.

Many of the recipients of the Anchor and WS medals also had the N.G.S. and/or the China 1842 medals, so it is worth keeping a lookout for these.

There has also been considerable doubt regarding the date of the change from WS to narrow suspender (NS) medals, taking a ribbon $1\frac{1}{4}''$ wide. One writer puts the date as 1850, but records show the WS medal being awarded up to Jan. 1875, and Capt. Douglas-Morris' researches show the earliest award of the NS medal to be in Feb. 1875, coinciding with the widening of eligibility under the amended regulations of 16 Dec. 1874. From Feb. 1875 to Feb. 1877 the medals appear to have been engraved, but with only a very few examples still showing the number of years, while from March 1877 they have been impressed, without years, in tall seriffed capitals.

With both WS and NS types, several *rev.* dies were in use. Most of the WS medals have a rectangular flag at the mainmast (with a somewhat convex surface) representing the flag of a full admiral; later issues have the flag almost triangular, while the later NS medals have a triangular flag with a raised outline (*Fig. 14*), incorrectly representing the much longer pendant worn by ships other than flagships. The last die of the WS and the first of the NS (probably the same) have a capital M at the right of the narrow exergue, just below the waves. These, and other details of rigging, are described in Capt. Douglas-Morris' excellent article*.

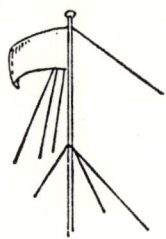

FIG. 14.
Masthead detail of the Naval L.S. & G.C. Medal – Queen Victoria issues. Left: first type, with wide suspender. Right: later types, with normal suspender.

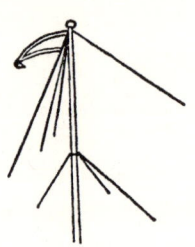

*op cit.,

Imperial Russia
Cross of St George, 4th Class
Silver Medal for Bravery, 4th Class.

Plate 14.

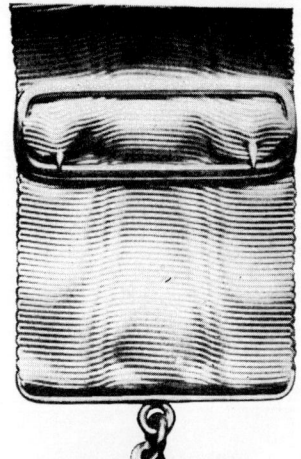

Turkey

Sultan's Gold Medal (Order of the Crescent), 1801

Order of the Mejedie, 4th Class, of the Crimean War period

Plate 15.

*Twentieth Century Issues*

These present no problems. The first George V type, showing the King in admiral's uniform, exists with both swivelling (early) and fixed (later) mounts, the latter persisting, through the 'coinage head' type and the George VI issues, until 1955, when the Royal Mint reverted to the swivelling pattern (which they first did in 1954 for the Military L.S. & G.C. Medal).

VOLUNTEER OFFICERS' DECORATION

To be complete, this should have a top brooch-bar ornamented with a horizontal oak spray. It is one of the few hall-marked awards, being made by a commercial firm and not by the Royal Mint. It was issued unnamed, but may frequently be found privately engraved (often by the recipient's regiment) with particulars of the recipient, sometimes in quite full detail.

The decoration was established by Royal Warrant of 25th July 1892, and on the accession of Edward VII, the central initials, VR, were, of course, changed to E VII R. In 1894 a similar decoration was instituted for Volunteer Officers in India and the Colonies, and differs from the home decoration only in the royal cipher, interlaced VRI or E VII RI.

COLONIAL AUXILIARY FORCES OFFICERS' DECORATION

This decoration is very similar to the previous, but instead of the oval oak wreath, it has an oval band lettered COLONIAL AUXILIARY FORCES. It was in use from 1899 to 1921. Most books give the width of the ribbon as $1\frac{1}{2}''$, as with other volunteer officers' decorations, but all the examples I have seen have a silver wire 'flat loop' suspender, made to take a ribbon $1\frac{1}{4}''$ wide.

VOLUNTEER LONG SERVICE MEDAL

This medal appears with, successively, the heads of Queen Victoria and King Edward VII. The Victorian issues for home troops have the *obv.* legend VICTORIA REGINA, and *rev.*, FOR LONG SERVICE IN THE VOLUNTEER FORCE. Many are unnamed, but impressed and engraved ones are quite common. Those for volunteers in India and the Colonies have the same *rev.*, but the *obv.* legend reads: VICTORIA REGINA ET IMPERATRIX.

177

For the Edwardian issues, both home and colonial issues are lettered, EDWARDVS VII REX IMPERATOR, while the Indian issue bears the title EDWARDVS VII KAISER-I-HIND.

The same medal appears with the head of George V, but not for home troops, as the Territorial Force Efficiency Medal had already replaced the home Edwardian medal in 1908.

### COLONIAL AUXILIARY FORCES LONG SERVICE MEDAL

Instituted in 1899, and in use until 1921, this medal may easily be overlooked owing to its similarity to the Volunteer L.S.M. The *rev.*, however, is slightly concave, and the legend, FOR LONG SERVICE IN THE COLONIAL AUXILIARY FORCES, is on an ornamental panel instead of on a series of ribands; it also has a crown above the legend, which does not appear on the home medal. Naming is either impressed or engraved.

### TERRITORIAL EFFICIENCY MEDAL

The first issue, with the head of Edward VII, had the *rev.* legend, TERRITORIAL FORCE EFFICIENCY MEDAL, with a swivelling ring suspension, as did the second issue with the head of George V. Later, in about 1920, a fixed ring was used. The third issue, also of George V with a fixed ring, had the shorter legend, TERRITORIAL EFFICIENCY MEDAL. This change took place after the Territorial Force became the Territorial Army, in 1921. It is, however, peculiar that in the *first* (1916) edition of Taprell Dorling's *Ribbons and Medals*, he gives the legend, both in the text and in the illustration, in its shorter form, while in his 1920 edition the longer style is given in both places, and this has been retained in subsequent editions, with no mention of the shortened legend.

The medal remained in use until the institution of the Efficiency Medal in 1930, with its designation scroll on the suspender, indicating by the word, TERRITORIAL, that it was granted to a unit in the United Kingdom; in the case of certain overseas units, the name of the Dominion or Colony appears on the scroll.

The Honourable Artillery Company has its own special ribbon for the Volunteer L.S.M., the Territorial Efficiency Medal, and the present medal, also for the officers' decorations, in the racing colours of Edward VII – half red, half dark blue, with narrow yellow edges – granted by royal permission; the widths are, of course, $1\frac{1}{2}''$ for the officers' decoration and $1\frac{1}{4}''$ for the medal. The original ribbons had corded edges.

## ROYAL NAVAL RESERVE L.S. & G.C. MEDAL

There are four identical medals with the familiar H.M.S. *Dreadnought*, and DIUTURNE FIDELIS reverse (apart from that with the ring suspension, which was the Royal Fleet Reserve L.S.M. until 1959), which can only be identified by their naming, and consequently might well be passed over in a batch of unribboned medals. By far the largest number are to the Royal Naval Reserve (with either a plain green ribbon, or, after 1941, green with white edges and white centre stripe); these are all designated R.N.R. in the naming.

With the same plain green ribbon until 1919, but later with its own ribbon of green centre and dark blue edges, separated by red stripes, is the Royal Naval Volunteer Reserve medal, identified by R.N.V.R. in the naming, and usually preceded by the name of the Division, thus: 1117 G. J. LANGLEY, SIG. BRISTOL DIV. R.N.V.R. Another variety of the medal, known as the Royal Naval Auxiliary Sick Berth Reserve L.S.M., worn with either of the R.N.R. ribbons, was awarded by the Admiralty, through the Commissioner-in-Chief of the St John Ambulance Brigade. It can only be recognised by the initials in the naming, R.N.A.S.B.R., and, in addition to naval medals, is often accompanied by the St John Service Medal; on occasions it has confused both collectors and dealers, who have thought that the first four letters referred to the Royal Naval Air Service. The R.N.A.S.B.R. was disbanded in 1949.

The fourth award is to the Royal Naval Wireless Auxiliary Reserve, and had the R.N.V.R. ribbon; the naming carries either the initials, R.N.W.A.R. or R.N.V.W.R.

With the amalgamation of the R.N.R. and the R.N.V.R., a common L.S. & G.C. Medal is now in use, with a ring suspension. From October 1959, the ribbon has five equal stripes, blue, white, green, white, blue.

## SPECIAL CONSTABULARY LONG SERVICE MEDAL

Instituted in August 1919, this medal has a standard sized straight suspender, made to take the normal $1\frac{1}{4}''$ ribbon, yet the actual ribbon used is $1\frac{3}{8}''$ wide – a peculiarity which has never been explained. The original issue, with the crowned head of George V, had the bar: *The Great War 1914–18*. Subsequent bars were issued, worded *Long Service* and the year of issue. The instructions issued with Long Service bars states that the first bar is to be sewn on the ribbon with a space one-eighth of an inch between the bottom edge of the ribbon and the bottom of the bar; subsequent bars are to be similarly sewn, with one-eighth of an inch clear between each bar.

The Elizabeth II issue includes a variety, instituted in 1956, with the *rev.* legend, FOR FAITHFUL SERVICE IN THE ULSTER SPECIAL CONSTABULARY.

### ROYAL NAVAL AUXILIARY SERVICE L.S.M.

This body was formerly the Royal Naval Minewatching Service. The medal was instituted in 1965, and both officers and ratings are eligible after twelve years' continuous service. The medal is of cupro-nickel, the *obv.* bearing the sovereign's head and titles, while the *rev.* has a naval crown and anchor in an oak wreath, with the surrounding legend, ROYAL NAVAL AUXILIARY SERVICE – LONG SERVICE. The ribbon, $1\frac{1}{4}''$, is in equal stripes of white, blue, white, each charged with a narrow green stripe.

### VOLUNTARY MEDICAL SERVICE MEDAL

This medal is awarded to members of the British Red Cross Society and the St. Andrew's Ambulance Association, for fifteen years' active efficient service. Naming is usually by impressed thin *sans serif* capitals, with forenames in full. When bars are awarded for further service (slide-on type), members of the B.R.C.S. have a small Geneva cross in the centre of the plain narrow bar, while those of the St. Andrew's Ambulance Association have a St. Andrew's cross (*Figs. 14a* and *14b*).

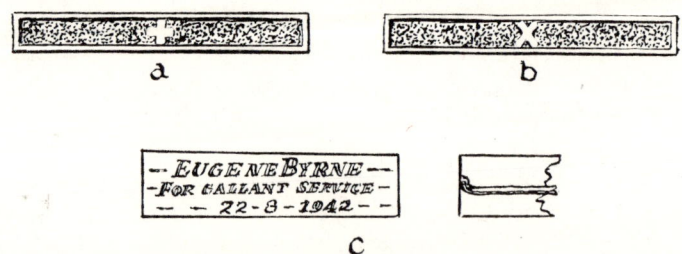

FIGS. 14a and b.
Bars to the Voluntary Medical Service Medal: a – for the British Red Cross Society; b – for the St. Andrew's Ambulance Association.
FIG. 14c.
Bar to the Liverpool Shipwreck & Humane Society Medal.

# 9

## Some Miscellaneous
## British Medals

*Ratings*         *Ranks and Units*

### Royal Humane Society Medals

Life-saving medals have long been undeservedly neglected by
collectors. They should, in fact, be in great demand, as the stories
behind them are most thrilling. In common with the awards of the
Royal National Lifeboat Institution, the Liverpool Shipwreck and
Humane Society, and the Shipwrecked Fishermen and Mariners'
Royal Benevolent Society, the medals of the Royal Humane Society
are not lightly given. In every case the recipient has really earned his
medal, risking his own life to save others, frequently in wild storm
conditions at sea. For those who want to collect 'medals with a
story' at reasonable prices, this series offers a most attractive field.

Founded in 1774, the Royal Humane Society issued large silver
and bronze medals for over ninety years. They were approximately
2″ in diameter (slight variations in size and details of design are
found in the various dies used), and were not originally intended to
be worn, but recipients often fitted them with rings, or other means
of suspension, and wore them from a deep blue ribbon. The inscriptions on *obv.* and *rev.* were, as now, in latin, with at first a
latinised form of the name of the recipient, but later medals show
the name, etc., in English.

In order to make the medals more suitable for wearing, the
size was reduced to 1½″, and many books, including publications
of the R.H.S., give the date of this as 1869 – the year in which the
Admiralty and the Army published permission for them to be worn
in uniform. However, according to a report of the Society's half-
yearly meeting, given in the *United Services Gazette* of 13th July
1867, new medals, 1½″ in diameter, which had been prepared for the
exclusive use of soldiers and sailors in accordance with the recom-
mendation of the War Office and Admiralty Board, were then ready
for delivery. It may well be that these small medals were not actually
released until finally authorised by the Services some twenty months

later (and it would appear, from the wording of the newspaper report, that civilian recipients would continue to receive the large medals, although there does not seem to be any evidence that this actually happened). Those who had already received a large silver or bronze medal could apply for a similar medal in the 'wearable' size; these were engraved on the edge (as now) with the same personal details which had appeared on the *rev.* of the large medal; this explains why a large and a small medal are frequently found for the same rescue, with an award date on the small medal earlier than that of its introduction. Some of these are marked DUPLICATE.

Owing to the long period of issue, the style of naming varies: on the small medals this ranges from neat small letters to very large, crude capitals. The silver or bronze buckles, worn on the ribbon as a brooch, have also varied over the years, some having two prongs while others have three.

Bars are awarded for further services, in the same metal as the medal (i.e. the recipient of a silver medal receives a silver bar if the subsequent award would have been a further silver medal, but he would be given a second medal, in bronze, if the deed is judged to be of that standard). These bars are of unusual scroll design, with the date of the award engraved at each side (*Fig. 15*). Collectors, and dealers too, have occasionally failed to recognise the bar as such, and have used it as a top suspender with the buckle affixed below.

The Stanhope Gold Medal, instituted in 1873 by a fund in memory of Captain Charles S. S. Stanhope, RN (himself a Silver Medallist of 1851), is given annually for the best Silver Medal case exhibiting the greatest gallantry during the previous year. The medal itself is of the same design as the normal medals of the society; up to 1936, it had a rectangular bar suspender, lettered STANHOPE MEDAL, but since that date it has had a scroll suspender of the same type as the other medals, with nothing to indicate that it is the Stanhope Medal except that the medal, suspender, and buckle are all in gold – and, of course, the ribbon is dark blue with black edges, separated by a narrow yellow stripe on each side.

FIG. 15.
Bar to Royal Humane Society Medals.

## Royal National Lifeboat Institution Medals

The gold and silver medals were authorised in 1824 (the first being presented in 1825), when the title of the body was *The Royal National Institution for the Preservation of Life from Shipwreck;* they bore the head of the Patron, King George IV. They were engraved on the edge with the name (and rank, if any) of the recipient, and the date voted, usually in large serifed letters. At this time quite a number of naval officers, redundant after the Napoleonic War, were serving with the coastguard, and received the medal for gallant rescues: a number of these recipients also received the N.G.S. Medal, 1793–1840, and it is worth checking up in the hope of bringing them together.

Until the middle of the nineteenth century, a second medal was given for a second award, but later a straight bar, rather clumsily fashioned, was instituted, lettered SECOND SERVICE (or as appropriate), with the date engraved on the *rev.*

The head of George IV was retained until 1862, and all my medals of this type have a small ring soldered at the top, and parallel with the rim, thus needing two more rings for the ribbon to lie flat, except the earliest (1829) and the latest (1855); the early medal is pierced and has two rings, while the late one has the 'dolphin' type suspender (but this may be a replacement). See *Plate 10.*

In 1862, the head of Queen Victoria, together with the modern title, replaced the original *obv.* design, but the familiar *rev.* of three sailors rescuing a comrade, was retained. A proper suspender, comprising two dolphins, was substituted for the soldered ring, and this has been in use ever since. The style of engraved naming is usually rather neater than earlier.

The third type of the medal was in use from 1902 to October 1912, with the head of Edward VII on the *obv.*, and a new *rev.* design of Hope buckling a life jacket on to a lifeboatman. During the reign of George V, his head appeared on the *obv.*, and the original *rev.* design returned. According to the authors of *Gallantry*, a bronze medal, of the same design, was instituted in 1917, for lesser, though still hard-earned, awards. Bronze examples of the Queen Victoria and Edward VII medals exist, however, but all that I have seen have been unnamed and thus may be only specimens, patterns, or proofs.

King George VI decided that, for the future, the sovereign's effigy should appear only on medals awarded by the sovereign, and consequently the present medal – the fifth type, and still retaining the original *rev.* design – bears the head of the founder of the Institution, Sir William Hillary, Bt. All medals have the same original ribbon of dull blue, but in recent years recipients of the gold medal wear a miniature badge depicting Hillary's head, on the ribbon when the medal itself is not being worn.

## Liverpool Shipwreck and Humane Society Medals

The various medals of this society are described in several medal books, and are generally familiar to collectors. One type, however, does not seem to be so well known, namely the oval medal, in use in the early 1870s and coming between the very large medals and the modern circular medal, $1\frac{1}{2}$″ in diameter. The oval medal measures $1\frac{1}{2}$″ across by 1·8″ long, and the *obv.* is similar to the modern medal, with a life-saving scene, and with the title and foundation date, 1839, surrounding it; the *rev.* has a plain centre encircled by two prolific oak branches; in the centre is engraved the recipient's name, rank, and ship, and the date of the award. Below the straight suspender bar (which takes a ribbon only 1·2″ wide) is a Liver bird – the emblem of Liverpool – and the mount on which it stands is hinged to a small clip riveted to the top of the medal. As with other medals of this society, the neat engraving on the edge is a story in itself. One example, to John Park, A.B., of S.S. *Batavia*, reads FOR GREAT COURAGE AND HUMANITY IN GOING IN THE BOAT IN A HEAVY GALE AND RESCUING 9 OF THE CREW OF THE CHARLES WARD ABANDONED 20 NOVEMBER 1872. (See *Plate 10*).

It would appear that this handsome medal was replaced by the present circular medal towards the end of 1874 (the secretary of the society has, I understand, suggested 1882, but this seems much too late). While we know that an oval medal was awarded to Charles Brown, mate of the yacht, *Virago*, on 25 September 1874, a circular medal is known dated February 1874. It is perhaps possible that this was a retrospective award (or even a replacement, although not so marked), as in May 1874 a tender for a supply of medals, including oval ones, was accepted from Elkington & Co. Ltd. Thus the oval medals could have gone on for a longer period, perhaps with an overlap, and evidence of late dates for oval medals and early dates for the circular medal would be welcome, to try to establish the precise date or period of the change.

Bars are given for subsequent awards, a modern example being a rectangular tablet (*Fig. 14c*) with a thin back strip for slipping over the ribbon; naming is engraved in sloping serifed capitals.

### Earl St Vincent's Medal, 1800

It is not immediately apparent, from its design, for what event this medal was issued, and enquiries from collectors on this point are quite frequent. The design is quite well known: *obv.* the bust of the Earl in naval uniform, within a laurel wreath and surrounding legend, *Earl St. Vincent's Testimony of Approbation, 1800*, and *rev.*, two figures shaking hands, described by most writers as a sailor and marine, but one semi-official publication calls them a naval officer and a bluejacket. The background is a hopelessly inaccurate Union Flag, which is neither the pre-1801 type, without the St Patrick's Cross, nor the modern 1801 design; around is the legend, *Loyal and True*. The diameter of the medal is 1·85″.

The medals were awarded by Admiral Earl St Vincent, to the crew of his flagship, H.M.S. *Ville de Paris*, as a reward for their loyalty and good conduct following the naval mutiny at the Nore in 1797. The medals are generally described as of silver, and most examples are in this metal, but other types are recorded, including gold, bronze, bronze-gilt, and silver-gilt. The scope of the award is also open to some difference of opinion; it is usually recorded as given to petty officers, seamen, and marines, but *The Times* of 21st April 1801, states that the medal was for "officers and seamen of the *Ville de Paris*". The medals are usually unnamed, but many recipients had their names engraved, and fitted a rim or frame and some method of suspension, for wearing. One, in silver-gilt, is known with a gold frame, glazed, with ring suspension, and named on the frame, *Given to the Rev. Cooper Williams, A.M. His Lordship's Domestic Chaplain.*

Although an unofficial award, this is an interesting medal, and worthy of a place in a collection of naval medals.

### Davison's Medals for the Battle of the Nile, 1798

These large medals, together with the next two, were issued privately, long before official campaign medals came into being, and they were, perhaps, of a 'commemorative' nature, but they were certainly worn by many of the recipients – officers and ratings alike. They are of considerable interest, and are well worth a place in the collection. Those that are named – provided one can reasonably feel that the naming is genuine – are of greater interest, especially as many of the recipients did not survive until the middle of the nineteenth century to become entitled to the Naval General Service Medal, and these were the only rewards they had for a long service career. Furthermore, the large size of the medals does not necessarily mean that they were not intended to be worn – the large Naval and Army Gold Medals, awarded to senior officers, were of similar size, as were the many medals issued by the Hon. East India Company.

Until the first China Medal was instituted in January 1843, no medals, as we know them today, were given to naval personnel for actions and campaigns, consequently the decision of Nelson's prize agent, Alexander Davison, to present, at his own expense, medals to the officers and crews present at the Battle of the Nile, was something of an innovation.

The medals are 1·85″ in diameter, and although some are found without mounts, like commemorative medallions, the majority have some form of suspension fitted – soldered loops or rings; steel clips with a ring; pierced for a two-ring suspension; set in a frame, with or without glass; and so on. Contemporary paintings often show the medal worn with a dark blue ribbon, about $1\frac{1}{2}$″ wide; sometimes it was worn from a long ribbon, round the neck, but others were worn from a buttonhole, similar to the Prussian Iron Cross, while a few are shown with a brooch buckle.

Admirals and captains received the medal in gold, while other officers received it in silver; it was given in copper-gilt to petty officers, and in copper, bronzed, to ratings. The impressed inscription on the edge, *A Tribute of Regard, From Alexr. Davison, Esq. St. James's Square.*, prevents any naming in that place, but some medals have the recipient's name and ship engraved in the upper part of the *rev.* In some cases these names also appear on the N.G.S. Medal Roll.

### Boulton's Medals for Trafalgar, 1805

Matthew Boulton, of the Soho Mint, Birmingham, emulated Davison's action, by giving medals of a similar type to Davison's Nile Medals, 1·9″ in diameter, to those taking part in the Battle of Trafalgar. The medals were given to Flag Officers in gold, those to other senior officers in silver, and junior officers and ratings received pewter medals. As before, they are frequently found set in a gold or silver rim, and glazed; there is generally a swivel ring on the rim, and a dark blue ribbon appears to have been worn.

It is reported that many of the ratings were disgusted with the base metal (and one must admit that it looks pretty poor), and threw their medals overboard.

### Davison's Medal for Trafalgar, 1805

This medal is in pewter, 2·1″ in diameter, and is usually set in a copper (or sometimes silver or gold) rim. It is reputed to have been given only to the crew of H.M.S. *Victory*, but examples have been noted as named (privately engraved, of course) to ratings from other ships. As with the pewter Boulton's medals, it is similarly related that many of the recipients threw them away, but such as were worn appear to have had the same dark blue ribbon.

### Naval Engineers' Medal, 1842-46

As it is sometimes possible to find an unnamed 'specimen' example of this very rare medal, it might be as well to mention that only eight were actually awarded. The recipients were: William Shaw, W. Dunkin (1842); W. Johnstone (1843); John Langley (1843); G. Roberts, James P. Rundle, James Urquhart (1845); and S. B. Meredith (1846). It will be noted that this list differs very slightly from that given in Gordon's *British Battles and Medals* (4th Edition, 1971), and is based on a list supplied by the Admiralty.

The medals had the name and rank (and, in some cases, the ship) engraved around the *rev.* The unnamed examples appear to be genuine contemporary strikings from the original dies (which are in the Royal Mint Museum), and are probably from unissued stock, a few of which may have found their way, by special favour in years gone by, into private collections which have since come on the market.

At one time there seemed to be some doubt as to whether Urquhart was awarded an Engineer's Medal, although a medal named to him, as 1st Engineer, H.M.S.V. *Columbia*, 1845, is in a collection in Australia, together with unnamed Baltic and China 1857 medals. However, official correspondence, quoted in *Seaby's Coin and Medal Bulletin*, 1950 (pp. 536-7), shows that the Record Office of the Admiralty thinks it extremely probable that the medal is genuine, as Urquhart, then serving in *Columbia*, was voted 'a medal' in 1845 for the invention of a Tide Gauge; also his award of the Baltic and China Medals, while serving in other ships, was confirmed.

**Canadian Memorial Crosses**

These oxydised silver crosses, first instituted by Order in Council, PC 2374, on 1 December 1919, and amended by PC 822 of 15 April 1922, were given to mothers and widows of Canadian soldiers and sailors killed or who died on active service, or who died subsequently as a result of such service. If both mother and widow were alive, two crosses were issued.

The cross is 32 × 32 mm., with slightly expanding arms, similar to the Military Cross but with slightly concaved ends to the arms. A Greek (or St. George's) cross is superimposed, with a crown beyond the top arm, and a maple leaf beyond the other three arms (similar to the crowns on the M.C.). In the centre is the royal cypher, GRI, intertwined. The whole cross is superimposed on a laurel wreath, the tips of which just overlap the top arm of the cross.

Suspension is by two small rings, with an 11 mm. violet silk ribbon, the badge being worn as a pendant round the neck.

The *rev.* is plain, and engraved with the number, rank and name, usually in two lines; those relating to officers have only rank and name.

A similar cross was awarded for World War II, but with the royal cypher, G VI R, in script and not intertwined, although up to 31 July 1941 crosses with the GRI cypher were issued. Several different dies were used, by four different firms, so minor differences of design and weight will be found. In January 1945 the suspension was changed from a ring to a bar suspender, and crosses awarded since 1953, in respect of those killed in later campaigns, have the royal cypher, E II R.

**General Gordon's Pewter Star, 1884**

This interesting but crude and entirely unofficial award was cast in pewter, by General Gordon, for distribution to his loyal native troops. It has been suggested that it was, in fact, struck in 1898 (Gordon was killed in January 1885), after the entry into Khartoum following the Battle of Omdurman. I have, however, a specimen, mounted in a frame, with a note stating that it was bought from an Arab soldier at Metemneh, in 1885 or 1886, by a Major Pierson (of the Royal Sussex Regiment). This officer, then a captain, served in the Nile Expedition of 1884–85, to relieve General Gordon; he did not serve in the 1896–98 campaign, and as the medal came from a reliable source, there is no reason to doubt that the date on the note is correct – not proof, admittedly, but reasonably satisfactory.

The 'medal' is about 2·15″ across, cast in a mould made from the Turkish Order of the Mejedie, which it reproduces except for the centre, which has a plain boss, supposed to be a grenade, in place of the *Toughra*, or Sultan's signature. The suspender has the usual star and crescent, and since the former is attached to the latter by only two points, it would seem that a specimen of the Crimean War period was used. The ring is cast in one piece with the star and crescent, and the 'ribbon' on my specimen is a coarse piece of faded red braid, $\frac{1}{2}$″ wide.

### Automobile Association – Patrol Service Awards

In 1956 the A.A. instituted two awards for acts of bravery and devotion to duty performed by their Patrols. As these are not generally known, and are not lightly awarded, a description may be of interest.

The Patrol Service Cross is awarded for bravery involving personal risk. It is in silver, 1·8″ across, and somewhat reminiscent of the D.F.C. The central medallion bears the well-known interlaced initials, AA, surrounded by PATROL SERVICE and two laurel sprays. The wings which normally appeared at the top of the A.A. badge are seen here on the horizontal arms of the cross. The *rev.* is also somewhat similar to the D.F.C., in that it is plain except for a thin central circle which, in this case, encloses FOR/BRAVERY. The ribbon is $1\frac{1}{4}$″ wide, yellow with a narrow black centre stripe and side

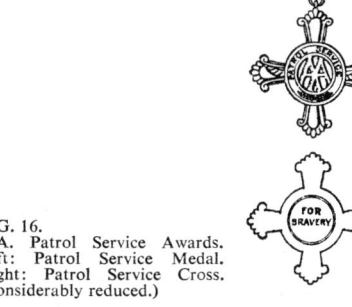

FIG. 16.
A.A. Patrol Service Awards.
Left: Patrol Service Medal.
Right: Patrol Service Cross.
(Considerably reduced.)

stripes, and there is a straight top-bar brooch, rectangular with a conventional laurel spray.

The Patrol Service Medal, also in silver, is given in cases of outstanding initiative or devotion to duty. It is 1½″ in diameter, with the interlaced AA surrounded by a laurel wreath, with wings above. Outside the wreath is the legend, PATROL SERVICE − AUTOMOBILE ASSOCIATION. The *rev.* is plain except for the legend, FOR MERIT. The 1¼″ ribbon is half yellow, half black, and the top-bar brooch looks like a double bumper bar with overriders (but I understand that this is purely coincidental).

In both cases ring suspension is used, and the decorations are engraved on the *rev.* with the recipient's rank, name, and the date of the award. They are worn on the right breast. Incidentally, the official description gives the colours of the ribbon as 'yellow and *bronze-blue*', but pieces of the actual ribbon used show the second as black − jet black.

### Swivelling Mounts on Modern Medals

From 1846, with the issue of the Sutlej Medal, until the end of the First World War, almost all our medals have had a swivelling mount or suspender. But from about 1920, with the need for economy, medals were made with a fixed suspender, starting with the British War Medal and other medals commemorating that war, although exceptions seem to have been made for the George V and George VI issues of the India General Service Medals.

As a result of this practice, certain medals of George V, such as the Army and Naval L.S. & G.C. and Territorial Efficiency Medals, and others, can be found with swivel mounts or later fixed mounts. Although of interest as minor varieties, no special importance or variation in value normally attaches to either type (except for post-war awards of the George V Military Medal (*q.v.*).; it is interesting to note that re-issues of earlier medals, such as the Queen's South Africa Medal, were also made with the fixed suspender (See *Plate 11*).

The Army and R.A.F. General Service Medal had always had the fixed mount until, in 1954, the Royal Mint were requested by the War Office to modify the mounts and to make them so that no part of the inscription or design of the medallion itself was covered. The eventual outcome was the general adoption of the type of clamp, attaching the mount to the medal, which the Royal Mint terms the 'three-pin mount'. To fix this type of clamp directly on to the medal rim, a swivel-type bar has to be used. (The foregoing details were kindly supplied by the Royal Mint, and their terminology has been retained.)

From 1955 onwards the Mint has been using this type of mount on the following medals (and doubtless others will follow): Africa G.S., Naval G.S., Army and R.A.F. G.S., Champion Shot of R.A.F., and the following Long Service and Good Conduct Medals: Naval, R.N.R., R.A.F., King's African Rifles, and R.W.A.F.F.

Although most of the George VI Army and R.A.F. General Service Medals are of the fixed type, late issues of the *Palestine 1945–48* may be found with swivel mounts. These medals are approximately 3 mm. thick – about ½ mm. thicker than those with the fixed mount.

### Ratings, Ranks and Units

Quite a number of medals bear ratings, ranks, and units, often abbreviated, which cause the collector some difficulty in interpretation.

Even medal rolls have produced misunderstandings; until comparatively recently, the rating shown in the N.G.S. Medal Roll as *L.M.* was consistently interpreted by some dealers and auctioneers as *Leading Man*, giving the impression that the medal was to a rating senior to *Ord.* or *A.B.* In point of fact, *L.M.* was lower than *Ord.*, as it denoted *Landman* or *Landsman* (both spellings are used, even in official publications), who was usually an impressed man and definitely not a *seaman*. The rating was abolished by Admiralty Order of 1st April 1853. There *was* a rating of Leading Man at that time, but he was a shore rating of civilian employment in dockyards, etc., and would certainly not have qualified, as such, for the N.G.S. Medal. The misinterpretation of *L.M.* is most probably due to confusing it with the later rating of *Leading Seaman*, which ranks between *A.B.* and *Petty Officer,*

Another rank which caused some difficulty was that impressed on an Army of India Medal (bar – *Ava*), to *Col. Midshipman*. This proved to indicate *College Midshipman*, i.e. one who had passed through the Royal Naval College, and was in use for only a short period. A similar naming on the N.G.S. Medal (bar – *Syria*) has been noted – *Coll. Mate.*

Medals with the rating, *Dom.*, have appeared in dealers' lists as awarded to a *Donkeyman* (which is a Merchant Navy rating), whereas the abbreviation indicates *Domestic* – a messman rating.

Some awards to naval petty officers are occasionally passed off as officers' medals, as the rating includes the term, *Captain*. As some of these namings omit the words, *of the*, we get such namings as *Capt. Hold*, *Capt. Mast*. The abbreviations vary, but the list of ratings given below should assist in deciphering them. Some of these *Captain* ratings have a *Second*, i.e. *Second Captain of the Forecastle;* several of the ratings have a *mate* and/or *crew*, such as *Carpenter's Mate*, *Carpenter's Crew*. (Captain of the Heads is not an official rating, and does not appear on any medal; for interpretation, ask any sailor).

The majority of puzzling naval ratings can be solved by reference to a *Navy List* of the period concerned, in the *Rates of Pay* section. There are a few which are not included, such as those peculiar to polar voyages, where we find *Ice Mate*, *Greenland Master*, *Ice Quartermaster*, *Harpooner*, *Dog Driver*, etc.

A study of the *Navy Lists* over a period, will show how and when ranks changed; thus in 1861, *Mates* are replaced by *Sub-Lieutenants*.

The following ranks and ratings (not all in use at the same time) may not be as well known as some, and their varied abbreviations may not always be clear at first glance:

Admiral's Cook
Admiral's Coxswain
Admiral's Domestic
Admiral's Steward
Armourer
Barber
Blacksmith
B.M. – Boy Mechanic, RNAS
Butcher
Captain of Quarter Deck Men
Captain of Forecastle,
   of Foretop, of Hold,
   of Maintop, of Mast,
   of Mizentop
Captain's Cook
Captain's Coxswain
Carpenter
Caulker
C.E.R.A. – Chief Engine
   Room Artificer

C.S.B.A. – Chief Sick Berth
   Attendant
Coll. Mate – College Mate
Col. Midn. – College Midship-
   man
Cd. Ck – Commissioned Cook
Cooper
Coxswain of the Barge, of the
   Cutter, Launch, Pinnace
Dom. – Domestic, 1st, 2nd,
   3rd Class
General Messman
Inspector General (of Hospitals
   and Fleets)
Inspector of Machinery
Keeper of Royal Apartments
   (a Domestic in H.M. Yachts)
Krooman
   (also Head Krooman)

Lamp Trimmer
Landman, Landsman
Lithographer
Musician
Naval Schoolmaster
Painter
Pensioner Writer
    (in home ships)
Plumber
Purser's Steward's Mate
Qualified Signalman
Ropemaker
Sailmaker
Seaman's Schoolmaster
Seedie (African native rating)

Ship's Corporal
Shipwright
Shoemaker
Signal Boy
Tailor
Tindal (or Seedie Tindal, or
    Tindal of Seedies – African
    native rating in charge of
    Seedies)
Tinsmith
Ward Room Steward
Writer (also Chief W. and 2nd
    W.)
Yeoman of Signals
Yeoman of Storeroom

*Chief Skipper*, *Skipper*, *Skipper Lieutenant*, and *2nd Hand*, are peculiar to the R.N.R. and R.N.V.R., while *R.N.A.V.* (rarely seen on medals) indicates the old Royal Naval Artillery Volunteers, and *R.N.A.S.B.R.* refers to the Royal Naval Auxiliary Sick Berth Reserve (and no connection with the Royal Naval Air Service, as the first four letters might lead one to think). These last initials are usually only found on R.N.R. long service medals, and are the only means of identifying what is virtually a separate medal.

Generally speaking, medals to the Army do not present as many difficulties in deciphering ranks as do the naval ones, but the initials of units, especially some of the colonial ones, are often obscure. Occasionally medals are found passing as awarded to officers, with the first word (or abbreviation) erased in such ranks as *Sgt.-Major*, etc. The following ranks may, perhaps, be unfamiliar:

2nd Captain (R.A. and R.E.)
Carriage Smith (Cpl C.S., etc.)
Clerk of Works (R.E.)
Collarmaker (also Cpl.-C; C-
    Major, etc.)
Conductor of Stores (Ord.
    Store Corps, etc.)
Corporal-Major, Corporal of
    Horse (Household Cavalry)
Corporal Artificer, Sgt. Art,
    etc. (R.E.)

Corporal Saddletree-Maker
Farrier (also F.Sgt., etc.)
Infirmary Sergt. (Corps of Mili-
    tary Labourers)
Garrison Sgt.-Major (Staff)
Master Gunner, 1st or 2nd
    Class (R.A.)
Regimental Quartermaster
    Corporal–Major (House-
    hold Cavalry)
Ridingmaster

Schoolmaster
Sergt. Artificer (R.E. or Corps
  of Ordnance Artificers)
Sergt. Farrier & Carriage Smith
Sergt. Photographer (R.A.)
Sgt.-Major Foreman of Works
  (R.E.)
Sgt.-Major Mechanist
Sergt. Saddler
Shoeing Smith; Jobbing Smith
Staff Collarmaker
Superintending Clerk
Tinsmith (Ord. Store Corps)
Trumpet-Major; Fife-Major
Wheeler (also Corpl. Wheeler,
  etc.)
Troop Sgt.-Mjr. Rough Rider

*Medical Dept.*
Apothecary
Captain of Orderlies
Purveyor (also in Purveyor's
  Dept, later A.S.C.)
Purveyor's Clerk
Hospital Assistant
Hospital Mate

*Commissariat Dept.*
A.C.G. – Asst. Commissary
  General
D.A.C.G. – Deputy ditto
Com. Clerk
Conductor of Stores
Barrack Q.M. Sgt. (C. & T.C.)
Superior Barrack Sgt.
  (C. & T.C.)

The number of abbreviations of units is legion. Many are, of course, well known, such as *K.O.Y.L.I.*, and *K.R.R.C.* Of the hundreds of others, those listed below are only a short selection, and may be encountered fairly frequently, although the initials are sometimes expanded; thus while one medal may be impressed *I.Y.H.*, others may have *I.Y. Hosp.*, or *Imp. Yeo. Hosp.*

| | |
|---|---|
| A.C. | Ambulance Corps |
| A.H.C. | Army Hospital Corps |
| A.M.1 GR. | Air Mechanic, 1st Grade (on BWM and Victory Medal, &c.) |
| A.P.D. | Army Pay Department |
| A.P.O.C. | Army Post Office Corps |
| ARTY. | Artillery (H.E.I.Co. Artillery on early Indian medals) |
| A.S.D. | Army Schools Dept. |
| A.S.R. | Army Scripture Reader (on QSA Medals) |
| A.W.C. | Army Works Corps (Crimea period only) |
| Assam V.L.H. | Assam Valley Light Horse |
| B.M. | Boy Mechanic, RNAS |
| B.M.D. | Bengal Medical Dept. |
| B.M.I. | Boulton's Mounted Infantry (NW Canada 1885) |
| Bo.N.I. or Bomb.N.I. | Bombay Native Infantry |
| BR.COL.RGT. | British Columbia Regt. |
| Br. Coy. | Bearer Company. |
| B.Y.C.H. | Buckinghamshire Yeomanry Cavalry Hussars (on Geo. IV Coron. M.) |
| C. & T.C. | Commissariat & Transport Corps |

194

| | |
|---|---|
| C.C.C.C. | Cape Colony Cyclist Corps |
| C.F.C. | Canadian Forestry Corps |
| C.M.M.P. | Corps of Military Mtd. Police |
| C.M.R. | Cape Mounted Riflemen (Sth. African campaign medals) Canadian Mounted Rifles – 5th Bn. Quebec Regt. (shown as 5–C.M.R. on 1914-18 War medals) |
| C.M.S.C. | Corps of Mil. Staff Clerks; also Cape Medical Staff Corps |
| C.O.A. | Corps of Ordnance Artificers |
| C.P.Div. (or Dn.) R.A. | Cinque Ports Divn., Royal Arty. |
| C.P.I. | Corps of Permanent Instructors |
| C.R.I. | Chinese Regt. of Infantry |
| CEYLON PL.R.C. | Ceylon Planters Rifles Corps |
| C.S.C. | Commissariat Staff Corps |
| C.S.E.F. | Canadian Siberian Expedy. Force (on BWM & Vic. M.) |
| D. & D. | Devonshire & Dorset Regt. |
| D.E.O.V.R. | Duke of Edinburgh's Own Volr. Rifles |
| D.M.T. (after town name) | District Mounted Troops (QSA & KSA) |
| E.B.S.R.V.R. | East Bengal State Rlys. Volr. Rifles |
| F.F. (on Indian medals, after regt., 51st Sikhs to 59th Scinde Rifles) | |
| | Frontier Force. On other medals, sometimes as above, sometimes Field Force |
| F.I.D. | Field Intelligence Dept. |
| F.M.R. | Frontier Mounted Rifles |
| G.G.F.G. | Governor-General's Foot Guards (Canada) |
| G.R. | Gurkha Rifles |
| G.S.C. | General Service Corps |
| G.T.R. | Gurkha Transport Regt. |
| H.C.C. | Hospital Conveyance Corps |
| HIGH. CYC. BN. | Highland Cyclist Bttn. |
| H.K.RGT. | Hong Kong Regt. |
| H.M.C.S.C. OF DERBY | H.M. Colonial Ship *Countess of Derby* (E&W Africa Medal) |
| I.A.C.C. | Indian Army Corps of Clerks |
| I.I.C.D. (on QSA Medal) | Believed to be Impl. Irregular Corps Detachment |
| I.M.D. | Indian Medical Dept. |
| I.M.R. | Imperial Military Railways (on QSA Medal) |
| I.M.S. | Indian Medal Service |
| I.R.V.C. | Imperial Rlys. Volr. Corps |
| I.U.L. | Indian Unattached List |
| I.Y.B. | Imperial Yeomanry Bearer Company |
| I.Y.H. | Imperial Yeomanry Hospital |
| L.I.V. | Light Infantry Volrs. (Modern T&AVR unit) |
| L.T. CORPS | Land Transport Corps (1854-57; afterwards Military Train) |
| M.E.S. | Military Engineers Services |
| M.F.A. | Mercantile Fleet Auxiliary |
| M.I. (after name of regt.) | Mounted Infantry |
| M.M.G.S. | Motor Machine Gun Service |
| M.M.R. | Mercantile Marine Reserve |
| M.P.D. | Military Prisons Dept. |
| M.S.C. | Medical Staff Corps |
| M.S.D. | Military Store Dept. |
| M.S.S.C. | Mil. Store Staff Corps |
| M.W.S. | Military Works Service |
| N.CYC.BN. | Northern Cyclist Battn. |
| N.I.M. | North Irish Militia |
| N.V.A.C. | Naval Volr. Ambulance Corps |

| | |
|---|---|
| O.H.A. | Osmanli Horse Arty. (On Crimea Medals; several British officers serving with the Turkish Army had medals so named) |
| O.I.C. | Osmanli Irregular Cavalry (See previous item) |
| O.M.D. | Ordnance Medical Dept. |
| ONT. RGT. | Ontario Regt. |
| P.A.V.G. | Prince Alfred's Volr. Guard |
| P.P.C.L.I. | Princess Patricia's Canadian Light Infy. |
| R.D.C. | Royal Defence Corps |
| R.G.J. | Royal Green Jackets |
| R.G.R. | Royal Garrison Regt. |
| R.H.F. | Royal Highland Fusiliers |
| R.H.G./D. | The Blues & Royals (R. Horse Guards & 1/Dragoons) |
| R.H. of CAN. | Royal Highlanders of Canada |
| R.M.F.A. | Royal Malta Fencible Arty. |
| R.N.A.S.B.R. | Royal Naval Auxiliary Sick Berth Reserve |
| R.N.W.A.R. | Royal Naval Wireless Auxiliary Reserve |
| R.N.V.W.R. | Royal Naval Volr. Wireless Reserve |
| R.R.F. | Royal Regt. of Fusiliers |
| R.R.W. | Royal Regt. of Wales |
| S.A.C. | South African Constabulary |
| S.A.I. RGT. | South African Irish Regt. |
| S. & A.H. | Used for a few months in 1881; later A. & S.H. – Argyll & Sutherland Highrs. Some LS&GC Medals were named to S. & A.H. |
| S.A.S. | Special Air Service Regt. |
| S.A.S.C. | South African Service Corps |
| S. & T.C. | Supply & Transport Corps (Indian Army) |
| S.A.U.L. | South African Unattached List |
| S.C. | Suffolk & Cambridgeshire Regt. (T&AVR) |
| S.C.I. (or I.S.C.) | Indian Staff Corps |
| SPT. (before number) | Sportsmen's Battn., Royal Fusrs. (1914-18) |
| STK. (before number) | Stockbrokers' Battn., Royal Fusrs. (1914-18) |
| S.R.Y. | Sherwood Rangers Yeomanry |
| T.B.M.E. CORPS | Tientsin British Municipal Emergency Corps (*ca.* 1900) |
| T.O.S. | Trucial Oman Scouts (GSM: Arabian Peninsula bar) |
| V.Q. | Voltigeurs de Quebec (NW Canada Medal, 1885) |
| W.I.R. | West India Regt. |
| W.W.Y. | Warwickshire & Worcester Yeomanry |

RAF 6-figure numbers beginning with 2, on BWM and Victory Medal, indicate ex-RNAS personnel.

From time to time the *Army Lists* have included several colonial units, e.g. *Hart's Army List*, 1859, shows the following:

1st, 2nd, and 3rd West India Regt. of Foot.

Ceylon Rifle Regt. (till 1873)

Cape Mtd. Riflemen (1828–70)

Royal Canadian Rifle Regt. (1841–70)

St. Helena Regt. (1842–63)

Royal Newfoundland Companies

Gold Coast Artillery Corps (1851–63).

# 10

# Foreign Decorations

In the space at our disposal it is only possible to deal with a very few selected foreign items. Mention is made of some of the decorations which collectors of British medals are likely to encounter in their groups, and some notes are included of a few interesting points which may not be generally known. It is only possible to include a few of the snags which might be met with, but it is hoped that even this restricted information will be helpful to collectors.

With foreign decorations the collector is faced with problems quite different from those connected with British awards, where the main difficulties lie with re-naming and with altered or unofficial bars. Very few foreign medals are named, apart from life-saving awards, and the snags one has to look out for are more in the direction of repaired pieces, missing or falsely added embellishments, and copies or replicas.

As regards orders, most British insignia are items which have actually been awarded to, and worn by, some recipient (even if he cannot always be identified); they cannot normally be bought, other than second-hand, from dealers or jewellers, although members of the Great Orders often had duplicate badges, sometimes set with precious stones, made for them by court jewellers. But for many years the practice in various foreign countries has been for recipients of the lower classes of orders and of decorations, to have to purchase their insignia. Consequently many high-class jewellers in Paris, Berlin, Vienna, and elsewhere (particularly in the 19th and early 20th centuries) manufactured insignia of all classes of all orders. These could, and still can, be bought by entitled recipients and collectors alike, so it is not surprising that even British insignia, from the Order of the Garter downwards, were included in their stocks. But *any* continental made example of a British order is merely an unofficial copy, and should be worth little more to a British collector than its gold or silver value. On the other hand, one cannot say that the badges of foreign orders are necessarily copies; if an example of, say, a South American order is found in a Paris or Berlin shop, the manufacturer could well have been one of the official makers to that order. Provided the details of design are correct – and they vary quite a bit, both in correctness of detail and standard of work-manship – the specimen is accepted by collectors, although one does not always know if it has been worn by a recipient or has come direct from a dealer's stock. Foreign collectors like to obtain, whenever possible, the diploma or other official document awarded with the insignia, and although (even if obtained from the recipient or his family) this does not prove completely who the owner was, it is very helpful, especially where a group, mounted as worn, is accompanied by all its relative diplomas.

There is one point on which I must warn collectors, and that is when foreign orders (and, in many cases, decorations) are described as *rare*. Unfortunately many items so described in dealers' lists are not rare at all, *although they may have been very sparingly awarded*. An example is the Baden Order of Loyalty (*Hausorden der Treue*), which was given only to ruling princes and to a very few noblemen. Genuine 'awarded' examples are certainly very rare, but since specimens were made for collectors by all these various firms in all the capitals of Europe, there are very many more examples on the market than were ever awarded. Consequently it does not seem really justifiable to fix the price by the number issued and describe it as *extremely rare*.

Generally speaking, the question of commercial manufacture and sale did not apply so much to foreign *medals*, except, perhaps, coronation and other commemorative medals, although in certain countries, particularly France and Belgium, one can buy commer-cially made examples of both past and modern campaign medals, Croix de Guerre, etc. In most countries campaign and long service medals have always been officially awarded to those entitled, and although few of them are named, they offer a much more satisfac-tory field to the collector who likes to feel that his medals have been won and worn by heroes.

One cannot stress too strongly the desirability of devoting as large a proportion of available funds as can be spared, for the build-ing up of a library of reference books. Admittedly literature in English regarding foreign awards is rather scanty, and the collector is strongly recommended to learn something of the language of any country whose decorations particularly interest him – it is not necessary to be able to speak it (although undoubtedly highly desirable), but the ability to read it will be sufficient. For the general collector, some knowledge of German, French and Italian or Spanish is most useful – even a schoolboy smattering of German and French, with the aid of a good dictionary (and it can even be an old one), will enable you to make good use of books in those languages.

### Foreign Awards Frequently Found in British Groups

The collector of British campaign medals will very soon come across groups containing at least one foreign item, even if it is only a bronze *Khedive's Star*, accompanying the Queen's medal for Egypt. Another class of foreign award, frequently seen in 1914–18 groups, is that for gallantry. These are all recorded in the *London Gazette*, indicating the granting of the award by the sovereign or president of the country concerned, and intimating our own King's permission for it to be accepted and worn. Consequently such items can be verified (although it means searching through the Index of each volume over a period of up to five years – this, however, is assisted by the fact that each foreign decoration is shown in the Index, with the names of recipients in alphabetical order); in the case of army personnel, awards are often listed in regimental histories.

It may not be generally realised that the award of an allied decoration does not necessarily imply that the deed of gallantry or meritorious service was actually performed in the country concerned, or in connection with its forces – although frequently this was in fact the case. In practice, a number of Crosses of St George of Russia were sent to the British Army in France, to be awarded for suitable acts of gallantry. The recipients, who undoubtedly earned their decoration, never went near Russia nor saw a Russian in the whole of their service. On the other hand, a man might receive a Russian, Italian, French, Belgian, or Serbian decoration for saving the life of an officer of the respective nationality, or for capturing a machine-gun post on one of those fronts.

Sometimes groups of medals are found with a foreign award which does not appear in the *London Gazette*. This does not necessarily mean that it has been spuriously added; sometimes the award of an Order or Decoration does not fall within the categories for which Royal permission is given 'to accept and wear'. In these cases, while the recipient can accept it, he may not wear it (although some do, on uniforms other than those of H.M. Forces, e.g. British Red Cross Society, and other private bodies). A good example of this is the Greek medal for the Balkan War, 1912–13, which was awarded to several British doctors and nurses who served with the Red Cross; some were also awarded Greek Orders (i.e. the Order of the Re-deemer), but these are not recorded in the *London Gazette*. In the case of a doctor, verification has been possible, by reference to the *Medical Directory*, and sometimes such awards are recorded in *Who's Who;* a few back numbers of this work can be very useful for reference. Many mid-nineteenth century awards of foreign Orders, etc., are given in *The British Roll of Honour*, by Prof. P. L. Simmonds (London, 1887); this is a most useful volume for checking groups of medals to officers and civilians, and may sometimes be found in secondhand bookshops.

## Austria

Most Austrian orders and military decorations have a special embellishment when awarded for war services, known as the *Kriegs-dekoration* (usually abbreviated to *KD*), and frequently there is a special form when the holder of an award with the *KD* subsequently receives a higher peacetime class of the same order. In this case the higher class has a special variety of the *KD* to indicate that it relates to a lower class of the order. In view of the many complications of this system, it is only possible to indicate the main features of each order or decoration. The *KD* does not apply to the Order of Maria Theresa, since this is essentially a military award and thus an embellishment is not necessary.

The Order of Leopold has for its *KD* a green enamelled laurel spray above the cross, half encircling the crown. From 13 December 1916 the order could also be awarded 'with swords' for bravery in action, and these are placed saltirewise between the angles of the cross.

The *KD* for the Order of the Iron Crown consists of two laurel sprays rising, one on each side, from the circlet, but for the *KD* of a lower class the laurel branches are set close to the central shield.

Incidentally, genuine insignia have a flattened ring of iron (usually rusted) set in the base of the circlet, representing the Iron Crown of Lombardy after which the order was named. Examples with a solid base to the circlet should be avoided.

As with the Order of Leopold, this order could also be awarded 'with swords' but they are set, crossed very flatly, above the badge and below the crown (but on the ribbon for the 3rd class).

When the Order of Franz Joseph was won in war, it was worn with the ribbon of the Military Cross of Merit – red and white horizontal stripes, with red (inner) and white (outer) edges – instead of the plain red statute ribbon. There were also other indications of the *KD*, too complicated to be briefly described. When awarded 'with swords', these were worn on the ribbon for the lowest class, *Ritter* or knight, and between the top of the cross and the crown for the higher classes.

The Military Cross of Merit, which could also be awarded 'with swords' on the ribbon for the lowest class, and set in saltire between the arms of the cross for higher classes, had a wreath appearing between the arms of the cross (and below the swords, if present) as its *KD*.

Cannon Cross, 1813–14

With the surrender of Paris to the Allies in March 1814, the Austrian Emperor, Franz I, instituted the *Metallenes Armeekreuz für 1813– 1814*, for the "Defenders of the Fatherland". Made from captured French guns, it is generally known as the Cannon Cross, and original examples measure 27 mm. across. It is a straight-armed cross *patée*, the arms being 15 mm. wide at the outside, with a narrow laurel wreath between the arms, and pierced in the angles. The field, on both sides, inside the slightly raised edge, is lacquered a dark green with the *obv.* and *rev.* inscriptions raised in the colour of the metal; the *obv.* has: GRATI (top) PRINCEPS ET PATRIA (centre) FRANC:/IMP.AUG. (bottom), and the *rev:* EUROPAE (top) LIBERTATE ASSERTA (centre) MDCCCXIII/MDCCCIV (bottom), meaning 'The thanks of Prince and Fatherland, Francis, Emperor, that the liberty of Europe is maintained, 1813/1814'.

The original suspension, set at right angles to the cross through an arc loop, has a central groove, and the original ribbon was 38 mm. wide, black with a 14 mm. yellow central stripe. The cross was normally worn at the buttonhole. Many later versions are found, and are sometimes gilded as, allegedly, "officers' crosses".

Much rarer is the somewhat similar Civil Cross of Honour, 1813–14, in gold or silver, of the same shape but without the laurel wreath, while the colours of the ribbon are reversed. However, the originals were slightly larger than the Cannon Cross, being 30 mm.

diameter, and many examples occur of the bronze Cannon Cross, having the wreath filed away, the green lacquer removed, and the cross being gold or silver plates. It is therefore essential to check the size first – if this is only 27 mm., then the Civil Cross is cetainly not genuine (but if it is 30 mm., then one must still be wary, as it still might be a copy).

*Medal Ribbons.* The distinctive triangular ribbon (also adopted by Hungary, Bulgaria, Serbia, Montenegro, etc.) came in about 1840, prior to which Austria used the straight 'threaded through' ribbon. Since Austrians have frequently been awarded German orders and decorations, one often finds a triangular ribbon on awards such as the Prussian Iron Cross, 2nd Class (usually watered, whereas the normal ribbon is unwatered), and this usually indicates an Austrian, or similar, recipient.

### Belgium

During the two World Wars, many Belgian awards were made to British personnel, particularly the Croix de Guerre, but the badges themselves present no difficulties to collectors, although (as with most foreign awards) minor differences of design will be noticed among examples of any particular period.

It should be noted that the *rev.* of the Croix de Guerre and the palm leaf emblems for World War I bore the royal initial, A (Albert I), while those for World War II bore L (Leopold III). Actually the original 1941 crosses and palm leaf emblems, made in London, had L III L, with the second L reversed, and both set at 45°, but after the war, in 1952, the palm leaf initials were changed to the plain script capital L (like a £ without the cross bars).

The Yser Medal, instituted in October 1918, is one which is well worth its place in any collection, especially if it is accompanied by other medals for the war which have obviously been worn by a recipient. Although we normally have no way of knowing to whom they were awarded, we know that the original owner served *with distinction* (a necessary qualification) between 17 and 31 October 1914, in the really heroic action of the Belgian Army against the invading German hordes, on the banks of the River Yser, when the Belgians lost a third of their army, killed, wounded or taken prisoner.

In 1934 a Royal Decree instituted the Yser Cross to replace the medal, to signify the honour in which the heroes of the Yser were held. The design and ribbon were as before, except that the circular medallion was now superimposed on a cross *patée* (all integrated). The recipient could not wear both the medal and the cross, and many preferred to keep their original medals – whether the fact that they had to purchase the cross had any bearing on their decision is not known.

In order of precedence, the Allied Victory Medal comes before the Commemorative Medal for the War, 1914–18, while the Yser Medal (or Cross) takes precedence immediately after the Croix de Guerre and before other campaign medals.

For World War II (1940–45 for Belgium) some fifteen or more awards were instituted. One late award was not authorised until December 1967, first appearing in 1969, and does not seem to have got into the current medal books. This is the *Medaille van de Militair, Strijder van de Oorlog, 1940–45*, or Medal for the Fighting Soldier of the 1940–45 War, for all members of the Belgian forces, and for foreigners who served with the exiled Belgian forces in England. It is a bronze Greek cross with segments of a circle in the angles of the arms. The *obv.* has a Roman sword, point uppermost, between the dates, 1940, 1945, while the *rev.* depicts the Belgian lion rampant, to left. The ribbon, 37 mm. wide, has a yellow centre, 11 mm. wide, flanked by three stripes in the national colours, occupying together 7 mm., and 6 mm. bright green edges. Since the several firms who were authorised to strike this medal had to work from a very rough drawing, it is not surprising that examples occur with various minor differences in the design.

Collectors of Belgian Orders will frequently experience difficulty in obtaining the correct 'commander' width of ribbon for badges worn at the neck. Although they may have been in use at one time, for many years the normal ribbon of 36 mm. has been used in place of the 'statute' ribbon of 55 mm. or 45 mm. Similarly, the statutes provide for special ribbons augmented with either a central gold stripe or gold side stripes, for awards for special merit during the First World War; certainly some of these were issued, but from an authoritative source in Belgium, I learn that by no means all the ribbons were actually manufactured, and in many cases the insignia were issued with the normal ribbon but with gold stripes stitched on.

*Belgian Cross (or Star) for Waterloo.* For details of this frequently mis-named award, see under Netherlands.

## France

The Orders, Decorations, and Medals of France cover a wide range, and the more important of these have been described briefly in several books in English, particularly in the many editions of Taprell Dorling's *Ribbons and Medals*. The two most usually seen in British groups are the Legion of Honour and the Médaille Militaire.

There are at least a dozen types of insignia of the Legion of Honour, and these are described in several French books. The two which mainly concern us here are those of the Crimean War period, and those for the First World War. The badges of the former are those of the Second Empire, which were, in fact, authorised under the Second Republic on 31st January 1852. The design is very similar to that of the fourth type of the First Empire, but the central medallion has: NAPOLÉON EMPEREUR DES FRANÇAIS whereas the earlier type abbreviates the second word to EMP. Also the crown (from which the badge is suspended) has eagles at the base of the

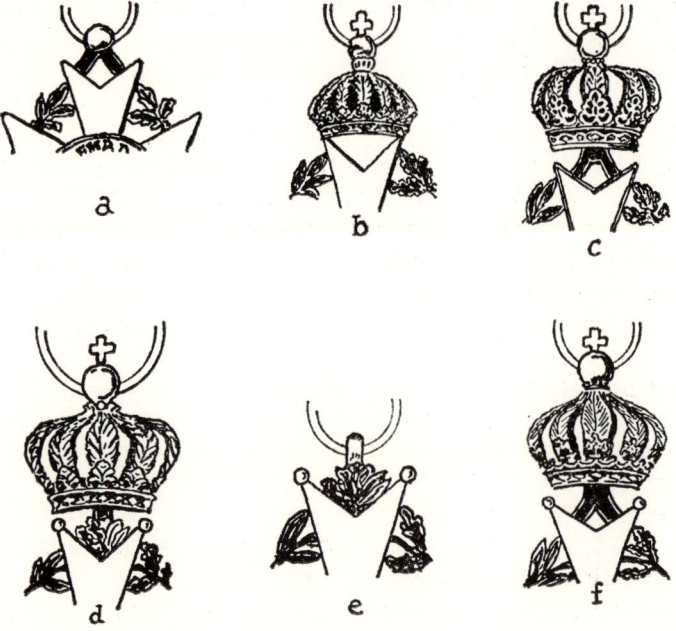

FIG. 17.
Details of some types of The Legion of Honour.
(a) First Empire; 1st type, 1804.   (b) First Empire; 2nd type, 1806.   (c) First Empire; 3rd type.
(d) First Empire; 4th type.   (e) Second Republic; 1st type, 1848.   (f) Second Republic 3rd type
Jan. 1852, and Second Empire, Dec. 1852.

arches in the Second Empire type, while the earlier one has conventional clusters of five leaves (rather like a five-leaved *fleur-de-lis*, if such a thing existed) (*Fig. 17* and *Plate 12*).

Awards made during the First World War were of the Third Republic type, with the female head of *La République* on the medallion, and the date, 1870, on the encircling blue riband. The present designs, of the Fourth and Fifth Republics, are almost identical, except that by decree of 27th February 1951, the date, 1870, has been removed.

Quite a number of awards of the Médaille Militaire were made to British soldiers during the Crimean War, and these are listed, by regiments, in Carter's *Medals of the British Army*, and in the Appendix of D. Hastings Irwin's *War Medals and Decorations* (4th Edition, 1910). The medal is the second type, with the head of Louis Napoleon on the *obv.*, while the *rev.* is lettered, VALEUR ET DISCIPLINE. The tail of the eagle surmounting the medal, stops short at the blue riband surrounding the central medallion (*rev.*), whereas on the first type it overlaps the riband and covers part of the centre.

The medals awarded during 1914–18 were those of the Third Republic, and, like the Legion of Honour, bear the female head. The eagle of the Imperial type has been replaced by a trophy of arms; in the early medals of this type, the trophy was soldered to the medal, but before 1914 this had been changed, and the trophy was hinged to the medal; also, whereas the *rev.* of the trophy on the first type of 1870, showed the design of all the component parts, the later ones had a plain *rev.* As with the Legion of Honour, the date, 1870, ceased to appear from 27th February, 1951.

The Croix de Guerre, or War Cross, was instituted on 8 April 1915, and bore two dates on the *rev;* these ranged from 1914/1915 to 1914/1918. British groups containing a Croix de Guerre should be checked against the *London Gazette*, or a regimental history (which may include honours and awards), for verification, at the same time making sure that the dates on the *rev.* are correct. An award made in, say, 1917 should have the dates, 1914/1917, but might have 1914/1916 (or even 1914/1915), according to availability, but one dated 1914/1918 is unlikely to be the original cross, unless the date of the award was very late in 1917 and the actual cross was not presented until well into 1918. While this is possible, it is rather unlikely and I would view such an example with some suspicion until verified.

Modern copies of the cross are still on sale in Paris, by the highly reputable firms who are authorised to manufacture French awards. They are naturally very 'new looking', with extremely sharp detail. On the contemporary crosses the figures on the *rev.* are usually somewhat worn, as they form the highest relief features and have constantly rubbed on the uniform.

As in Belgium, the French Allied Victory Medal is worn *before* the War Commemorative Medal. The official medal has, on the *obv.*, the standing figure of Victory with arms and wings raised, holding aloft an olive branch and a laurel wreath. The *rev.* has a cap of liberty flanked by the initials, R – F, below which is a 5-line inscription, LA/ GRANDE GVERRE/POVR LA/ CIVILISATION/ 1914–1918. Another design is found, however, which is presumably unofficial (since it is not mentioned in *Décorations Officielles Françaises*, nor in Delande's *Décorations – France et Colonies*), and is probably a rejected design. The *obv.* has a frontal figure of Victory, with downward pointing wings, holding in her outstretched hands a sword and an olive (or laurel) branch; near the edge, bottom right, is the signature, C. CHARLES. The *rev.* has a central 3-line inscription, LA GRANDE GUERRE/ POUR LA CIVILISATION/1914–1918, with laurel sprays above and below. Unlike the official medal, this one does not have R.F. to indicate the country of origin. It is interesting to note, however, that the *obv.* design is, in fact, that used for the Cuba version of the Victory Medal (but with a *rev.*, of the Cuban arms and a Spanish inscription).

## Germany

One does not often encounter a group of medals to a British recipient which contains a German award, although quite a number of Orders were awarded to officers during the nineteenth and early twentieth centuries (in addition to a number of courtesy medals given by visiting royalty to members of the Royal Household staff). With the outbreak of the First World War, the royal permission to 'accept and wear' was, of course, withdrawn, but it is interesting to note that the uniform worn by Admiral Jellicoe at the Battle of Jutland, still bore the ribbon of the Order of the Red Eagle of Prussia!

The most famous German award is, of course, the Iron Cross, and it is not always realised that until Hitler revived it, in 1939, as a German Order, it had previously been Prussian, not German, always being awarded by the King of Prussia (although from 1871, he also happened to be Emperor of Germany), Furthermore, it was not a permanent award, being instituted in 1813 for the Napoleonic Wars, discontinued until revived in 1870, for the Franco-Prussian War, and revived again in 1914. It has been awarded to a number of British subjects, a few of whom have received it with the black ribbon with white side stripes, as combatants; most of the awards were made with the white ribbon with black side stripes, to medical officers. With this latter ribbon, the decoration is often quite incorrectly described (even in some German books) as the *civil* Iron Cross; the Iron Cross is essentially a military decoration, but when awarded to non-combatant troops or to civilian personnel serving with the forces, the white ribbon was used.

Recipients of the 1870 Iron Cross who were living in 1895, received a 'jubilee' addition of an oakleaf cluster, with the figure 25, worn just above the ring of the cross, while any who qualified for a further award of the cross in the 1914–18 War, received a bar bearing a miniature Iron Cross and the date, 1914; this was worn on the ribbon, just above the oak leaves.

Holders of the 1914 Iron Cross who were nominated for the Hitler Iron Cross of the same class, continued to wear their original cross with the addition of an emblem, dated 1939, with the Nazi eagle and swastika.

Copies of all issues of the Iron Cross – Prussian and Third Reich types – exist, including near-contemporary copies of the 1813 and 1870 issues. Especially with these last two, one must be very wary, as genuine 1813 crosses are extremely rare (despite the fact that 10,000 of the 2nd Class were issued, probably even more), and original 1870 ones are certainly very scarce. Copies usually have the raised details – crown, initials, figures, etc., in lower relief than the originals, the crowns are often flattened in outline, being almost oval, while the edges of the relief designs are not usually as sharp as the originals. Sizes vary, but as an example, the 1870 Iron Cross, 2nd Class, is usually 41–42 mm. across, and a copy has been noted at 43 mm., with a ring only 10 mm. in diameter instead of 15 mm. (or, at any rate, 13–16 mm.).

Over 5,000,000 of the 1914 Iron Crosses were issued, made by several different firms, consequently diameters varied from 41·5 mm. to 44 mm., the majority being about 43 mm. Some have a silver rim made in two parts and welded to enclose the iron centre; others, probably made late in the war, were stamped in one piece of metal, coloured black in the centre and silvered on the rim.

Occasionally a smaller model, approximately 35 mm. in diameter, may be encountered, especially of the 1870 cross, known as the *Prinzen* size, and alleged to be for wear by any young princes to whom it had been awarded. It has also been recorded as having been worn in undress uniform and in civilian clothes; its precise status does not appear to have been specified, and Hessenthal & Schreiber do not include it in their book.

With the re-introduction of the Iron Cross, effective from 1 September 1939 – this time as a German order – various enlargements and embellishments were authorised, so that in addition to the 2nd Class, 1st Class and Grand Cross, there were the Knight's Cross, Knight's Cross with Oak Leaves, with Oak Leaves and Swords, with Oak Leaves, Swords and Diamonds, and with Golden Oak Leaves, Swords and Diamonds (of which only one award was made).

Copies exist of all these 1939-45 types, and of the modern de-nazified types, without swastika. After the war, the Third Reich insignia were not allowed to be worn, but in 1957 certain awards (excluding those for Nazi Party service, SS service, etc.) were permitted provided all Nazi emblems were removed. Before the modern re-designed types appeared, the original decorations were worn with the swastika filed off, consequently crosses are now on the market which are perfectly genuine Third Reich awards, but the filing of the swastika has been done just recently, to make them appear as authentic 1957 provisional insignia.

Some terrible copies, or forgeries, of Third Reich decorations and medals are being made in Spain and offered for sale there and in Portugal at £4–£6 each; they include the Iron Cross, War Merit Cross, Order of the German Eagle, Russian (East Front) Medal and others.

ORDER OF THE RED EAGLE

Perhaps the most interesting of the many orders of the German States is the Prussian Order of the Red Eagle. In its various classes, from Grand Cross down to *Ritter* (knight), with crown, with swords, with swords on the ring, with brilliants, with oakleaves, with St. John's Cross, with bow, with Jubilee button for 50, 60, or 70 years, with special designs for non-Christians, its insignia number well over

100 varieties, some with the statute ribbon of white with red-orange side stripes (appearing as reddish brown in some wartime weaves), some with a black ribbon with two or three white stripes.

In recent times copies have been seen, not only on the continent but in Britain as well, of several of the 1813–15 campaign medals of the German States, particularly of Hesse, Prussia and Oldenburg. It is impossible to describe how to distinguish these from the originals, since there are several varieties on the market – one can only say that most of them look "too good", without the signs of wear which the originals usually show (although this can be faked), but on several the lettering and such details as the crown or wreaths are not as sharp as they should be. Compared with the genuine medals there are many minor points of difference, and unless a collector has access to original medals for comparison, the only answer is to buy only from a reputable *and experienced* dealer. Such medals bought at market stalls or from junk shops are more than likely to be these copies.

### Italy

During the latter half of the nineteenth century, and up to the end of the First World War, quite a number of Italian awards were made to British subjects. The Sardinian War Medal for the Crimea was the first to be given in any numbers, and the recipients are listed in the Appendix of D. Hastings Irwin's *War Medals and Decorations* (4th Edition, 1910), while Carter's *Medals of the British Army* lists the army recipients. Since this medal is not common, and the names and units are engraved in the *rev.* field, a number of faked medals exist, sometimes using a restrike. The original medal is of silver, 33 mm. in diameter. The *obv.* bears the designer's initials, F.G., at the bottom; as the *obv.* wording is AL VALORE MILITARE (*for military valour*), the much commoner general medal which goes by that name, instituted in 1833 and in use for a century, is sometimes passed off as the Crimea one, with the name of a British recipient re-engraved over the erased original. However, the Crimea issue has on the *rev.*, SPEDIZIONE D'ORIENTE (*Eastern Expedition*), and, at the bottom, the dates, 1855✱1856, with a small six-petalled rosette between the two years. Copies of the medal exist, and one omits this rosette, while another has a star (i.e. with pointed members instead of rounded ones). The naming is usually in running script, in the centre of the *rev.*, and is thus easily imitated. Suspension is by a narrow silver flattened loop or 'lug' at the top of the medal, in the usual Italian style (*See Plate 13*).

There are several later examples of the Italian Medals for Military and Maritime Valour having been awarded to British personnel, the latter medal usually for saving the lives of Italians or rendering services to Italian ships in distress. During the 1914–18 War, the bronze Italian War Cross was widely given, but was issued unnamed and does not call for comment; its presence in a British group can, of course, be verified from the *London Gazette* (*See Plate 13*).

The Messina and Reggio earthquakes, in December 1908, brought the award of the silver medal, specially struck for the occasion, to many British sailors who rendered assistance, and royal permission was given in 1912 for this medal to be worn in uniform. The ribbon is green, with a white centre stripe and white edges, and the medal is somewhat smaller than our normal size – only 32 mm. in diameter. The medals were issued unnamed (in a case), but many British naval recipients had them named privately. Nearly 5,000 medals were awarded, to all the crews of the battleships *Duncan* and *Exmouth*, the cruisers *Euryalus*, *Lancaster*, *Minerva* and *Sutlej*, and the destroyer *Boxer*, also to those of the crews who had actually landed from the battleship *Canopus* and the cruisers *Philomel* and *Aboukir*. In addition some 400 medals were awarded to members of the mercantile marine and 12 to the army.

### Netherlands

THE SILVER CROSS FOR 1813–1815. On the 50th anniversary of the institution of the Military Order of Willem, the Dutch King, Willem III, instituted by Royal Decree of 10 May 1865, the *Zilveren Kruis van 1813–1815*, for the veterans of the campaign against Napoleon, including the Battle of Waterloo.

This is a rather thin and poorly made five-armed silver cross, 35 mm. in diameter, with shallow V-ends to the arms. The arms have a smooth border enclosing a pitted field. The central medallion has '1813' on one side, and '1815' on the other, in smooth figures on a hatched ground. The ribbon is orange-yellow, watered, with narrow white side stripes, and should be 27·5 mm. wide.

In many medal books this award is quite incorrectly described as 'the Belgian Cross for Waterloo' or (as in Gordon's *British Battles & Medals*) as 'the Belgian Star', but without any question the award is *Dutch*, not Belgian, and was not just for Waterloo. It must be admitted, however, that the majority of the 5,000 survivors who received the cross were, in fact, Belgians by the time it was instituted, but they were Dutchmen in 1813–15, as Belgium had not then become independent. Another incorrect factor is that the ribbon is often described, and has been manufactured, as *light brown*, unwatered, with white side stripes.

THE HASSELT CROSS, 1830–31. The award which we know as the Hasselt Cross is called by the Dutch, *Het Metalen Kruis* (the metal cross), and should be 29 mm. in diameter; the same applies to the variety awarded to volunteers, which has VRIJWILLIG on the *obv.* upper arm of the cross. While the six-striped ribbon of the former is in orange-yellow and Nassau blue, that of the latter has green in place of blue. The crosses were made from the metal of two cannon captured at the battle of Hasselt on 8 August 1831.

One sometimes finds these crosses embellished with an oval bronze wreath, 18 × 12 mm., between the top of the cross and the ring; these are unofficial additions, to indicate an Honourable Mention in an Order of the Day. Crosses are also found gilded or lacquered green, again an unofficial embellishment, and forbidden by an Order of 2 March 1832. Copies, particularly of the volunteers' cross, exist, usually thinner than the genuine cross, with variations in the detail of the W and crown on the *obv.* and in the inscription on the *rev.*

THE EXPEDITION CROSS. Generally known as the *Expeditie Kruis*, the official name of this award is the *Kruis voor Krijgsverrichtingen* (Cross for War Operations), and it probably comes second only to our Naval General Service Medal, 1793–1840, for a record in number of clasps – 33 in all, covering from BALI 1846 to TIMOR 1942 (although none was awarded between 1927 and 1942). The clasp, ATJEH 1873–1896, not only covered actions in the area between 1891 and 1896, but replaced five earlier clasps with various dates from 1873 to 1890, thus reducing the number of clasps to borne on the ribbon.

Various dies were in use during the long life of this medal, which was introduced in 1869, with clasps retrospective to 1846. It was made in German silver, 38 mm. in diameter, with the portrait of Willem III (unaltered in Wilhelmina's reign), and a plain *rev.* Copies exist in proper silver, not to deceive collectors but to provide recipients with a 'better class' medal, in the same way that British copies of the Turkish Crimea Medal were made and sold by military tailors.

The last issue, authorised on 29 October 1942, was struck by the firm of Stokes, of Melbourne, with the clasp, TIMOR 1942, for guerilla fighters against the Japanese on that island, and was also awarded to members of the Royal Dutch Navy who eventually carried them back to Australia.

THE HONOURABLE MENTION. Until the institution of the Bronze Lion, in 1944, the highest award below the Military Order of Willem was the *Eervolle Vermelding*, or Honourable Mention, for bravery in action. Although such mentions in Orders of the Day were made from 1815 onwards, there was no visible emblem until 1877, when a gilt crown, 23 mm. tall, was introduced, to be worn on the ribbon of the Expedition Cross, immediately below the clasp for the campaign concerned (for subsequent awards a gilt figure indicating the number of mentions, was worn below the crown). The order was retrospective for survivors, and examples are known of a Hasselt Cross with a gilt crown on the ribbon.

The Honourable Mention was also awarded in World War II up to 1944, and was worn on the ribbon of the Bronze Cross (instituted, 11 June 1940) or the Flying Cross (instituted, 28 August 1941.)

**Russia (Imperial)**

Russian awards are not common in British groups, except for the early part of the First World War. When Orders were given (usually St Vladimir, St Anne, and St Stanislas, and less frequently St George), they were usually in gold, and the enamel work is delightful. A common mistake is to confuse the *Cross of St George* with the Order itself (a mistake which one often finds in regimental histories and auction descriptions). The Cross, in its four classes – the first two in gold, and the third and fourth in silver – although of similar design, is not enamelled as is the Order, below which it stands. The class of the Cross is indicated on the lower arm of the *rev.*, thus: 3 CTEⅡ and 4 CTEⅡ for the third and fourth classes, respectively; some examples have only the word, CTEⅡ in raised letters, leaving the number of the class to be engraved on issue. Those issued early in the war had a distinguishing number impressed in double-lined figures on the *rev.* horizontal arms, thus: 127–302. Since many examples are found without numbers, and some of these are of inferior workmanship, one may assume that either they are unofficial copies, or the prevailing conditions towards the date of the Russian collapse, influenced the standard of production. Certainly they do not command as good a price as the earlier numbered examples of good style; one cross, alleged to be the original issued to a British soldier, is obviously made of brass, with most of the silvering rubbed off (*See Plate 14*).

### Serbia

A large number of Serbian decorations were awarded to British troops during the Great War. According to Serbian regulations, all these should be worn with a plain red watered ribbon (the ribbon of the Order of the Karageorge Star 'with swords'); it is possible that this was applicable only to Serbian subjects, as many of these awards appear in British groups, worn with the normal statute ribbons, but in other cases it is obvious that the British recipients used the plain red ribbon.

It should be noted that the so-called *Gold* Medal for Zeal is actually of bronze-gilt, although many recipients have long treasured it as gold.

### Turkey

The long succession of Turkish awards to British personnel started with the Sultan's Gold, or Silver, Medal (also known as the Order of the Crescent, but apparently regarded by the Admiralty as a medal and not an Order), in 1801. The sizes quoted in most medal books are for the gold medals, 2·1″, 1·9″, 1·7″ and 1·4″ diameter, and 1·4″ for the silver medals (for N.C.Os), but some discrepancies occur in individual specimens, the workmanship of which is rather poor. Since these medals are unnamed, it is difficult to identify the army and navy recipients, but when one is found in company with the N.G.S. Medal with *Egypt* bar, reference to *Haultain's Navy List* will show if the recipient was entitled to the gold medal. At one time I had a pair consisting of the N.G.S. Medal with bar, *1 June 1794*, and the Gold Medal; reference showed that he was entitled to both, and would have had the *Egypt* bar as well, had he lived until 1850, when that bar was authorised (*See Plate 15*).

The Order of the Mejedie was founded in 1852, and has been widely awarded to British personnel on several occasions, the most important of which are the Crimean War, the Egypt and Sudan campaigns of 1882–89, and the re-conquest of the Sudan, 1896–98.

It is not difficult to verify the award of this Order, as they appear in Navy and Army Lists, several medal books, etc. It is, however, important to see that the badge is the correct one for the period. The 5th Class is the one most frequently found, and those given for the Crimean War can be distinguished by their rather crude suspension ring (*Fig. 18* and *Plate 15*), by the centre of the *rev.*, which is convex and held in place by four small claws, and by the red star of the suspender, which is joined to the crescent by only two points. Those given towards the end of the nineteenth century are of better workmanship, and have a square suspension ring; the centre of the *rev.* is concave (and might or might not have a 'hallmark' or cartouche with an arabic inscription), while the star in the suspender has four points joined to the crescent. Also the groups of rays are sometimes pierced with tiny holes; the silver is of a 'whiter' type than that of the Crimea period, which is darkish in tone. Several of the later badges have a zig-zag mark filed into the back of one of the groups of rays; its purpose is not known, but one theory is that it was to prove that the badge is of silver and not plated.

FIG. 18.
Order of the Mejedie: reverses of 5th Class. Left: Crimean War period. Right: later types.

The ribbon of the Mejedie varies somewhat in the early badges, some pieces of obviously contemporary ribbon have wide dull green *edges*, while others (including also the later issues) have a narrow bright green stripe near each edge.

**Conversion of A.H. to A.D., and** *vice versa*.
To convert the Moslem year, A.H., to the Christian equivalent, deduct 3% of the A.H. figure and add 622. Thus, referring to the *Tokar* clasp on the Khedive's Star:–

| | A.H. | 1308 |
|---|---|---|
| less 3% | | 39 |
| | | ———— |
| | | 1269 |
| add | | 622 |
| | | ———— |
| | A.D. | 1891 |

For the reverse calculation, deduct 622 from the A.D. year, add 3% of this difference, then add 1:—

| | A.D. | 1891 |
|---|---|---|
| deduct | | 622 |
| | | ———— |
| | | 1269 |
| add 3% (38) + 1 | | 39 |
| | | ———— |
| | A.H. | 1308 |

The above formula may be one year out in some cases, depending on the month concerned.

# APPENDIX A

# Bibliography

## A Short Bibliography of Works useful to the Medal Collector

(Note: *The abbreviation, ANSM, refers to the American Numismatic Society's Monographs, with the appropriate number.*)

### 1. Books on Medals as such

Abbott (P. E.) and Tamplin (J. M. A.). *British Gallantry Awards.* LONDON, 1971. 359pp., incl. 8 col.pl. and 196 other illustrations. An outstanding contribution to works on British medals.

Burke (Sir Bernard). *The Book of Orders of Knighthood and Decorations of Honour.* LONDON, 1858. 411pp. 99 col.pl.

Carter (Thos.). *Medals of the British Army and how they were Won.* LONDON, 1861. First published in 3 vols., later bound up together. Enlarged and revised, 1893, with 656pp. 26 col.pl. A useful book, with details of actions and units present. (Reprinted 1973).

Cole (Lt.-Col. H. N.). *Coronation and Royal Commemorative Medals, 1887–1977.* LONDON, 1977, 68 pp., illus. 2 coloured plates. Very useful in its own field.

De La Bere (Brig. Sir Ivan). *The Queen's Orders of Chivalry.* LONDON, 1961. 212pp. 12pl. An authoritative survey.

Dorling (Capt. H. Taprell). *Ribbons and Medals.* LONDON, 1916 onwards. Enlarged and revised edition, 1974. 359pp., incl. 24 col. pls. of ribbons, numerous illus. The best general book for beginners, covering British and foreign awards.

Elvin (C. N.). *A Handbook of the Orders of Chivalry, War Medals, and Crosses.* LONDON, 1892. 172pp. 32pl. (some coloured). Not well arranged. Contains much miscellaneous information.

Gordon (Major L. L.). *British Battles and Medals.* ALDERSHOT, 1947. The 3rd edition, 1962, is much better than the first two. Deals only with campaign medals – no Orders, decorations, or long service medals.

The 4th edition, LONDON, 1971, has been revised by E. C. Joslin, and is the best book for the general collector of British medals.

Hall (Donald). *British Orders, Decorations and Medals*, St. Ives (Cambs.), 1973. 96pp. Numerous col. illus. Does not cover long service medals.

Hieronymussen (Paul). *Orders, Medals and Decorations of Britain and Europe*. London, 1967. 256pp. 450 colour photographs and other line drawings. An excellent survey of existing awards.

Irwin (D. Hastings). *War Medals and Decorations*. London, 1890. The 4th edition is the best, 1910, 536pp. 18pl. A most useful book for the beginner and general collector; gives lists of units engaged and considerable other information.

Joslin (E. C.). *The Standard Catalogue of British Orders, Decorations and Medals*. London. 3rd edn. 1976. 63pp. Col.Fpce., 70pls. (39 in colour).

Joslin (E. C.). *The Observer's Book of British Awards and Medals*. London, 1974. 191pp., 8 col.pls., numerous illus.

Johnson (S. C.). *The Medal Collector*. London, 1921. 320pp. 8 coloured pl. of ribbons, and numerous other pl. and drawings. Supersedes his earlier *Medals of Our Fighting Men* (1917). Both rather elementary.

Kerr (Major W. J. W.). *Notes on War Medals, 1794–1840*. Exmouth, 1948. 36pp. 1pl. A valuable little book, with notes on M.G.S., N.G.S., and Army of India Medals.

Long (W. H.). *Medals of the British Navy*. London, 1895. 450pp. 21 coloured pl. One of the best books on naval medals, with full details of actions and ships engaged.

Mayo (J. H.). *Medals and Decorations of the British Army and Navy*. London, 1897. 2 vols., 617pp. 55 coloured pl. A valuable work, with authoritative details of the institution of each medal. Does not deal with the actions or units engaged.

Měřička (Vaclav). *The Book of Orders and Decorations*. London 1976. 248pp., incl. 32 col. pls., numerous illus.

Payne (Dr A. A.). *Handbook of British and Foreign Orders, War Medals, and Decorations*. Sheffield, 1911. 811pp. 60 illus. A catalogue of his collection, with many useful notes.

Poulsom (Major Neville W.) *The White Ribbon*. London, 1968. 216pp. 9pl. An excellent survey of all the polar medals and expeditions, with medal rolls of each. Indispensable to all interested in polar medals.

Pownall (Henry). *Korean Campaign Medals, 1950–53.* LONDON, 1956 (but dated 1954). 10pp., illustrated. Reprinted, with additional information, from the series in Spink's *Numismatic Circular*, June–Sept. 1956. 1 col.pl. of ribbons.

Purves (Alec A.). *Orders and Decorations.* LONDON, 1972. 160pp., numerous col. illus. (Hamlyn All-Colour Paperbacks, No. 91). An overall general survey.

Purves (Alec A.). *The Medals, Decorations and Orders of the Great War, 1914–1918.* LONDON, 1975. 199pp., 7 col.pls. of ribbons, 24 b/w pls., illus. Covers the Allies and associated countries, the Central Powers, neutral countries and the emergent nations.

Risk (James C.). *British Orders and Decorations.* ANSM. NO. 106, 1945. 124pp. 76pl. A useful general survey. (Reprinted, LONDON, 1975).

Risk (James C.). *The History of the Order of the Bath and its Insignia.* LONDON, 1972. 214pp., col. fpce., 28pls. (3 in colour). An authoritative and important work.

Sandwich (Earl of). *British and Foreign Medals Relating to Naval and Maritime Affairs.* H.M.S.O., 1937. 308pp. 27pl. Supplement, 1939, 96pp. 2nd Edition, 1950, enlarged and revised. A fully detailed description of the large collection of medals, medallions, and tokens, in the National Maritime Museum, Greenwich. Almost a condensed version of the Marquis of Milford Haven's large work on Naval Medals.

Smyth (Sir John). *The Story of the Victoria Cross, 1856–1963,* LONDON, 1963. 496pp. 17pl. Now the standard work on the V.C.

Smyth (Sir John). *The Story of the George Cross.* LONDON, 1968. 208pp. 17pl. A companion volume to the previous item.

Steward (W. Augustus). *War Medals and Their History.* LONDON. 1915. 407pp. 153 illus. A revised edition appeared in 1918, entitled, *The A.B.C. of War Medals.* Extremely useful books both for the beginner and general collector, with some details of participating units, naming of medals, some foreign awards, etc.

Tancred (George). *Historical Record of Medals Conferred on the British Navy, Army, and Auxiliary Forces.* LONDON, 1891. 483pp. 24pl. (some coloured), and other illustrations. In addition to official medals, it also describes regimental medals, and is generally regarded as the standard work on the latter. Although useful, is badly arranged and there is no index.

Tozer (Charles W.). *The Insignia and Medals of the Grand Priory of the Most Venerable Order of the Hospital of St. John of Jerusalem.*

LONDON, 1975. 80pp., col. fpce., 3 col. pls., illus. An authoritative work.

Trost (L. J.). *Die Ritter- und Verdienstorden, Ehrenzeichen, und Medaillen.* VIENNA, 1910. 14½″ (horizontal) × 10¾″ 200pp. 40pl. Text in tabulated form. More comprehensive than any previous work, but there are some inaccuracies and omissions.

Werlich (Robt.). *Orders and Decorations of all Nations.* WASHINGTON, 2nd edn., 1974. 476pp., 5 col. pls. An ambitious work, lavishly illustrated, but like the first edition, contains many mistakes.

Wilkins (Philip A.). *The History of the Victoria Cross.* LONDON, 1904. 443pp. Many photos of recipients. A useful book. (Reprinted 1969).

Wilson (Sir Arnold) and McEwen (Capt. J. H. F.). *Gallantry.* LONDON, 1939. 498pp. No illus. Describes fully British awards for gallantry, military and civil, with brief notes on foreign awards. An extremely good book.

*The following list of works dealing with individual foreign countries, is but a short selection from the hundreds available.*


## AUSTRIA

Falkenstien (J. von). *Imperial Austrian Medals and Decorations.* SAUSALITO, CALIF/PLANTATION, FLA., 1972. 180pp., col. pl. of ribbons, illus. A useful book, but excludes orders.

Měřička (Vaclav). *Orden und Ehrenzeichen der Österreichisch-Ungarischen Monarchie.* MUNICH, 1974. 304pp., 60 magnificent col. pls., numerous illus. A sumptuous work.

Procházka (Roman, Freiherr von). *Österreichisches Ordenshandbuch.* MUNICH, 1974. 160pp., 101pls. illustrating over 600 items. An important work.


## BADEN

Volle (H.). *Badens Orden.* FREIBURG-i-BR., 1976. 188pp., 24pls. (incl. 1 col. pl. of ribbons). Covers orders, decorations and medals from the 18th cent. to 1934.


## BAVARIA

Leser. (J. & O.). *Die Ritter- und Verdienstorden . . . des Königreichs Bayern.* STRAUBING, 1910. 253pp. 18pl.

219

Schreiber (G.). *Die Bayerischen Orden und Ehrenzeichen.* MUNICH, 1964. 200pp. 6pl. 138 illustrations of medals.

## BELGIUM
Quinot (Henri). *Recueil Illustré des Ordres de Chevalerie et Décorations Belges de 1830 à 1963.* BRUSSELS, 1963. 328pp. Many plates. This is the 5th edition, the earlier ones, from 1930, being entitled, *Recueil Illustré des Décorations Belges et Congolaises.*

## CENTRAL AMERICA
Guille (Lionel F.). *The Decorations and Medals of the Central American Countries,* STEVENAGE, 1952 23pp. No illus. Publication No. 2 of the Orders and Medals Research Society.

## DENMARK
Jørgensen (Capt. P. J.). *Danish Orders and Medals.* COPENHAGEN, 1964. 124pp. Illustrated. Text in English.

## FINLAND
(Ministry of Foreign Affairs) *Les Ordres Nationaux de la Finlande.* HELSINKI, 1975. 70pp., 7pls. (5 in colour).

## FRANCE
*Décorations Officielles Françaises Contemporaines.* PARIS, 1956. 291pp. 80pl. An authoritative work, published by the French Mint. Supplement, 1967. 27pp., incl. 6pls. (5 in colour).
Delande (M.). *Les Décorations de France et ses Colonies.* PARIS, 1934. 104pp. incl. 51pl.
Gillingham (H. E.). *French Orders and Decorations.* ANSM, NO. 11, 1922. 110pp. 35pl.
Gillingham (H. E.). *Notes on the Decorations and Medals of French Colonies and Protectorates.* ANSM, NO. 36, 1928. 62pp. 31pl.

## GERMANY
Doehle (Dr H.). *Orden und Ehrenzeichen im Dritten Reich.* BERLIN, 1940. 100pp. 4 col.pl. of ribbons and many half-tone illustrations. Enlarged and revised (with coloured illustrations) in 1941, entitled, *Orden und Ehrenzeichen in Gross-Deutschland.*
Hessenthal (Dr W. H. E.). and Schreiber (G.) *Die Tragbare Ehrenzeichen des Deutschen Reiches.* BERLIN, 1940. 563pp. 32pl. Des-

cribes in full detail all medals, but gives names only of Orders. It is now almost unobtainable, and very highly priced.

Klenau (Arnhard, Graf). *Grosser Deutscher Ordenskatalog bis 1918.* MUNICH, 1974. 228pp. Fully illustrated; covers orders, decorations and medals of all the German States to 1918.

Klietmann (Dr K. G.). *Pour le Mérite und Tapferkeitsmedaille.* BERLIN, 1966. 104pp., 19 plates. Covers the awards for bravery and merit of Germany (incl. the German States) and her allies. First published in 1955 under the title: *Für Tapferkeit und Verdienst,* 64pp. 8pl. (4 in colour).

Klietmann (Dr. K. G.). *Deutsche Auszeichnungen.* BERLIN. Part 1: 1971. 21pp., 18pls. (incl. 1 in colour of ribbons). Part 2: 1971. 333pp. History and documentation of the awards listed and illustrated in Part 1. Part 3: 1972. *Anhalt.* 63pp., 5pls.

Krantz (H. U.). *Orden und Ehrenzeichen der Bundesrepublik Deutschland.* 1958. COLOGNE/HERFORD, 1958. 241 and 19pp., incl. 10pl. (9 in colour) and numerous illustrations.

Littlejohn (D.) & Dodkins (Col. C. M.). *Orders, Decorations and Medals of the Third Reich.* MOUNTAIN VIEW, CALIF., Vol. 1, 1968; 231pp. (incl. 4 col. pls. of ribbons), illus. Vol. 2, 1974. Illus., some coloured.

Prowse (A. E.). *The Iron Cross of Prussia and Germany, 1813-1945.* WELLINGTON, NZ., 1970. 62pp., incl. 10pls. A useful survey.

## GREECE

Dimacopoulos (George D.). *Greek Orders and Medals,* Vol. 1. ATHENS, 1961, 78pp. 20pl. A authoritative survey.

## ITALY

Bascapè (G.). *Gli Ordini Cavallereschi in Italia.* MILAN, 1972. 524pp., 16 col. pls., numerous illus. Also includes Order of Malta, the Vatican orders, San Marino, etc.

Ceschina (R. E.). *Gli Ordini Equestri del Regno D'Italia.* 3rd. Edn. MILAN, 1938. 175pp. 15 col.pl.

Gillingham (H. E.). *Italian Orders of Chivalry and Medals of Honour.* ANSM, NO. 20, 1923. 146pp. 34pl.

## LUXEMBURG

Schleich de Bossé (J. R.). *Les Distinctions Honorifiques au pays de Luxembourg, 1430–1961.* LUXEMBOURG, 1962. 48pp. 36pl.

## MEXICO

Gillingham (H. E.). *Mexican Decorations of Honour.* ANSM, NO. 89, 1940. 53pp. 17pl.

Perez-Maldonado (C.). *Condecoraciones Mexicanos y su Historia.* 1942. 212pp. Half-tone illustrations of every medal.

## NETHERLANDS

Bax (Dr W. F.). *De Nederlandse Ridderorden en Onderscheidingen.* ROTTERDAM & THE HAGUE, 1951. 57pp. 6 col.pl. A reliable work, dealing with existing Orders and modern medals.

## ROMANIA

Klietmann (Dr K. G.). *Phaleristik – Rumänien.* BERLIN, 1975. 131pp., 16pls. Text in German and English.

## RUSSIA (Imperial)

Hurley (C.). *Russian Orders, Decorations, and Medals.* LONDON, 1934. 90pp. 13pl., some coloured. Very little on medals; deals only with Imperial awards, mainly Orders. Contains list of British recipients.

## RUSSIA – USSR

Kolesnikov (G. A.) & Rozhkov (A. M.). *Ordena i Medali, SSSR.* MOSCOW, 1974. 270pp., 36 col.pls. Supplement (tipped in), 4pp., incl. 2 col.pls.

## SCANDINAVIA

Areen (E. E.). *De Nordiska Ländernas Officiella Belönings-Medaljer.* STOCKHOLM, 1938. 287pp. 203 illustrations, some coloured. Covers medals only, of Norway, Sweden, Denmark, Finland, and Iceland.

Berghman (A.). *Nordiska Riddareordnar och Dekorationer.* MALMÖ, 1949. 249pp. 71pl. (some coloured). Deals chiefly with the Orders of Norway, Sweden, Denmark, Finland and Iceland.

## SOUTH AMERICA

Gillingham (H. E.). *South American Decorations and War Medals.* ANSM, NO. 56, 1932. 178pp. 35pl.

## SPAIN

Gillingham (H. E.). *Spanish Orders of Chivalry and Decorations.* ANSM, NO. 31, 1926. 165pp. 40pl.

Puente y Gomez (F. F. de la). *Condecoraciones Españolas.* MADRID, 1953. 608pp. 88 col.pl. A sumptuous work.

## UNITED STATES OF AMERICA

Gibbons (C.). *Military Decorations and Campaign Service Bars of U.S.A.* NEW YORK, 1945. 100pp. col.pl.

Kerrigan (E. E.). *American War Medals and Decorations.* NEW YORK, 1971: LONDON, 1973. 173pp., 4 col.pls., illus.

National Geographic Society. *Medals and Insignia of the Armed Forces of the U.S.A.* Various issues of the *National Geographic Magazine,* with coloured illustrations; Dec. 1919; June 1943; Oct. 1943; Dec. 1944.

Robles (P. K.). *United States Military Medals and Ribbons.* RUTLAND VT./TOKIO, 1971. 187pp., incl. 44 col.pls.

## 2. Books Useful for Verifying Medals

Abbott (P. E.). *Recipients of the Distinguished Conduct Medal, 1855– 1909.* LONDON, 1975. 112pp., 2pls.

*Burke's Handbook to the Order of the British Empire.* LONDON, 1921. (Edited by A. Winton Thorpe). 704pp. 5 col.pl. (of insignia). Gives dates and categories of all awards, incl. many short biographies; extremely useful for verifying awards of the Order of 1914–18 War period.

Cook (F. & A.). *The Casualty Roll for the Crimea, 1854–55.* LONDON, 1977. 286pp. incl. 21pls., maps, plans. A sumptuous volume, listing all Army (with number, rank and name) and Naval Brigade personnel killed, wounded, missing, etc., with much additional information.

Dalton (C.). *The Waterloo Roll Call.* LONDON, 1890. 256pp. 4pl. 2nd (revised) edn., 1904. 296pp. Details of all officers present, and complete Muster Roll of 2nd Dgns. (Royal Scots Greys). Reprinted 1971.

Gould (R. W.) & Douglas-Morris (Capt. K. J.). *The Army of India Medal Roll, 1799–1826.* LONDON, 1974. 123pp. Includes officers and ORs of the British Army, Indian Army officers, Naval officers and ratings (RN and Bombay Marine).

*Honours and Awards of the Old Contemptibles, 1914–15.* LONDON, 1971 (reprint of the 1915 edn.). 58pp. Covers Navy, Army, Indian Army and Colonial Forces.

Lummis, **W. M.** & Wynn, **K. G.** *Honour the Light Brigade*. LONDON, 1973. 320pp., 16pls. A record of the services, etc., of officers and OR's of the Light Brigade at Balaclava.

*Medal Roll of the 50th and 97th Regiments (Royal West Kent), 1793–1881*. GUERNSEY, 1928. 66pp. 1pl.

*Medal Roll of the Royal Highland Regiment (Black Watch), 1801–1911*. EDINBURGH, 1913. 350pp. 4pl.

*Medal Rolls of the Naval General Service Medal, 1793–1840, and Army of India Medal, 1799–1826*. These exist only in manuscript or typescript, but several reliable "editions" are known, and are occasionally offered by numismatic dealers, or in auction sales.

*Military General Service Medal Roll, 1793–1814*. A printed edition was compiled by the late Lt.-Col. Kingsley Foster, and published in Germany in 1947, 650pp., 1pl. Other manuscript or typescript copies exist (see previous item).

*Naval Honours and Awards, 1939–40*. LONDON, 1942, 276pp. 13pl. (1 in colour). An official publication.

Simmonds (Prof. **P. L.**). *The British Roll of Honour*. LONDON, 1887. 560pp. 3 col.pl., and other illustrations. A descriptive account of the recognised Orders of Chivalry in various countries, and gives lists of Orders awarded to British subjects and to Royalty. Very useful to collectors for verifying groups to eminent recipients, civilian and H.M. Forces.

*The Navy List*. This official publication started in 1814, and although its contents have varied considerably, contains much useful information, especially where officers' careers are concerned, although individual services are not shown. At some periods lists of gallantry and life-saving medals are shown.

*Haultain's Navy List*. From 1839 to 1845.

*The New Navy List*. From 1846 to 1856. Conducted by Joseph Allen, RN.

*Lean's Royal Navy List*. From 1878 to 1917.

These series of unofficial navy lists give the services of officers, active and retired, and usually mention the award of medals, etc.

Markham (Clement **R.**). *The Arctic Navy List*. LONDON & PORTS-MOUTH, 1875. 62pp. Gives a list and details of all officers who took part in Arctic and Antarctic Expeditions, from 1773 to 1873, also the 1875–76 Expedition. Very useful for verifying officers' groups containing the 1818–55 Arctic Medal.

*A List of Gunners, Boatswains, and Carpenters of H.M. Royal Navy.* An official publication, published from 1860 to 1893. Contents and title vary slightly.

Capper (Lieut. H. D.). *Royal Naval Warrant Officers' Manual, 1910.* Contains lists, with war services, historical notes, etc.

Oaklands Book Division (Pubr.) *South Africa Field Force Casualties, 1899–1902.* ILFORD, 1972. 740pp. A reprint of the official lists originally published in Cape Town. Includes killed, wounded, prisoners, etc., by regiments.

O'Byrne (W. R.). *A Naval Biographical Dictionary.* LONDON, 1849. 1400pp. Biographies of all officers, Lieutenants and above. A 2nd edition, in folio size, started publication, in parts, in 1861, but unfortunately ceased at *Giles;* not only does it specify medals awarded, but (unlike the 1st edition) it includes Masters, Mates, Surgeons, Engineers, Chaplains, Paymasters, R.M. Officers, etc.

*The Army List.* This official publication started in 1779. Towards the end of the 19th century, services of regular officers are given (incl. medals). For holders of temporary commissions during the 1914–18 War, refer to the *Monthly Army List*, as the quarterly one gives only regular officers. The Monthly List also gives, at intervals, awards of decorations such as M.C., etc.

*Hart's New Annual Army List.* LONDON, from 1840 to 1916. Gives details of all active and retired officers, with services, medals, etc.

*South Africa, 1899–1902. Officers and Men of the Army and Navy Mentioned in Despatches.* 2nd edn., LONDON, 1902. 132pp. Includes lists of honours and awards to Nov. 1902, with brief citations in some cases. Reprinted 1971.

*List of Officers of the Royal Regiment of Artillery, 1716–1899.* 4th edn., LONDON, 1900. 274pp. A revised edition of Kane's work (with similar title, first published in 1815), with details of services and medals. A new edition was published in SHEFFIELD in 1914, as Vol. II, covering the period from June 1862 to June 1914; 405pp.

\*    \*    \*

In addition to the works listed above, many regimental histories include lists of awards for gallantry, while back numbers of regimental magazines often include similar data, also lists of detachments sent on special service – useful when only a few men of a regiment received a particular medal or bar.

## 3. Books for Background Information

Chichester (H. M.) and Burges-Short (G.). *Records and Badges of the British Army.* LONDON, 1895. 3rd Edn. (undated, but *c.* 1900), 942pp. 24 col.pl., many line drawings. Gives a brief history of every unit in the army. Reprinted 1970.

Norman (C. B.). *Battle Honours of the British Army.* LONDON, 1911. 500pp. 8pl. 4 maps. Covers actions from 1662 to 1902; gives numbers of casualties of regiments, and much other data. (Reprinted 1971).

*Short Histories of the Territorial Regiments of the British Army.* H.M.S.O., 1905. (Edited by R. de M. Rudolf, of the War Office). 726pp. Deals with each infantry regiment individually, from the Royal Scots to the Royal Dublin Fusiliers (i.e. 'territorial' by county titles, etc., not the modern T.A.). Includes names of awards of the V.C. and D.C.M., some with brief citations.

"Centurion". *Men Whose Fathers were Men,* LONDON, 1925, 99pp. Subtitled, *A Story of a Hobby.* A fascinating introduction to medal collecting, which ought to be in the hands of every collector. Published by A. H. Baldwin & Sons, Ltd. A short supplement, 22pp., was issued a few years ago, undated, entitled: *More 'Men Whose Fathers were Men': Their Medals and their Message.*

Perry (Ottley L.). *Ranks and Badges in Her Majesty's Army and Navy.* LONDON, 1887. 402pp. A most useful book, with much unusual miscellaneous information. A 2nd Edition appeared in 1888, 417pp., revised and enlarged, entitled *Ranks, Badges, and Dates in H.M. Army and Navy.*

\*     \*     \*

In addition to the above, many books provide interesting and useful information to the medal collector, making his medals mean something more than just silver or bronze pieces. These include regimental histories, accounts of campaigns – official and otherwise, personal diaries of both officers and other ranks, etc. The following are but a very brief indication of the types of books suggested:

Bryant (Arthur). *The Years of Endurance, 1793–1802.* LONDON, 370pp. Maps.

Bryant (Arthur). *Years of Victory, 1802–1812.* LONDON, 1944. 500pp. Maps.

Doyle (A. Conan). *The Great Boer War*. LONDON, 1900, and many later editions. The later editions, in large format, with better maps, are to be preferred.

Fleming (Peter). *Bayonets to Lhasa*. LONDON, 1961. 319pp. Illus. The story behind the Tibet Medal, 1903–04.

Jerrold (Douglas). *The Royal Naval Division*. LONDON, 1923. 368pp. Plates and maps. Even 1914–18 War medals have a story, and this is one of many books recommended.

*The Autobiography of Sergeant William Lawrence*. LONDON, 1886. 250pp. Edited by G. N. Bankes. A fascinating story of life in the ranks throughout the Peninsular and Waterloo Campaigns, by one who survived to receive his M.G.S. Medal with ten bars (40th Foot).

Warner (Oliver). *The Glorious First of June*. LONDON, 1961. 184pp. Illus. This, and other volumes in this Batsford series, will prove interesting reading for owners of the N.G.S. Medal.

*The War, or Voices From the Ranks*. LONDON, 1855. 220pp. Small 8vo. Extracts from letters home from officers and men. A very vivid account of life and action in the Crimea.

# APPENDIX B

## Auctioneers Specialising in Medal Sales

The following firms specialise in medal sales, and collectors may either attend personally or entrust their bids to an agent, usually either one of the leading medal dealers or to the auctioneer himself:

Glendining & Co. Ltd., 7 Blenheim Street, New Bond Street, London W1. (Tel. 01–493 2445)

> Their conditions of sale state: "Each lot is believed to be genuine, but should any lot prove to be a forgery, or reprint, or wrongly described in the catalogue, the purchaser is at liberty to take or reject it, provided always that notice of such rejection be made and the lot returned within seven days from date of sale."

Sotheby Parke Bernet & Co., 34–35 New Bond Street, London W1A 2AA. (Tel. 01–493 8080). Similar conditions apply.

Wallis & Wallis, 210 High Street, Lewes, Sussex. (Tel. 3137)

> A number of medal lots are usually included in their frequent sales of arms, armour, militaria, coins, etc. Their conditions of sale do not include a clause as above, but they say in a letter "We think you will find that we always act fairly in any case where medals have proved to be forgeries or not as described in the catalogue. We have always made available to purchasers the choice of either retaining or returning the medals to us and being refunded with the full purchase price. We feel we cannot be fairer to our purchasers than this."

(NOTE: In earlier editions a list of leading British medal dealers was included, all of whom are prepared to guarantee all medals sold by them. With the large increase in the number of dealers, it has not proved possible to ascertain in every case whether they are prepared to give this guarantee, and in order to avoid giving offence by omitting reputable dealers, it has been thought advisable to omit the list altogether).

# APPENDIX C

## Societies for the Medal Collector

THE following information was correct at the time of writing, but changes are bound to occur. If prospective members have any difficulty in tracing a society, no doubt any of the leading medal dealers will be able to assist.

### The Orders and Medals Research Society (Founded 1942)

Hon. General Secretary: N. G. Gooding, 11 Maresfield, Chepstow Road, Croydon CRO 5UA.

Meetings are normally held at the Society's premises in E Block, Duke of York's Headquarters, King's Road, Chelsea, SW3, on the last Saturday afternoon in each month. Visits and other special meetings are arranged at intervals, and the society publishes an illustrated quarterly journal, *Orders & Medals*. A substantial library is available to members.

There are also provincial branches at Manchester (Hon. Sec. D. L. Thompson, 45 Moss Lane, Bramhall, Stockport SK7 1EQ) and at Retford, Notts. (Hon. Sec. T. Driver, 3 Atholl Crescent, Doncaster DN2 6HZ).

### The Military Historical Society (Founded 1948)

Hon. Secretary: J. W. F. Gaylor, 7 East Woodside, Leighlands, Bexley, Kent, DA5 3PG.

Meetings are held at the Centre Block, Duke of York's Headquarters, King's Road, Chelsea, London SW3, and visits are arranged to regimental depots and museums, and other places of military interest. The society caters for those interested in medals, badges and buttons, uniforms, and other aspects of the history and traditions of H.M. Forces. An excellent library is available to members, and the society publishes an illustrated quarterly magazine.

There are also provincial branches as follows: West Midlands, East Midlands, Southern, South-East, Merseyside and East Anglia.

## The Birmingham Medal Society (Founded 1964)

Hon. Secretary: Mrs J. Done, 4 Mossfield Road, King's Heath, Birmingham 14.

The Society holds regular meetings; for details apply to the Hon. Secretary.

# Lists of Plates and Illustrations

# Index

## (a) General

## (b) Orders, Decorations, and Medals

233